Praise for *Kidnapped by the Junta*

'Julian Manyon's heart-thumpingly powerful book is history told from the closest and most frightening quarters. He was both witness and near-victim to the darkness that enveloped Argentina in the 1970s and 1980s. And now, across the gulf of the years, and with fresh access to fascinating documentation, he records the carnage of the Falklands War of 1982, kicking away many widely held assumptions. His account of state terror and global geopolitics is by turns pulse-quickeningly tense and richly illuminating.'
Sinclair McKay, author of The Secret Life of Bletchley Park

'Shocking, terrifying and revealing. Ground-breaking history, expertly told – a dramatic new insight into the Falklands conflict.'
Roger Bolton, BBC journalist and broadcaster

'Drawing on a huge tranche of recently declassified US documents, Julian Manyon authoritatively nails the Argentine Junta's regime as one of the most depraved and deluded of modern times. After reading this book, packed with so much graphic new detail, I feel more fortunate than ever to have escaped Argentina with my life.'
Ian Mather, former defence correspondent of The Observer

'A gripping story, brilliantly told ... a compelling account of a dark period of modern history.'
Stephan Shakespeare, founder and CEO of YouGov

KIDNAPPED BY THE JUNTA

INSIDE ARGENTINA'S WARS WITH BRITAIN AND ITSELF

JULIAN MANYON

ICON

Published in the UK in 2022 by
Icon Books Ltd, Omnibus Business Centre,
39–41 North Road, London N7 9DP
email: info@iconbooks.com
www.iconbooks.com

Sold in the UK, Europe and Asia by
Faber & Faber Ltd, Bloomsbury House,
74–77 Great Russell Street,
London WC1B 3DA or their agents

Distributed in the UK, Europe and Asia by
Grantham Book Services, Trent Road,
Grantham NG31 7XQ

Distributed in Australia and New Zealand by
Allen & Unwin Pty Ltd, PO Box 8500,
83 Alexander Street, Crows Nest, NSW 2065

Distributed in South Africa by
Jonathan Ball, Office B4, The District,
41 Sir Lowry Road, Woodstock 7925

Distributed in India by
Penguin Books India,
7th Floor, Infinity Tower – C, DLF Cyber City,
Gurgaon 122002, Haryana

ISBN: 978-178578-852-9

Typeset in Adobe Text by Marie Doherty

Printed and bound in Great Britain by
Clays Ltd, Elcograf S.p.A.

Contents

To my son Richard for his steady encouragement throughout and to my dear wife Caroline without whose help this book could not have been completed.

ABOUT THE AUTHOR

Julian Manyon was a journalist specialising in international stories for more than 40 years, starting in Vietnam. He covered the Falklands War in Argentina for Thames Television's *TV Eye* and then became a long-serving foreign correspondent for ITN, winning numerous awards for his work. He lives with his wife on their small farm in the south of England.

List of illustrations

Interviewing President Leopoldo Galtieri hours after the kidnapping.

A secret report by the CIA stating that the kidnapping had been done by 'a paramilitary group' linked to the secret service.

The first military Junta which seized power in March 1976.

The Junta which lost its war with Britain.

Uniformed troops and police suppress dissent in the streets.

A massive demonstration in support of the Junta's seizure of the Falkland Islands.

Mothers and Grandmothers of the 'disappeared' protest in the Plaza de Mayo.

Aníbal Gordon, kidnapper, torturer and murderer, soon after his arrest in 1984.

Allen 'Tex' Harris, the American diplomat appalled by the regime's use of torture and murder.

Mario Firmenich, leader of the Montoneros revolutionary group.

HMS *Antelope* sinks after the detonation of two unexploded bombs.

Argentinian soldiers captured at Goose Green are guarded by a British Royal Marine.

Automotores Orletti, where Aníbal Gordon ran a secret torture and murder centre.

The cellar at 3570 Bacacay Street where victims are said to have been tortured.

Intelligence officer and torturer Miguel Ángel Furci awaits sentencing in a Federal Court.

CHAPTER 1

——

Swallowed

AMID ALL THE DRAMAS of the career in journalism that I had so much desired, I had not expected to have an hour to contemplate my own imminent execution.

As the car rolled forward at a deliberately steady pace, I lay constrained and helpless on my back in the rear footwell, a cloth over my head blocking almost all vision, a man's knee jammed against my neck pinning my head against the back of the seat in front and a hard, tanned hand holding an automatic pistol pressed against the side of my head.

The words were in Spanish but even with my fragmentary knowledge of the language I could understand them. 'Quiet,' the harsh voice said, and then with a short gesture of the pistol, 'When we get where we are going, I will kill you with this.'

It was May 12th, 1982, in the age before training courses in hazardous environments and psychological counselling. As I briefly reflected on the mess in which I found myself, only unhelpful thoughts occurred.

I had been close to death before. So determined had I been to become an international journalist that more than a decade earlier I had launched myself as a freelance in Vietnam. There, following the American invasion of Cambodia in a battle too obscure for mention in the history books, I had survived the destruction of a Cambodian Army battalion by the North Vietnamese Army and Viet Cong, as untrained Cambodian youngsters were ambushed and shot down by terrifyingly effective NVA regulars charging with fixed bayonets. As night fell an American airborne gunship trying to save their allies added to the chaos and terror by firing long red streams of tracer fire, which appeared suddenly and silently in the darkness, followed by a deafening roar as the sound of the machine guns caught up. I had saved myself by playing dead while communist troops sprinted past around me, and I found out in that paddy field what it is to tremble uncontrollably. In the end, as dawn broke, I was able to crawl out alive.[1]

This was different but, if anything, even more terrifying: a slow steady progress through moving traffic in the streets of Buenos Aires as I lay helpless and unable to affect my fate in any way. In the jargon of the Argentinian secret police which I learned later, I had been 'swallowed' and 'walled in'.

There were three men in the saloon car that carried me: the driver, a man in the front seat operating a radio on the dashboard and the man holding the gun to my head who appeared to be their commander. Brief incomprehensible radio messages were occasionally exchanged.

One thing was very clear: the men who had seized me and who now held my life in their hands were professionals in the art of kidnapping. In the early afternoon, together with the other members of our British television team, I had emerged from the Argentine Foreign Ministry after a failed attempt to interview Minister Nicanor Costa Méndez, the Oxford-educated civilian described by some as the 'evil genius' of the military regime. Costa Méndez, who walked with the aid of a stick, had been angered by the press of journalists and my insistent questions and brushed us off with an infuriated wave of the hand. Minutes later, as we stepped into the tree-lined square outside the handsome colonial-style building and got into our car, I was suddenly swept up in a series of events that seemed to happen in slow motion but in reality occurred at lightning speed: another car, which I remember as being grey in colour, cut in front of us forcing us to stop and disgorged strongly-built men clad in sharp suits. They seized me with firm hands while shouting, 'Police!' Suddenly I was looking up at trees we had been passing and, before I could make any real attempt at resistance, I was propelled into the back of their vehicle. A pistol was pressed against my head. I had no idea what was happening to the rest of the team. I just knew that they weren't there.

The doors slammed shut and in a motion that immediately terrified me, the men produced what appeared to be custom-made leather thongs with which they expertly tied the door handles to the door locks in this pre-electronic vehicle. As I dimly realised amid the shock and mounting panic, this made it virtually impossible for me or any other victim, no matter how desperate, to kick open a door. It was a practised routine which these men had clearly carried out many times before.

The car, built by the Ford factory in Argentina, was called a Falcon, a solid, practical model that was already notorious as the vehicle of choice of the secret police. It moved quietly through the streets which despite the war with Britain were choked with traffic. As was their aim, the kidnappers had achieved complete control. Resistance was beyond my power and would, in any case, have been futile and probably fatal. From beneath the cloth covering my head I caught occasional glimpses of the upper storeys of some of the buildings we were passing, the fine old ones in the centre, then more modern structures as we began to move towards the outskirts of the city.

Suddenly I saw gantries carrying familiar yellow signs advertising the Lufthansa airline and realised that we were passing the international airport where we had arrived some ten days before.

'Look,' I said in broken Spanish-English to the man holding the gun to my head, 'In my pocket I've got dollars. Please take the money and throw me out here.'

No word came in reply but I felt a horny hand force its way into my trouser pocket searching for the money, some $800, which he silently removed. Without the slightest change of pace, the car rolled on. When I made another attempt to speak I was silenced with a slap. Then, as our car seemed to move through traffic, my knees were struck with the pistol butt to make me pull them down beneath the level of the window.

But as my kidnapper scrabbled for the money he had given me a brief glimpse of his face. I was too frightened to look at him calmly with a view to recall but something remained lodged in my memory all the same.

CHAPTER 2

War

I N MAY 1982 the eyes of the world were fixed on events taking place at one of the most remote and obscure points on the planet. So little-known were the Falkland Islands that some of the British servicemen hastily dispatched there had initially believed that they were being sent to islands north of Scotland rather than to the middle of the South Atlantic. Even the then Defence Secretary, Sir John Nott and the Chief of the General Staff, Lord Bramall, later confessed to similar ignorance when they both told a seminar in June 2002 that at the outset they had had no clear idea of exactly where the islands lay.[1]

In my case, though claiming no greater knowledge, I was at least in the right continent when the crisis erupted in late March. Together with a crew from Thames Television's current affairs programme *TV Eye* I was filming a report on the elections in war-torn El Salvador, the second time I had been sent to that beautiful, unfortunate land on the north-west coast of Latin America. Our team included cameraman Ted Adcock, a dashing figure and winner of awards for his work, soundman Trefor Hunter, quiet, reserved and highly professional, and our producer, Norman Fenton, a canny, bearded, Scots-accented veteran of the television industry. Together we filmed blown bridges and murder victims lying in the street and took cover as an election office came under fire. Then came a telephone call from our Editor in London.

Mike Townson was a man possessed of a curious charisma with his stocky, overweight frame and heavy lips. He had always reminded me of a tribal chieftain making his dispositions from the substantial chair behind his desk. Now his instructions were brisk and to the point. Some Argentines had landed on a British-owned island called South Georgia. It was becoming an international crisis. We should leave El Salvador immediately and head for Buenos Aires. 'Try to keep out of trouble,' he said helpfully.

We had no idea how British journalists would be received in Argentina and it was agreed that our team would split up and make our way there by different air routes, in my case via Miami and Santiago in Chile. In fact, even though our journey took place just as Argentine troops were landing on the Falkland Islands, we experienced no difficulty with passport control or customs in Buenos Aires and were soon reunited. Following journalistic instinct, we quickly boarded yet another aircraft and flew to Comodoro Rivadavia, a southern oil town in Argentina's tapering cone that ends near Antarctica and one of the key locations from which the invasion of the Falklands was being staged. There we had our first brush with the reality of trying to cover events in a country with which Britain was now effectively at war.

Within a few minutes of our arrival in the somewhat barren settlement, we were arrested by secret policemen dressed in plain clothes and equipped with pistols and walkie-talkies. They told us that Comodoro Rivadavia was now a military zone and escorted us to a local hotel where, as soon as we checked in, all the telephones were cut off to prevent us making outside calls. We were then told that we must leave the area by 10am the following day. Early next morning, in our desire to get at least a few images from the trip, we attempted to film a view of the ocean, looking in what we imagined was the direction of the Falkland Islands, and were immediately arrested by armed soldiers. Fortunately they were appeased by our promise to leave the town and we were permitted to return to the local airport, where we saw exactly why security was on such high alert. The runway was now lined with troops with their packs and rifles waiting to board C-130 transport aircraft for their flight to the Falklands. It was visual evidence that the Argentine Junta had no intention of backing down and was instead doubling up on its bet of seizing the islands.

We were able to fly back to Buenos Aires and in retrospect had been extremely fortunate. A few days later, three other British journalists, Simon Winchester of *The Sunday Times* and Ian Mather and Tony Prime of *The Observer*, ventured even further south and were also arrested. However, they were charged with espionage and spent the next twelve weeks as the war was fought sharing a cell in an unattractive Argentine prison which also housed thieves and murderers. It has occurred to me to wonder whether the relative ease of our own return to the capital produced in my case a certain over-confidence that contributed to our later near-disaster.

With the clarity of hindsight we were dangerously naive. Reporting on a war from the enemy's capital held obvious perils, but even as the British task force assembled and set out we were among those prey to the widespread belief that this confrontation would end without serious bloodshed. Our first days in Buenos Aires only served to strengthen the sense of unreality.

Even as the crisis gathered pace the Argentine capital remained a captivating city which symbolised the country's extraordinary history: the elegant centre with its fine French-style neo-classical buildings, punctuated by florid Art Nouveau masterpieces, all products of the astonishing building boom between 1880 and 1920 when Buenos Aires was one of the fastest-growing cities in the world and Argentina, fuelled by its vast agricultural hinterland, seemed destined to become one of the world's richest countries.

It was a land originally seized by Spanish soldiers and fortune-hunters who had exterminated or driven out most of its indigenous Amerindians – now just 2% of the population – and was then filled by waves of European immigrants ranging from Italian slum-dwellers to English landowners, Russians trying to escape Tsarism or revolution and yet more Spaniards, often peasants from Galicia or the Basque country. There were also Japanese hungry for opportunity who set up their own Spanish-speaking tribe. In similar fashion to the United States, this was a country built by tough-minded incomers and indeed the sheer volume of immigration was second only to the US. The resulting architectural styles of Buenos Aires reflect the utopian ambitions of the designers as well as their foreign heritage, and speak more to aspiration than to a reality in which boom was regularly followed by crushing economic bust. On Avenida Rivadavia, named after the first President of Argentina, we saw the two splendid Gaudí-influenced masterpieces: the Palace of the Lilies and the other fine building next door, which bears on its façade a legend reading, 'There are no impossible dreams'. But in the outlying areas beyond the centre, the miles of often crudely built housing and commercial blocks testified to the struggles and disappointments of what was painfully becoming a Latin American megapolis.

In May 1982, as the British task force sailed towards the Falklands – or as Argentines call them Las Malvinas, using the name given to them by French explorers who were in fact the first to settle the islands – many in Buenos Aires found themselves dreaming of national fulfilment. Raising the Argentine flag over those windswept outcrops would finally transcend dictatorship, terrorism and the never-ending economic crisis in which inflation had reached 150% and the peso was almost valueless. There was intoxicating drama in the rallies in front of the Presidential Palace, the Casa Rosada or Pink House, known in the Anglophone community as the Pink Palace, where General Leopoldo Galtieri, leader of the military Junta who had ordered the seizure of the islands after only four months in power, appeared on a balcony in the style of Argentina's earlier cele-brated leader Juan Perón and delivered a nationalist clarion call to a vast, excited crowd. In the streets were columns of cars with driv-ers flying the Argentine flag and sounding their horns, and all over the city an excited buzz fed off the newspaper headlines announc-ing Argentina's preparations for air and naval war and the certainty of their victory. I was welcomed to the offices of the leading news-paper *Clarín* by its Foreign Editor Roberto Guareschi, as the paper's journalists pounded the metal typewriters of that era to produce yet more optimistic copy. In remarks that were typical of the coun-try's mood but seem tragically out of touch in the light of events, Guareschi told me that Margaret Thatcher and the British govern-ment appeared confused: 'They don't know whether to use force or not. First they say they might use it. Then they say they wouldn't use it. I guess that all this is only to be tough before negotiations ...'

Like many Argentines Mr Guareschi had convinced himself that Mrs Thatcher would negotiate a settlement: 'I don't give much importance to the public British proposals,' he told me. 'I guess that in the end at the negotiation table the proposals will be more realistic.'

Argentines with an interest in history like our excellent inter-preter/researcher Eduardo harked back to another war in the early

1800s between British troops and the Spanish colony that is now Argentina, a war that is completely forgotten in Britain but is taught religiously to every Argentinian schoolchild. Two successive attacks were launched by a British force that had been granted extraordinary freedom of action by London. In the spirit of those times it was an openly piratical mission seeking commercial control not of a few remote islands but of the increasingly prosperous area around the River Plate and the growing hub of Buenos Aires itself. The assault was driven on by reports that a large shipment of Peruvian silver had just arrived in the town but, contrary to the expectations of the operation's commanders who had hoped to enrich themselves with prize money and had even reached agreement on how to divide it, they met with fierce resistance from local militias and, in the end, suffered a crushing defeat. 'People here are not that soft, effeminate race they are in old Spain,' a British officer said ruefully. 'On the contrary they are ferocious.'[2]

Now hailed in Argentina as a landmark victory, the war with Britain opened the way for the country to declare independence from Spain nine years later in 1816.

In 1833 Britain successfully asserted her naval power by seizing full control of the Falkland Islands, where the British had first landed more than 100 years earlier, and removing some of the small number of Argentinians who had settled there. For the now-powerful British Empire this was little more than a geopolitical footnote that scarcely registered in the public's consciousness, but for the new nation of Argentina it became a running sore. Economic relations between Britain and Argentina grew and prospered, with Britain for many years effectively controlling the Argentine economy, but Argentines continued to hark back to their first triumphs over the redcoats. The bodies of several hundred British soldiers, mostly

Scottish Highlanders, are said to be buried under Avenida Belgrano in central Buenos Aires and the colours of the British 71st Regiment of Foot, together with two Royal Navy banners, are still held at the Santo Domingo convent. In 1982 the lesson that many Argentines drew from this was that victory over Margaret Thatcher's task force, however well-equipped and heavily armed, was possible.

Lucia Galtieri, the wife of the dictator, attended prayers at a church which was a bastion of resistance to the British Army in 1806. Afterwards she told us of the emotional attachment Argentinians felt for the islands: 'The Malvinas are not just a myth. They are a longing, a desire ... Everybody in Argentina agrees that the Malvinas should again become part of our national patrimony.'

'Las Malvinas son argentinas' were the words on every lip and, a little surprisingly, they were often accompanied by smiles of welcome when we identified ourselves as British journalists seeking to report their views of the war.

Above all the city itself still had the energy for which Buenos Aires was famous. This, as any Argentine would tell you, was the country that had produced Formula One's greatest racing driver in Juan Manuel Fangio, five times world champion in the tournament's first decade, as well as footballers who had won the World Cup and dazzled soccer fans everywhere, a country which each year on December 11th celebrates a national day of Tango. At the end of April 1982, cafes were packed and restaurants full of people feasting on the country's legendarily massive and surprisingly tender steaks washed down by flagons of hearty red wine, an elixir which for many bred ebullient optimism. The military men we were able to interview were more restrained in their assessments but absolutely uncompromising in the message they wished to convey. Admiral Jorge Fraga, a cheerful balding expert in sea warfare from the Argentine Naval

College, claimed to be heartened by the relatively small size of the British task force, which included fewer than 5,000 combat troops in defiance of the traditional military formula, which would give the Argentine soldiers now entrenched in the Falklands a key strategic advantage. His thinking clearly reflected the beliefs of the military Junta which he served: 'You know that invasion needs seven soldiers attacking for each one defending, so I think that to have success the British will need about 40,000 soldiers. If not they will lose men and ships and maybe suffer disaster.'

I then asked him a question which seemed obvious even before the events that followed. Could the result in fact be a disaster for the Argentine Navy? I received a chilling reply: 'Maybe our Navy too,' he said, 'but our objective is to stay in the islands and we are going to stay.'

Prayers and rhetoric were soon to be replaced by the frightening drumbeat of war. On May 1st a giant RAF Vulcan bomber, flying at extreme long range from Ascension Island with the help of repeated air-to-air refuelling, struck Port Stanley airfield and cratered the runway with one of its 1,000lb bombs. This was followed by another raid on the airfield by Royal Navy Sea Harriers. Hours later, Argentinian Air Force jets attacked the Royal Navy task force, causing limited damage to two British ships. Twenty-four hours after that, the Royal Navy struck in clinical and devastating fashion. The antiquated Argentine cruiser *General Belgrano* was torpedoed and sent to the bottom by the British nuclear submarine HMS *Conqueror* with the loss of 323 lives.

Britain's sinking of the *Belgrano* has been hotly debated, a debate which continues to this day. Was the out-of-date warship – which as the USS *Phoenix* had survived the Japanese attack on Pearl Harbor and then served in the Pacific theatre throughout the Second World

War before being sold to Argentina – sailing towards the British task force or away from it? Did it constitute a threat that required a British nuclear submarine to fire torpedoes which blew a massive hole in the side and cut the warship's electrical power supply, making any attempt to pump out the millions of gallons of onrushing seawater impossible? Was it significant that the *Belgrano* was outside the naval exclusion zone which Britain had declared, in light of London's warning that even ships outside it could be attacked? Was this a British war crime or was the Argentine Admiral Juan Lombardo, the Commander of the South Atlantic theatre of operations, who the day before had ordered all naval forces to attack the British, guilty of sending hundreds of his seamen to their deaths through a naive underestimation of the Royal Navy's strength? How much weight should be given to the statement by the *Belgrano*'s commander, Captain Hector Bonzo, who said in a later interview, 'It was absolutely not a war crime. It was an act of war, lamentably legal'?[3]

I do not intend to contribute to this argument, which reached a bitter climax when Mrs Thatcher's husband Denis accused BBC producers of being 'Trots' and 'wooftahs' after they broadcast a celebrated television confrontation between the Prime Minister and a critical and well-informed member of the public a year after the sinking. What I can personally testify to is the surge of shock and grief which ran through Buenos Aires when reports of the sinking were confirmed after being initially denounced as 'lies' by the Junta. At our hotel young women, who normally worked there cheerfully, appeared close to tears. It took almost 48 hours for what had happened to become clear, hours in which men struggled and drowned or froze to death in the chill waters of the South Atlantic, hours in which a terrible pall of sorrow and growing apprehension hung over the city.

On May 4th the Argentine government issued a statement on the sinking:

At 17 hours on 2 May, the cruiser ARA *General Belgrano* was attacked and sunk by a British submarine in a point at 55° 24' south latitude and 61° 32' west longitude. There are 1,042 men aboard the ship. Rescue operations for survivors are being carried out ...

That such an attack is a treacherous act of armed aggression perpetrated by the British government in violation of the UN Charter and the ceasefire ordered by United Nations Security Council Resolution 502 ...

That in the face of this new attack, Argentina reiterates to the national and global public its adherence to the ceasefire mandated by the Security Council in the mentioned resolution.

In fact diplomacy was already failing with the unsuccessful visit and brusque departure of the US Secretary of State Alexander Haig and it rapidly became clear that what the Junta meant by adherence to a ceasefire was, in reality, bloody retaliation. Even as the government's statement was distributed to journalists a pair of Argentina's most advanced aircraft, the French-built Super Étendards, headed for the British task force carrying two of the country's small stock of five lethal missiles, the name of which soon entered the English lexicon, the Exocet. As one of the pilots popped up from sea-skimming level to fix the target, the ship he locked on to was the destroyer HMS *Sheffield*. The results shocked Britain and the world. Twenty Royal Navy sailors died and the ship, which had cost £25 million in 1971, was wrecked and then lost when it sank while under tow.

In Buenos Aires a jubilant Junta turned on the printing presses to rush out thousands of copies of a poster to rally the nation. It showed a Union Jack riddled with bullet holes and the legend, 'Fight to the Death'. The glamorous Argentine news presenter, Magdalena Ruiz Guiñazú, told me of her sorrow at the growing number of dead and injured but said, 'We are at the point of no return.' The Junta's official spokesman Colonel Bernardo Menéndez told me with jutting jaw that sovereignty over the islands 'No es negociable' – it is non-negotiable.

The pugnacity of the Argentine Junta surprised many who did not know the recent history of the country. These were men who had been at war in a savage but little reported conflict for more than seven years and already had much blood on their hands. The Generals and senior officers were men who had ordered the torture and often the murder of leftist subversives whom they had kidnapped on the street or dragged from their homes. It was a 'Dirty War' against many of their own people, a war that they regarded as a holy struggle against Marxist terrorism and which had extended into brutal suppression of all and every vestige of opposition in Argentina, be it in the form of terrorist gunmen, the leaders of organised labour, or intellectuals, many suspect in the eyes of the military for being Jewish, who advocated an alternative vision for the country's future. Their victories against these opponents had bred hubris, with some in the Junta's leadership claiming that they had won the first battle of the Third World War.

The terrorism they had set out to suppress was real enough. It was fuelled by repeated economic crises, with money rendered almost worthless by inflation rates of 500–600%. This gave the terrorists relevance as they evolved into a peculiarly Argentine breed inspired, it was said, by the writings of the Marxist philosopher Frantz Fanon, who had delivered his infamous eulogy of terrorism: 'Violence frees the [individual] from his inferiority complex and makes him fearless and releases his self-respect. Terrorism is an act of growing up.' The fact that Che Guevara was by origin an Argentine added some glamour to the cause.

In the early 1970s Argentina was plunged into a dark tunnel of violent lawlessness. One of the key landmarks on the road to full-scale repression had been the shocking murder in 1974, when the elected civilian government of Isabel Perón was still in power, of Argentina's police chief Alberto Villar and his wife Elsa, killed by a bomb hidden aboard the cabin cruiser they used at weekends on the River Plate. Responsibility was claimed by the Montoneros, a left-wing group which proclaimed its allegiance to the now-dead dictator Juan Perón who had mobilised and motivated the working classes, but which was in fact one of the Marxist revolutionary groups surging throughout the Latin American continent, financing itself through highly lucrative acts of kidnapping and extortion. The police chief was known for carrying his own hand grenades on a belt around his waist but they were of little use on this occasion. The powerful explosion lifted the cabin cruiser 30 feet in the air and the bodies of Villar and his wife were found floating in the river.

Operating in parallel and occasional competition was the People's Revolutionary Army or ERP, a smaller but well-organised Trotskyite group that believed in the propaganda of the deed. At an early stage they had tried to ignite a classic guerrilla war in the rural province of Tucumán in the north-west of the country but found themselves unable to match the Army's firepower and resorted to urban terrorism. Their attacks on the regime were fewer in number than those of the Montoneros but no less spectacular. They included a well-planned attempt in 1977 to assassinate the Junta's then leader,

President Jorge Videla, by placing a powerful remote-controlled bomb in a culvert beneath the runway of the Buenos Aires municipal airport, shortly before an aircraft carrying the President and high-ranking officials took off. The attack only succeeded in damaging the runway. According to the US Defense Intelligence Agency it was a 'near miss'.[4] The same DIA document suggests that together the ERP and the Montoneros carried out well over 1,000 terrorist attacks between 1974 and 1979.

General Jorge Videla had seized power in 1976 in the sixth military coup which Argentina had experienced since 1930. A three-man Junta made up of the heads of the Army, Navy and Air Force installed themselves, promising to restore stability. Videla had already made their intentions clear in a speech to the Conference of American Armies in the Chilean capital of Montevideo the year before. He said: 'As many people will die in Argentina as is necessary to achieve order.'[5]

Once in power, Videla had tried to cultivate the image of a humble man who could save the country. But while the new military leaders sought at first to present an apparently reasonable image to the outside world, their security forces stepped up the already brutal campaign against the insurgent threat. Argentina's still functioning judicial system and conventional police forces were brushed aside in favour of special units using the crude tools of kidnapping, torture and murder. With an ideology embracing fierce nationalism extending at times into fascism and a fervent Catholic faith, the armed forces had always considered themselves the guardians of the Argentine flame. Now they set up what can only be described as a killing machine which dealt with its victims with frightening efficiency, turning them into a legion of the 'disappeared'. It was a ruthless struggle in which a particularly murderous branch of the security forces was led by a violent career criminal who had earlier carried out one of the most spectacular bank robberies in Argentina's history and who joined the secret police directly from prison. He had been given the power of life and death over the perceived opponents of the Junta and it was he that we would encounter in that square in Buenos Aires.

The progress from anti-terrorist operations to systematic secret slaughter was chronicled by a few brave journalists such as Robert Cox, the Editor of the English-language *Buenos Aires Herald* (now sadly defunct). Cox, who had settled in and loved Argentina, felt he had to leave the country in 1979 to save his life. The 'Dirty War' was also brought to international attention by the growing number of mothers of the young men and women who for whatever reason had been targeted as suspect and vanished into the maw of the machine and who now demonstrated every week, becoming known as the Mothers of the Plaza de Mayo, after the square in front of the Presidential Palace where they gathered.

The bloodshed was also systematically recorded by operatives of the Central Intelligence Agency (CIA) reporting to Langley, Virginia from their offices at the US Embassy in Buenos Aires. Hundreds of their reports, including some dealing with our case, have now been released by the US government. The revelations they contain are at the heart of this book and what they make clear is that the CIA was extraordinarily well informed and able to follow the Dirty War on a virtually daily basis as the number of killings steadily mounted.

The many events covered in this secret reporting included ghastly actions by the security forces near the small town of Pilar, a place with which we would soon become acquainted in terrifying circumstances. Pilar had become a macabre landmark, following the discovery soon after the Junta came to power of 30 mangled corpses in a field nearby. Twenty of the victims were male, ten female and the bodies had been blown up with dynamite, leaving them almost beyond recognition, but it turned out that the dead were Montonero suspects who had been in police detention. They had apparently been killed by the security forces in reprisal for the murder of retired General Omar Actis, who had been appointed head of the committee organising the forthcoming football World Cup. The CIA stated that the killers, who on this occasion came from 'operating levels of the Argentine Federal Police', apparently believed that 'the public display of the thirty bodies in response to the killing of General Actis would cause the ERP and Montoneros to reassess the advisability of engaging in further terrorist actions in the near future.'[6]

The CIA report also described the reaction of the new President, General Videla:

> President Jorge Videla is annoyed that the bodies were left so prominently displayed and has ordered that this not occur in the future. Videla considers that such a type of situation reflects adversely on the good name of Argentina both within and outside the country. Videla's objection is not that the thirty people, who were purportedly involved with the Montoneros, were killed, but that the bodies appeared publicly.

As the Dirty War progressed, many other security forces operations remained horrifyingly brazen. The released American documents include a graphic description of the kidnapping of several members of the Mothers of the Plaza de Mayo and two of their supporters, French nuns named Alice Domon and Léonie Duquet.

> On Saturday 10th [December 1977] ... Mrs Devisente was picked up a block from her house at 8.30 in the morning and thrown

into a Ford Falcon kicking and screaming. Later in the same morning a French sister accompanied two gentlemen from her house and drove away with them.[7]

These abductions caused diplomatic protests from both the French government and the Vatican. The Argentine security services then arranged to supply the local press with photographs supposedly showing the two nuns in the hands of Montonero terrorists, although these were widely dismissed as fake. The US Embassy carried out its own investigation and Ambassador Raul Castro finally sent his report to Washington:

> A source informs the Embassy that the nuns were abducted by Argentine security agents and at some point were transferred to a prison located in the town of Junín which is about 150 miles west of Buenos Aires.
>
> Embassy also has confidential information obtained through an Argentine government source (protect) that seven bodies were discovered some weeks ago on the Atlantic beach near Mar del Plata. According to this source, the bodies were those of the two nuns and five mothers who disappeared between December 8 and December 10, 1977. Our source confirmed that these individuals were originally sequestered by members of the security forces acting under their broad mandate against terrorists and subversives.[8]

It was clear that, in spite of the professed Catholicism of the regime and its operatives, religion and even the Vatican's protests counted for little. In Buenos Aires gunmen targeted St Patrick's church after a young priest, Father Alfredo Kelly, had preached about the need for social justice in Argentina. The armed men broke into the parish house where three priests and two seminarians lived. The gunmen made them kneel as if they were praying and shot them dead. A message was daubed in blood on the wall: 'This is what happens to those who poison the minds of our youth.'[9]

Attention focused on Argentina and the horrors taking place there when the country hosted the 1978 football World Cup. But the protests of human-rights groups were brushed aside as the bankrupt nation staged a spectacle which sent soccer-crazy Argentines wild with joy and captivated fans around the world. In front of President Videla and his guest of honour, the former US Secretary of State Henry Kissinger, whose support had long been of immense value to the Junta, Argentina triumphed in the final against Holland with Mario Kempes, 'the Matador', scoring two of Argentina's three goals. Meanwhile, outside the stadium, the number of victims continued to mount. The Junta finally admitted that 6,500 people were 'missing' in its war. Amnesty International put the true figure at that stage at more than 25,000.

By the turn of the decade the military were claiming victory over the terrorist groups and the numbers of 'disappearances' declined. But the Junta made no move to restore democracy. It was determined to hold on to power and knew no other way than the use of its secret police to suppress opposition. Even as General Galtieri sent troops to the Falklands and sought to motivate the nation for confrontation with Britain, teams of 'dirty warriors' continued their work at home. We had a glimpse of their operations at a Peronist labour demonstration which, unusually, had been permitted by the regime in order to express support for its 'Malvinas' campaign. In a square in the capital, several hundred people waved placards and chanted anti-British slogans as they laid wreaths at

a monument to workers' rights. On the fringes of the demonstration we saw a number of men dressed in suits sitting in several
of the signature grey Ford Falcon cars. As it ended they got out
and with cool self-assurance collected up a selection of the placards and leaflets that had been distributed among the crowd and
wrote down the names of people who had signed the commemora-
tive wreaths. Perhaps unwisely, we filmed them going about their
business and then a short time later went to the scene of the latest
known 'disappearance' where, in a rundown street on the outskirts
of the city, a young leftist called Anna Maria, pregnant with her
soon-to-be-born child, had been kidnapped a few weeks before.
Eight days after the kidnapping her body had been found nearby
with two bullet wounds, one in the head, the other in the stomach.
We filmed the location unaware as we did so that, according to the
now-released CIA documents, we ourselves were under surveillance by the secret police.

We had already met the man who was officially in command
of much of Argentina's security apparatus, the Interior Minister,
General Alfredo Saint-Jean. Unlike the famously bad-tempered
Foreign Minister the grey-haired Saint-Jean was calm, almost
avuncular, as he welcomed us in front of a large oil painting which
adorned the wall of his office. A broad panorama, it showed uniformed sabre-wielding Argentine cavalry riding down fleeing
Amerindians on one of the country's vast open plains. The Minister
explained with some satisfaction how the indigenous populations
had been dealt with – leading, he claimed, to the establishment of
a coherent European-based society without ethnic discord. He then
turned to the crisis with Britain.

'We are a peace-loving nation,' he told me without a hint of
irony, 'But don't misunderstand me. Argentinians will not renounce

their rights to the islands. Argentina will negotiate but only as far as dignity will allow.'

Off-camera the Minister responded to our concerns about our own safety. He assured us that we were welcome in Argentina and that no one would interfere with our work. 'If you have any difficulties, telephone me here at the Ministry,' he said, writing down his direct number on a piece of paper.

But at that moment it was the Minister's repeated use of the word dignity that resonated and seemed a key to understanding the dictatorship's behaviour in this crisis.

With Argentinian troops preparing to defend their positions on the islands against what now seemed to be an inevitable British assault, defence of the nation's dignity depended heavily on the pilots of the country's motley collection of combat aircraft, organised in Air Force and Naval squadrons who alone could now challenge Britain's supremacy at sea. These were the men that the Junta celebrated as its noblest fighters and they were to show the world another side of the uniquely contradictory Argentinian character, combining both the potential for savage brutality with a belief in courage and chivalry. Untried in aerial combat, they were to display bravery and skill that even the British task force commander, Admiral Sir John 'Sandy' Woodward, would acknowledge. 'We felt a great admiration for what they did,' he would later say.

On May 12th, almost 500 miles from the capital of the Falklands, Port Stanley, at the Argentine Air Force base at Río Gallegos near the windswept southern tip of the country, where bleak open spaces meet treeless horizons under grey leaden skies, ground crews were preparing eight jets for an attack on the British fleet. The planes were American-made Douglas A-4 Skyhawks, a design from the 1950s which had played an important role in the Vietnam War and in the Middle East, but was now becoming dated. Unable to carry any of Argentina's small stock of Exocet missiles, each Skyhawk was loaded with 500lb or 1,000lb unguided 'iron' bombs, Second World War vintage weapons which had to be released at close range and would depend for success on the pilot's bravery, skill and luck. Some of the aircraft were also in poor condition with their ejector seats known to be unreliable.

First Lieutenant Fausto Gavazzi, recently married, was one of eight pilots suiting up for what some of his fellow officers believed would prove to be a suicide mission. In a chilling dress rehearsal hastily arranged as the British task force assembled, Gavazzi's squadron had taken part in mock attacks on one of the two Type 42 destroyers that Britain had sold to the Argentine Navy in the 1970s. These ships, designed for an air-defence role, had recently been refitted with Seacat anti-aircraft missiles similar to those carried by the Royal Navy, and a series of low-level simulated bomb runs had shown the Skyhawks being repeatedly shot down by the system. However, in the attacks on May 1st Argentinian Dagger aircraft, originally Mirage V jets designed in France and assembled and sold to Argentina by Israel, had carried out low-level attacks on British ships. The bombs had missed and only inflicted limited damage and one of the Daggers had been shot down by a Harrier. However, the fact that they had got through to their targets had encouraged Argentine commanders to order major attacks by the Skyhawk pilots.

On May 12th the plan was simple in conception but difficult and perilous to execute. After take-off the heavily laden Skyhawks would extend their range by refuelling from one of Argentina's two US-built KC-130 airborne tankers and then fly at sea-skimming level to find the British fleet. Though the weather was fine the pilots were to some extent flying in the dark. Without reliable long-range aerial reconnaissance they had only a general idea of where the British warships were. Radio messages from their troops in the Falklands, reporting that the British were now shelling them with their naval guns, suggested that there were ships quite close to the shore. The mission was to release their bombs at the closest range they could manage and then speed away at the lowest possible altitude before British missiles and guns could lock on and destroy them.

On that day the word *dignidad* – dignity – was undoubtedly a powerful motivator for the men flying the Skyhawks but for me, lying in the footwell of the Ford Falcon with a cloth over my eyes and a gun to my head, I must admit that it was not the most urgent thought in my mind.

CHAPTER 3

End of the Road

I HAD ALMOST got used to the steady motion of the vehicle and my cramped position in it when it came to a sudden halt. We were in some sort of lay-by and to my surprise Trefor, our sound record-ist, was pushed into the car. We were made to sit next to each other on the back seat and told to be silent and keep our eyes closed. We drove on into the countryside for what seemed an eternity. Then on what appeared to be a dirt track the car stopped again. Brusquely we were shoved out and saw other cars with more gunmen, who were guarding Ted, our cameraman. Of Norman there was no sign. Disconcertingly, Ted was taking off his clothes.

The sinister convoy had halted on the corner of a vast field stretching away into the distance. I saw the courage which my two colleagues were showing and tried to take heart from it.

The three of us could say no more than a word of recognition before being told to shut up. Trefor and I were instructed in bro-ken English to turn away from the gunmen, empty our pockets of our possessions and take off our clothes – though, strangely, not our underpants. I was asked some questions about the contents of my notebook but I don't know if I gave any coherent replies. The three of us stood cold, almost naked and virtually numb with fear while the commander's radio crackled sporadically behind us. I was in no condition to understand fully what our kidnappers were saying or doing but it seemed that they intended to kill us. In the words of Ted Adcock: 'They brought out a rifle and they pointed at it, and they said to walk down the road. One had to turn one's back on the rifle and walk away from it and I guess that's quite scary. It was tough.'

We walked slowly and silently, three abreast, away from the gunmen. Trefor was next to me and I found myself holding his hand. Behind us I heard the unmistakable double-click from the loading mechanism of the rifle, a sound that I had heard often enough in Vietnam. There was no way to run and nowhere to hide. At any second the bullets would hit us and the light of life would go out. In a recent conversation to assist in the preparation of this book, Ted kindly shared his memories with me. 'I was praying that they would shoot me first,' he now says. 'That way I wouldn't know it was happening.'

Then there was a sound. It was not the crash of a rifle or the crack of a pistol. It was the sputtering of a car engine starting up, then another, then a third. Wheels crunched on soil but we stood still, looking away, not daring to turn round. When we did, we were alone.

Instead of lying in pools of blood after the sort of execution that had taken place so often in Argentina, we were standing near-naked in a field, in the middle of a country at war with Britain.

As Trefor put it in his characteristically understated fashion: 'There were a few sighs of relief when they drove away.'

I think all three of us felt the same elation of survival. As emotion surged we grinned and laughed and felt what can only be described as joy.

Those moments have come back to me many times since: the sheer terror, the happiness of survival and the ultimate absurdity of our situation.

In a nearby unattended farm building, we found empty fertiliser sacks to wrap around our waists, but these did little to improve our appearance and our plight seemed to frighten the farmers who drove up in a pick-up truck not long afterwards.

One, however, seemed more amused than concerned. 'Today my birthday,' he announced in surprisingly good English, 'I didn't think I get three naked Englishmen.' He drove us to the nearest town which was called Pilar, though at the time the name meant nothing to us, and took us first to an Army base where the troops made it clear that they wanted nothing to do with us. The helpful farmer then dropped us at the local police station. There, still uncomfortably half-naked, I sat in a plastic chair in front of the young commander and attempted to explain how we had arrived in his office. It was evident that insofar as he understood my fragmentary Spanish he didn't believe a word of it.

The police commander developed his own theory: Argentina was at war with Britain. Plainly we were from the British military and were part of a Special Forces operation that had gone wrong. Our nakedness, though puzzling, was doubtless just another British ruse. Our physical condition was surprisingly poor for members of a commando unit – with the best will in the world none of our team could be said to have resembled an elite paratrooper – but perhaps Britain was scraping the bottom of the barrel.

'*Periodistas*' (journalists), I told him repeatedly, '*secuestro*' (kidnap). I begged him to lift the telephone which sat on his desk in front of him and call the Interior Minister, General Alfredo Saint-Jean, who would vouch for us. After what seemed an eternity of futile exchanges the commander dialled a number, said something to whomever answered the phone and sat back with a disbelieving expression on his face.

Twice in my career I saw someone salute a telephone. The other occasion was in Soviet-era Moscow where in the middle of an interview with a senior official at the Ministry of Defence a large old-fashioned telephone without a dial suddenly rang on his desk. This was the fabled *vertushka*, through which instructions to the upper echelons were issued on a downward-only basis and the caller in this case could only be the Minister of Defence himself. The official stood, took the receiver in his left hand and, disregarding our presence, saluted with his right while listening intently to what was said.

On this occasion in the small town of Pilar, the police commander's behaviour indicated that he had got through to the man at the top. He suddenly stood to attention bolt upright, saluting, and said repeatedly, 'Yes, my General. Yes, my General. It will be done.' It turned out that the Interior Minister was already aware of our disappearance, having been alerted by our producer Norman Fenton who, aided by his remarkable sixth sense, which we had frequently discussed in the past, had evaded the kidnapping and managed to contact the Minister, who had apparently reacted to the news with fury and now issued his instructions. In the Pilar police station officers who had been sullen suddenly fell over themselves to make us more comfortable. Military-style fatigues were produced to cover our nakedness and hot drinks were prepared as the atmosphere turned to bonhomie.

'The Minister is sending his own car,' the Commander assured me, 'It will be here soon.'

A very large limousine accompanied by six motorcycle outriders duly arrived an hour later and we began the journey back to Buenos

Aires in splendid fashion. What we did not know as we reclined in the comfortable vehicle driving us back through the fields around Pilar was that this was an infamous location, where the security services continued to leave numbers of their victims in the Dirty War. It seemed that the convenience of proximity to the capital and speedy access down the Pan-American Highway made this a practical dumping ground – something our kidnappers had seemed to know well. Our case was unusual in that we were still alive.

In our reports from Buenos Aires we had already described the fears spreading in the sizeable British community in Argentina as the war turned hot. David Huntley, married to an Argentine and father of two children, was not one of the wealthy Anglo elite but a hotel worker earning the equivalent of £40 a week. He told me of whispered insults from fellow workers and of his fears every time he boarded a bus. He said that he and his family would leave the country if they could, but lacked the means to do so.

David's fears were not irrational. Just how dangerous and unpredictable the situation in Buenos Aires had become, and how lucky we were on May 12th, has become clear in previously secret CIA documents now released by the US government and which I have examined in detail. Until their disclosure, there were few clues as to what was taking place in the complex world of Argentina's spies and executioners as the conflict with Britain intensified.

What we now know from the American documents is how Argentina's secret world was organised and some of the murderous plans it had drawn up in the event of full-scale war with Britain. The CIA analysts identified the key department responsible for black operations as the 601st Intelligence Battalion of the Argentine Army. This special unit, whose activities were shrouded in secrecy and widespread fear, had been for years at the centre of the Dirty War, collecting information on opposition groups and employing death squads to eliminate them. The battalion had already been repeatedly highlighted in secret American reports as a key component in the Junta's torture and killing machine. A diagram of its structure drawn up by the CIA[1] shows that in 1982 it consisted of eight task forces, each responsible for individual terrorist groups such as the ERP or Montoneros, others handling 'Labour, students and religious activities', 'political parties' and 'exterior activities' which apparently meant foreign operations and control of foreigners in Argentina. A defined chain of command led through the Army's G2 intelligence section all the way to General Galtieri himself. However, the question posed by our kidnapping and other events was how much real control the General was able to exercise, and what view he took of the deadly plans designed by his subordinates as the British task force set sail for the Falklands. It has taken almost 40 years for the details to be revealed in a now-declassified report to Washington from the CIA station in Buenos Aires. According to the American intelligence officers, the 601st was readying itself to murder some 500 British residents in Argentina.

The key document is a CIA report dated Monday April 12th, 1982, the day that Britain imposed a 200-mile maritime exclusion zone around the Falklands and one month before our kidnapping. In it, a CIA operative who appeared to be receiving information from a well-placed source inside the Argentinian military reported on actions taken the previous evening by the 601st Intelligence Battalion.

Headlined 'Contingency Plans For Violence Against US and British Citizens', the CIA report gave specific details of what it said were the Intelligence Battalion's plans and actions it had already taken: '[O]n the early evening of 11th April teams from the 601st Battalion were moving into position to be ready to take immediate action to "disappear" 500 British subjects in Argentina as soon as hostilities begin ...'

The report explains that, 'In the terminology used by the 601st Battalion, "disappeared" does not mean put in jail ... disappeared probably means killed.' It says that detailed plans had been made to blame the attacks on left-wing Montonero terrorists, something which the Battalion had frequently done in the past during the Dirty War.

The report also outlines 'contingency plans' by the operational arm of the Army Intelligence Service to 'disappear' US citizens in Argentina 'if the US Government adopts the British position in regard to the dispute in the Falkland Islands.'[2]

In fact, by May 12th war had begun, the US government was making its position in support of Britain increasingly clear and Congress had adopted Resolution 441, which called for 'the immediate withdrawal of Argentine troops from the islands' and offered unrestricted assistance to Great Britain, but so far the apocalyptic secret plans had not been carried out. Instead we had been kidnapped, terrorised, humiliated but, at the last moment, spared. In another incident a US journalist had also been seized, in his case beaten up, but also left alive.[3]

Even then it was evident that what had happened to us stemmed from the extraordinary tensions and confusion that the Argentine Junta was suffering at a crucial moment as it became increasingly apparent that Britain was not going to back down and that its act of seizing the Falklands would almost certainly end in a war for which it was, in reality, unprepared.

A further CIA document reported divisions in the Junta, with senior Air Force officers who were now carrying much of the burden of the war, said to be unhappy with the attack on us.

'Senior levels of the Air Force were deeply disturbed by the temporary kidnapping of foreign journalists in Buenos Aires,' reported the anonymous CIA officer. 'Air Force General Officers knew that the kidnappings were carried out by members of the 601st Intelligence Battalion, the operational arm of the Army Intelligence Service ... Air Force officers privately commented that it appeared as though President Leopoldo [Galtieri] were being undermined by the intelligence apparatus of his own military service by its permitting such unfortunate behaviour at the worst possible moment.'[4]

On the evening of May 12th we were still recovering from that 'unfortunate behaviour'. We had no knowledge of the discord inside the Junta or the diplomatic chess taking place behind the scenes but simply realised that we had been in the hands of Argentina's 'dirty warriors' and had somehow survived the experience. We had not been 'disappeared'. Instead we were alive, heading back into Buenos Aires in a comfortable government limousine with a faultlessly polite driver and wondering what explained our kidnapping, the mock execution and now the VIP treatment. Had we been chosen as a target? Was the intention simply to frighten the foreign press or was it a sign that the military Junta was losing control of the men in its own ranks? Would we be able to continue our coverage of what had become the most important crisis Britain had faced for a generation?

It was not until we reached Buenos Aires that we learned of what was in reality the most important development of the day. The liner *QE2*, hastily converted from luxury passenger vessel to troopship, had set sail from Southampton in front of crowds waving handkerchiefs and Union Jacks. Manned by a volunteer crew, it carried a further brigade of 3,000 British soldiers from the Welsh and Scots Guards and the Gurkhas and would now head with some twenty other rapidly commandeered ships for the Falklands to reinforce the task force and enable it to recapture the islands. The task force commander, Admiral 'Sandy' Woodward, would later recall this day as the crucial watershed moment when the wording of his orders from London underwent an all-important change. Where they had read, 'Prepare to land with a view to repossessing the Falklands', they now instructed him simply to 'repossess the Falklands'.

After May 12th, said Woodward, 'we were all pointing in the same direction, we were all agreed where we were going.'[5]

There was no mistaking the orders. The question which still remained was how the Argentine Junta would respond.

CHAPTER 4

Dictator

For a brief moment in Buenos Aires our team of journalists was the story. Bereft of our own equipment which had been taken by the kidnappers, we were besieged by cameras and questions. Watching a surviving video recording of the impromptu press conference as I tried to describe the experience of having a gun held to my head for an hour and fearing that we were about to be murdered still sends a chill down my spine. 'It was the most terrifying experience of my life,' I said without exaggeration. Amid the journalistic hubbub the discomfiture and embarrassment of Junta officials who had been rather belatedly instructed to turn on the charm was plain.

A message arrived from the Foreign Minister, Nicanor Costa Méndez, who had earlier rejected our request for an interview with a display of irritation, waving his hand angrily in my direction. Now his staff said that he would be at our disposal the following morning and indeed, when our meeting eventually took place, the Minister put on one of the most unctuous performances I have ever encountered in a politician, even complimenting me on my interviewing style. 'A very well put question,' he told me at one point with a sly grin. It seemed that the Foreign Minister had grasped that kidnapping and threatening to murder journalists was perhaps not the best way to improve the Junta's image at a moment when Argentina needed all the friends she could get.

The most extraordinary reversal of our fortunes came shortly after our return to the capital when we were informed that we would be received that evening at the Presidential Palace, the Casa Rosada, by President Galtieri himself. This bizarre if journalistically exciting invitation was, it seemed, intended as a dignified form of apology for our treatment lest it become a further impediment to what the Junta clearly still believed were diplomatic efforts to resolve the crisis. What it also appeared to demonstrate, however, was that Galtieri and his advisors could feel the ground moving beneath their feet but had no clear idea of what to do.

It could be argued that Galtieri's behaviour throughout this period was a textbook illustration of the weaknesses of a military dictatorship in confrontation with a historically based parliamentary democracy. Crucial decisions were taken, often with self-defeating speed, by a small, narrow group of men motivated by individual ambition and short-term expediency, based on instinct or prejudice and with very little analysis of the possible difficulties and consequences. Thus Galtieri, who had come to power only four months before in December 1981, took the decision to seize the islands on the basis of a promise made to the head of the Navy, Admiral Jorge Anaya, as a means of winning his support, and as what he saw as a way out of the formidable and growing difficulties confronting his regime. The economy was again in a state of near-collapse with inflation rocketing and the peso once more on the road to worthlessness. The Junta had killed thousands of its own people but it had not succeeded in silencing opposition to its rule, recently expressed in a massive and violent street demonstration in front of the Presidential Palace only days before the Falklands operation was announced. Triggering national fervour about the 'Islas Malvinas' seemed to offer a way forward.

Rational analysis might have suggested that a waiting game would have left Argentina with a far stronger hand. In Britain Margaret Thatcher's government was facing its own considerable economic difficulties and further painful defence cuts were on the cards. The two 'Harrier-carriers', *Hermes* and *Invincible*, which played such a pivotal role in the eventual campaign were due to be decommissioned, *Invincible* sold off to Australia and the 30 year-old *Hermes* scrapped. Without them Britain's operation to recover the islands could not have taken place. On the Argentine side, they were only part way through the acquisition of advanced Super Étendard jets from France. Only five of the air-launched Exocet missiles they would carry had been delivered and their ranging and firing systems had not yet been married to the aircraft by the French technicians whose services were part of the contract and who would be withdrawn as soon as hostilities began. Argentina would later hail as a triumph of their own technical improvisation that their pilots had been able to fire the missiles at all.

In 1982, with the hawkish Republican President Reagan replacing the Democrat President Carter in the White House, Argentina could also hope for improved supplies of vital American weaponry and spare parts after years of arms embargoes applied with President Carter's approval in protest at the Junta's human-rights abuses.

Galtieri's decision to ignore these and other military realities and occupy the islands rested on two core beliefs, both of which turned out to be completely wrong: that Britain was now a declining power and that the United States would be unwilling to alienate the most important Latin American nation, which is how Argentines saw themselves, as well as US allies in the rest of the continent and would therefore, if it did not support him, observe some sort of diplomatic neutrality. Encouraging this belief were the close ties that still existed between the military regime and branches of the US defence establishment which shared similar strongly anti-communist world views.

The British task force commander, Admiral 'Sandy' Woodward, spoke of his surprise on discovering that sympathy for the Junta among senior American military officers extended to NATO's Supreme Allied Commander Atlantic (SACLANT), Admiral Harry Train II. Train explained briskly that Admiral Jorge Anaya, the Junta's most hard-line member and commander of Argentina's Navy, was his son's godfather.[1]

Behind the scenes Argentina had greatly assisted US efforts against left-wing movements in Latin America, in particular the Sandinistas in Nicaragua, where the Argentinian military had provided weapons and advisors to the US-backed Contra rebels and the insurgents in El Salvador. Buenos Aires had also become the headquarters of, and driving force behind Operation Condor, which set out to eliminate leftist 'subversives' throughout the continent. All this had bred beliefs that the American diplomat, Allen 'Tex' Harris, who had a controversial tour as Human Rights Officer at the US Embassy before the Falklands War, had become familiar with in his dealings with the Argentine military:

[T]he Argentine military had all gone to the [US military] schools. They had all been to Fort Benning ... they all had very warm memories of 'my days at Fort Bragg, Tex. Let me tell you how great you guys were and how much fun we had and all the good parties.' There was a lot of goodwill that was built through the hard work of defense relationships, but when these guys were at Fort Bragg and the School of the Americas and all the other things, they were there during the Nixon years or before when anti-communism was key. The senior officers had been there as more junior officers, so their training in the United States was all based on Americans as being great friends and joining us in this very significant movement of anti-communism.[2]

General Galtieri himself had strong US links, having received part of his training at the US Army's School of the Americas in the Panama Canal Zone, which had set him on the path to eventually becoming Argentina's Army commander and a member of the ruling Junta. Before assuming the presidency in December 1981 he visited Washington twice and his reception, which included a meeting with President Reagan, could only have encouraged him to believe that he was among friends and may have bred a fatal over-confidence. American officials described him as a bulwark against communism and Reagan's then National Security Advisor, Richard Allen, called him a 'magnificent general'.[3] It was a somewhat overblown description of a man with a career in military engineering who after his fall from power would be indicted for his part in the murder of some twenty Montoneros seized near the border with Brazil in 'Operación Murciélago' (Operation Bat) in the province of Rosario where he was Army commander. The bodies of the twenty were never recovered but it was alleged that, after being tortured, the prisoners were drugged and thrown from aircraft flying over the South Atlantic.

In a now partially released CIA profile of Galtieri[4] written for the highest levels of the US administration as the Falklands crisis grew, the General is said to have 'vigorously conducted a successful campaign against the well-entrenched leftist insurgency'. In the declassified version the details of this are then blacked out; however, a striking assessment of Galtieri's personality can be read.

He is described as 'blond, blue-eyed and handsome', with the image of 'a Caudillo, the acme of heroic leadership in Latin America – the man on horseback.' The profile, entitled 'Galtieri of Argentina: Decisive and Unyielding', emphasises the General's firmness in language curiously reminiscent of 1930s profiles of an earlier, German dictator:

> Galtieri prides himself on his ability to be decisive and to take action. His iron will and unbending determination are hall-marks of his character. He equates indecision, temporizing and compromise with weakness ... Priding himself on being decisive and firm, Galtieri is harshly critical of those who do not display these attributes.

In 1981 Galtieri had used these qualities to bludgeon his way to the presidency, attacking his immediate predecessor and former patron, the physically ailing General Roberto Viola, for his inde-cision on key issues including the Falklands. Seemingly anointed by his warm treatment in Washington, he emerged as the new leader after apparently making his secret promise to the Navy com-mander, Admiral Jorge Anaya, that he would, if necessary, launch a military operation to seize control of the islands. Inconclusive dis-cussions between Argentinian and British diplomats shortly after he took power served only to infuriate Galtieri. The official com-muniqué after the talks described them as 'cordial and positive', but the new dictator's hand was visible in a warning from Buenos Aires that unless there was a quick solution, it would choose a 'pro-cedure which better suits its interest'. His response to rumours, subsequently shown to be unfounded, that the British were mov-ing a nuclear-attack submarine from Gibraltar to the South Atlantic

– which would complicate any naval operation – was to accelerate planning for the invasion.

Along with the other members of the Junta, Galtieri was convinced that Britain was greatly diminished and that her evasive responses to Argentina's renewed demands for negotiations on sovereignty were no more than a sign of weakness. He was encouraged in this belief by reports from London which appeared to suggest that the Conservative government would consider some sort of transfer of sovereignty and negotiated lease-back arrangement for the islands, even though this idea had met with an extremely hostile reaction from the still strong pro-Falkland islanders lobby when it was raised in the House of Commons. Clearly the General, accustomed to the use of brutal and violent methods to suppress dissent, could not imagine that the views of fewer than 2,000 islanders (or 'kelpers') would be allowed to play any serious part in the resolution of the issue in Argentina's favour. What he did know was that his sudden seizure of the Malvinas had transformed his standing with the Argentinian public almost overnight.

Two days before his move on March 30th, some 50,000 supporters of the Labour movement and opponents of the regime had marched to the Plaza de Mayo in front of the Presidential Palace to protest at the economic chaos engulfing the country and the continuing repression that kept the Junta in power. Chanting 'Galtieri, hijo de puta' (Galtieri, son of a whore) they clashed with police and more than 3,000 people were arrested.

Just over a week later the same square overflowed with more than 100,000 jubilant people chanting the President's name with passionate approval, as they waved national flags and banners proclaiming 'Long live our Navy' to celebrate the capture of the Malvinas. Argentine television showed the General struggling to get through the euphoric crowd with many trying to embrace him.

An announcer's voice boomed: 'His Excellency the President of the Nation has come out to greet his people!' and thousands cheered.

When Galtieri made his address it was a grandiloquent rallying call for national unity. '[T]he Argentine nation has risen,' Galtieri declared, 'the whole nation, spiritually and materially. We know full well that we have the backing of a people aware of their destiny, aware of their rights and obligations, a people who for a long time aspired for the return of the Malvinas Islands, Georgia and South Sandwich Islands and their zone of influence to the national territory.'

And in language whose meaning was clear to his audience, Galtieri claimed to rise above the fratricidal bloodshed of the Dirty War: 'The important step which we have just taken was done without taking any political calculations into account. It has been taken in the name of each and every Argentine citizen ...'

Then in words that were clearly intended as a rallying call but only served in the end to box him in, Galtieri said he was ready for war with Britain: 'If they want to come, let them come. We will present them with a battle.'

Little remarked upon, but still notable, was Galtieri's repetition of a very particular phrase, 'their zone of influence', when referring to the islands and the surrounding seas which Argentina was also insisting were its territory. Though neither the General nor any of the other principal Argentinian figures in the crisis made direct mention of it, it was universally understood that the Falklands/Malvinas sat at the heart of a zone which contained, and still contains, immense potential wealth. This had been described clearly a few years earlier in a US Defense Department briefing paper for senior officials in Washington, entitled 'The Stakes in Argentina', which is now among the declassified secret documents that I have been able to review. The paper provides this clear summary:

The US Geological Survey has estimated that Argentina's vast continental shelf – four times larger than the US Atlantic shelf – is potentially one of the world's richest oil bearing areas. The USGS puts an upper limit of 200 billion barrels to the shelf's oil potential – more than double existing proved reserves in the Western Hemisphere.[5]

The Falkland Islands sit at the heart of this immense if putative hydrocarbon wealth. Galtieri publicly denied any such mercenary considerations and spoke only of his regime's recurring watchword – *dignidad*. But CIA analysts noted his earlier statement before becoming President: 'We are not inclined to permit the smallest interference in the search for and exploitation of the wealth of our continental shelf from those who agree to return to us islands which are Argentine by historic heritage and legitimate right.' In other words, the vision of the future that Galtieri was presenting to the Argentine people was control of the Falkland Islands' oil wealth without any obligation to share it with Britain. There is no doubt that officials in London and, pivotally, in Washington were keenly aware that the implications of this conflict went beyond the question of national dignity and into the possession of what might be immense and vital resources that could even influence the future prospects of the world economy.

As the British task force established itself around the Falklands and further reinforcements moved south, some of the biggest questions continued to surround the character and likely reactions of the Argentine dictator whom, in the aftermath of our kidnapping, we were now about to meet. The CIA profile that spoke of Galtieri's strength and decisiveness had also pointed to extremely serious flaws:

Galtieri is a heavy drinker, sometimes consuming four or more Scotches before lunch. When drinking he becomes more out-spoken and argumentative and is given to occasional angry tirades. Galtieri is also a heavy smoker which, combined with his heavy drinking, heightens the risk to his health. He suffered a heart attack in 1973 at age 47 from which he appears to have recovered. The heart attack has not deterred Galtieri from con-tinuing his intense hard-driving ways.

This warning of impulsive, even out-of-control behaviour appears to reflect the experiences of US President Ronald Reagan himself. On the afternoon of April 1st, as Washington confirmed that an Argentinian flotilla led by the country's single aircraft carrier was nearing the Falklands, Reagan had attempted to telephone Galtieri to urge him to think again. The Argentine leader declined to take the call, a refusal some American officials put down to intoxication.

Four hours later Reagan got through and, according to talking points of the call that have been released, formally asked Galtieri for his 'absolute assurance' that he would not invade the islands the following morning, telling him that doing so would 'wreck' his country's relationship with the United States. Galtieri replied that 'time had run out' and then, in a surprisingly crude attempt to pres-sure both the US and British governments, declared that Argentina would feel free to use its resources unless its sovereignty over the Malvinas were recognised that very night. Galtieri declined Reagan's offer to use his 'good offices' to try to resolve the crisis.[6]

Two weeks later, as the British response became clear, Galtieri telephoned Reagan in a ham-fisted attempt at personal conciliation. Both Argentines and North Americans shared a common heritage of struggle against colonialism, the General claimed, seeking to cast the British as the villains of the story, but he offered no concrete moves to end the crisis and Reagan's National Security Advisor gave a curt appraisal: 'We read Galtieri as a worried man, but one not yet ready to retreat from previously established positions.'[7]

According to a CIA report from Buenos Aires the General's erratic handling of the all-important relationship with Washington had horrified a number of 'moderate' senior officers in the Argentine Army who 'believed that Galtieri was offensive to the US President during the latter's phone call on the night of 1 April, and this rudeness led the US Government to be less sympathetic to Argentina.'[8]

It was against this turbulent background, in which the Argentine President was under increasing pressure as he was forced to confront the consequences of his decision to seize the islands, that we entered the Casa Rosada, making our way past the tall plumed guardsmen in their braided and tailed 18th-century uniforms that would not have seemed out of place in an Italian opera. As we were guided into an ornate lift which would take us to the Presidential chambers, I received a surprising hint of what to expect – or perhaps what Galtieri's staff feared might happen. Our escort, a smartly uniformed Naval officer, leant towards me and whispered: 'Señor Manyon, you should know that today is Navy Day.'

Evidently I looked puzzled.

'On Navy Day our President has the habit of having a little DRINK.'

The last word was heavily emphasised and it seemed that the officer was warning me that Galtieri was drunk, a warning that appeared even more eccentric later when I learned that May 12th is not in fact Argentina's Navy Day, which actually falls five days later on May 17th. Before we could digest the information, the lift doors opened, giving on to a long and splendid gallery, at the end of which the undeniably impressive figure of the Argentine President in full uniform could be seen striding towards us with his staff.

Our camera equipment was still in the hands of the gunmen who only hours before had kidnapped and threatened to kill us, but a cameraman from Argentine Television was on hand to record our encounter with the President and kindly agreed to film it in a way suitable for our needs. Curiously, the officials surrounding Galtieri who were supposedly masterminding the confrontation with Britain included no one who spoke good English. An Argentine newspaperman who happened to be in the palace volunteered his services and with his help I was able to conduct what turned out to be a world-exclusive interview.

Galtieri was physically imposing and almost too ebullient as he shook my hand warmly and offered his apologies for what had happened to us on behalf of 'the people, the government and the nation of Argentina'. Journalism, he said, was 'a contribution to peace among men'. But his response to my first question – who had carried out the attack against us – was oddly uncertain and punctuated with long pauses.

'Against ...? Ah ... against you ... See ... Ehmm ... I think it must be a very small group ['un grupo muy reducido'] which is not contributing to the objective of peace.'

Then, with noticeably exaggerated gestures and slurring his words slightly, he made a fulsome apology for our kidnapping, describing it as 'regrettable' and promising 'on behalf of the Argentine people' that it would be investigated. His central message, however, was what appeared to be a slightly modified position on the Malvinas.

'Sovereignty is, was and always will be the objective of the Argentinian people. We will not give up this objective but we can talk with a view to achieving it in a reasonable time.'

I asked him if he was prepared to pull down the Argentinian flag on the islands to get negotiations started.

'No Señor.' And after a long pause which hinted at a degree of uncertainty, 'But it can be discussed.'

Finally I asked him if he could guarantee that the people of the Falkland Islands would not be subjected to the sort of brutal treatment that we had suffered earlier that day. Galtieri responded by raising his hand theatrically in the manner of someone swearing an oath.

'I swear it,' he said.[9]

As I will discuss in a later chapter, this was perhaps a crude attempt at some sort of diplomatic *démarche* but it was too ambiguous, came too late and was soon to be swept aside by events. Galtieri did his best to exude unshakeable confidence but he must already have known that the march towards full-scale war was close to unstoppable and that he had committed an irretrievable blunder. His decision to invade had briefly won him 98% approval in a Buenos Aires opinion poll but it was based on an illusion of military strength that could not be sustained.

Inside the Casa Rosada official photographers set off their flashbulbs and I did my best, in a way that today seems faintly comical, to avoid appearing as if we were collaborating with the leader of the nation with which we were at war. Pictures show me with arms folded in front of the seemingly friendly dictator who may have imagined that he was scoring some sort of public relations success. But even receiving our team of kidnapped journalists served to expose the violent factionalism inside his regime and it was clear to outside observers that the promise to investigate our kidnapping could not be kept. Two days after the event the CIA received information making clear that inquiries into the event were 'casual':

The implication of this information is that no serious attempt is currently underway to identify and punish the persons responsible for the kidnapping of the journalists. It is not clear whether the leadership of the Army or the President is aware of the casual nature of the investigation underway.[10]

In fact, as Galtieri and the men around him knew all too well, our kidnapping was just the latest reminder of a ledger which they were now doing everything possible not to open: the thousands of terrible crimes that the Junta had committed and which now served to trap it in its extreme nationalist policies. Defeat at the hands of Britain, or even any significant step back that involved loss of the cherished national 'dignity', could open the way to loss of power and prosecution for countless murders, abductions, rapes and cases of appalling torture all committed in the name of a holy crusade against communist subversion but which had left survivors and relatives calling for justice and revenge. A heavily redacted analysis from the US Director of Central Intelligence put our case in context:

> President Galtieri has pledged to bring the guilty to Justice, but he is unlikely to order a speed-up of the investigation, much less order other steps that could prove embarrassing to the Army, and ultimately to the Junta itself.[11]

As if to cushion these realities as we left the Casa Rosada at one o'clock in the morning the Interior Minister, General Alfredo Saint-Jean, stepped in. Argentines had a habit of eating late, he told me. Would we now care to join him for dinner?

CHAPTER 5

Dinner with the Junta

IT IS ONE OF the undoubted attractions of a career in journalism, and something of a cliché, that, amid the dross of trivial, sensationalised stories, the manipulations of cynical politicians and the all too numerous grey executives making decisions out of careerism or fear, it can just occasionally provide the 'hack' with a front-row seat in the theatre of history. The challenge given the suddenness and unpredictability of these opportunities, and the very superficial knowledge journalists like myself all too frequently arrive with, is to take full advantage of such opportunities or even understand their meaning.

A number of dramatic episodes on which I have reported still live with me both as a source of pride that I was able to gain extraordinary access and interview remarkable people, and of frustration that I understood so little of what was taking place before my eyes and could have produced work that was more important and, dare I say it, profound. I find myself wishing that I could relive specific hours or days equipped with at least a sense of what the future held but that is, of course, impossible.

One such story that took place a little after the events I am describing in this book, was the extraordinary three-day period that I and a camera team spent inside a Soviet nuclear-missile base, just before the fall of communism. Our presence there, which I believe was unique and never repeated, was the result of luck, persistence and the remarkably persuasive talents of our Russian fixer, Volodya, who somehow convinced the senior officers of the Soviet Strategic Rocket Forces that granting us access would advance the cause of *détente* in which many Russians at that stage genuinely believed. Still more extraordinary was that after filming the missile silos and bunkers in the base deep in a Siberian forest to which we were assigned, we discovered, by listening to the BBC World Service on a small short-wave radio that I carried and was permitted to use, that Soviet President Mikhail Gorbachev would that evening address the Russian people on television to announce further moves in arms limitation talks with the United States. Surprisingly our host, the young and highly intelligent base commander, had no knowledge that this was due to take place. Showing exceptional dynamism that instantly gave the lie to clichés about Russian bureaucracy, he delayed our celebratory departure dinner that he had organised and drove us in his jeep through the blacked-out base complex to the *Kommandny Punkt* – the underground command centre where officers sat in front of dated-looking screens with their hands not far from still-terrifying levers and buttons. There we were permitted to film Gorbachev's address and interview the men about it afterwards.[1] I remember in particular the young officer who told me that he was ready to carry out any orders he was given but that he nonetheless hoped that his job would become redundant: 'I would like my son to remember my profession of missile engineer as a profession that has disappeared ... that has become ancient history.'

When I think about that moment today, I am nagged by a feeling of having fallen short. I asked all the obvious questions but perhaps not all the right ones. Perhaps I should have tried harder to get at the inner feelings of men who lived with such frightening responsibilities, who had been trained to regard us as enemies but showed no sign of hating us. Perhaps I should have grasped more clearly that the communist world they were defending was about to fall apart along with the rule of Gorbachev himself. Certainly in all the years I later spent living in Russia, sometimes reporting on their military as it became bogged down in the war in Chechnya, it was an opportunity that was never repeated.

I have similar feelings about the dinner that took place in Buenos Aires in the very early hours of May 13th, 1982. We were to sit down with senior officers of a military regime known internationally for its crimes against its own people, which had now sunk a British warship in the South Atlantic and whose agents had kidnapped and terrorised us. I hesitate to compare the Argentine Junta with Nazism in the Second World War, even though some of its members were unconcealed admirers of it – the scale of the Argentinian version was so much smaller, the ambitions lesser, though still including belief in the creation through war of a race of Argentinian 'supermen' (as the historian Rogelio García Lupo recorded),[2] and the fundamental ethos inescapably Latin, capable of extraordinary brutality but perhaps not of the cold, organised relentlessness of the German model. Hunting for an imperfect analogy it was perhaps as if we had interviewed the Italian Duce, Mussolini, and were then dining with his senior officers at a time when their belief in his dictatorship had not yet given way to disillusionment in their struggle against the British Army in the North African sands. In today's world there are doubtless some who would regard our acceptance of the Interior

Minister's invitation with disapproval. In my case, still grateful for survival and running on a surge of adrenalin, I was happy to accept and Ted, Trefor and Norman did likewise.

It turned out that the Minister had arranged a private room at one of the city's most celebrated steak restaurants, the appropriately named 'Los Años Locos' – The Crazy Years – a reference not to Argentina's current state but to the more joyful Roaring Twenties. The restaurant had actually closed shortly before it received the Minister's call, but staff were ordered to return – some arriving by motorcycle or Vespa at the same time that we did – and the kitchen was fired up again. Awaiting us inside was a bevy of senior officers dressed in full, splendid uniforms, who welcomed us with old-fashioned courtesy.

Even in the middle of the night Argentine appetites did not appear to moderate and we were soon confronted with massive platters of the misleadingly named 'baby beef', slabs of astonishingly tender steak that had seemingly come straight from the pampas to the plate, along with bottles of fine Argentinian wine to wash it down. The Minister himself took on an avuncular air as he led a toast to us and apologised once again for what had happened. There followed lengthy if slightly incongruous statements from our hosts about the historic friendship between Argentina and Britain and their sadness at Mrs Thatcher's refusal to recognise Argentina's legitimate historical claim to the islands. There was also the repeated insistence that, now that lives had been lost in the *Belgrano*, their country must defend its honour and, yes, dignity.

Halfway through the dinner there was a knock on the door and a smart young officer entered carrying a silver salver on which was an envelope which he presented to the Minister. General Saint-Jean read the message it contained and turned to me: 'Señor Manyon, this message says that we have sunk your carrier the *Invincible* with an air strike.' Then with an expression which mingled both excitement and a degree of doubt, he said, 'Can this be true?'

Obviously I had not the slightest idea and felt distinctly uncomfortable as the Argentinian officers raised their glasses in front of us to what they now hoped would be a war-winning victory. In fact what became clear in the following days was that this announcement illustrated the confusion of war amplified by the poor reconnaissance capability which was to prove one of the fatal flaws in the Argentine war effort. There had indeed been a determined air attack on the British task force, the partial success and great cost of which were to set a pattern for the conflict. On the previous day, while we were in the hands of our kidnappers, eight near-obsolete A-4 Skyhawk jets, which had last seen serious service in Vietnam, had taken off with their pilots strapped into possibly defective ejector seats. Each plane carried two 500lb unguided bombs.

According to the former senior Argentine Air Force officer, Rubén O. Moro,[3] in his frequently contentious but nonetheless important history of the conflict from the Argentine side, the Skyhawks were in two formations codenamed 'Oro' (Gold) and 'Cuña' (Wedge), a formation which was dictated by the need for mid-air refuelling by the all-important American-supplied KC-130 tanker aircraft. The plan was to attack the Royal Navy task force in two consecutive sea-skimming raids.

The target they managed to locate was not in fact the carrier *Invincible* but the destroyers HMS *Brilliant* and HMS *Glasgow*, the second of which was engaged in shelling Argentine troops near Port Stanley. The jets of 'Cuña' carried out the first low-level attack but immediately came under fire from the newest air-defence system carried by the task force, British Sea Wolf missiles fired by *Brilliant*. Three of the four Argentinian planes were destroyed and the fourth pilot missed his target. Ten minutes later the Skyhawks of 'Oro' came in for a second attempt. *Brilliant*'s Sea Wolf computer system briefly malfunctioned and one of the Argentine pilots, Lieutenant Gavazzi, managed to hit the *Glasgow* amidships with one of his two bombs. In a great stroke of good fortune, it failed to explode on impact but smashed its way right through the ship, leaving two large holes in its sides. Gavazzi tried to escape by turning sharply to the north and flying towards what he may have imagined was the greater safety offered by Argentine air defences on the Falklands. However, with little coordination between Argentine forces in the air and on the ground, his own troops opened fire on him and he plunged to his death. The final toll of the operation from the Argentinian point of view, when they were able to establish what had really happened, was both heartening and deeply sobering. The *Invincible* had not been hit. A British destroyer had been put out of action but four of the eight Argentinian pilots had died and four of their eight aircraft lost, an unsustainable attrition rate of 50%.

In 'Los Años Locos' our uniformed hosts had yet to learn how treacherous and misleading the fog of war could be. Radiating satisfaction at the claimed destruction of the British flagship, the Interior Minister and his fellow officers continued to behave with great cordiality while seeking to persuade us that Argentina would triumph in what they called 'La Guerra de Las Malvinas'. The truth was that they were already losing the Falklands War.

From first to last, Argentina's Air Force and their Naval fliers were the instrument of most of their success. Acting with an almost kamikaze-like determination, their pilots flew into the teeth of one of the most potent air-defence systems of that era and managed to destroy or heavily damage a distressingly large number of British ships. Following the *Sheffield* and the *Glasgow*, the *Ardent, Antelope* and *Sir Lancelot* were all hit. Particularly shocking were the loss of the destroyer HMS *Coventry* and the *Atlantic Conveyor,* a converted civilian transport which was sent to the bottom by one of Argentina's last Exocets with valuable Harriers and virtually all the task force's Chinook helicopters in its hold. A final air-inflicted tragedy was the destruction of the *Sir Galahad* in which 46 British servicemen died in a fireball that incinerated the vessel. But in the end none of this was enough to halt the well-conducted and unstoppable British operation to recapture the islands.

At our dinner with the Junta the airmen were the 'holy warriors' of their cause and it was here, once again, that I encountered the extraordinary emotional leap that the Argentine military mind was able to make between use of the most brutal methods and a self-image of purest chivalry exemplified by the pilots who were showing their willingness to take the most extreme risks. The historian Hugh Bicheno, with his considerable knowledge of Latin America, describes the attempt to understand the Argentine cause as like 'stepping through the looking glass, into a reality too weird for most to comprehend'.[4] We had stepped through that looking glass, or rather been forcibly rammed through it by our kidnapping, and had glimpsed the disturbing and deadly reality on the other side. If I had been more courageous, or perhaps more foolish, I would have asked the Minister and his acolytes how they could claim the right to provide government for the British Falkland islanders when the most powerful and ever-present law-enforcement body in Argentina consisted of squads of men in anonymous grey suits equipped with Ford Falcon cars and pistols. I could also have asked him to try to explain the fate of about 100 Argentine journalists who had up to that moment been murdered or 'disappeared' (the distinction generally reflecting whether or not the body had been found) by the Junta and its servants. I could have asked him why he thought it appropriate to give a prominent role in the South Atlantic campaign to the internationally notorious Lieutenant Commander Alfredo Astiz, who had taken part in the murder of nuns and priests in 1977. (He had been sent in the first stage of the operation to lead the occupation of South Georgia and, despite his promise to fight to the death, had immediately surrendered to British forces.) I could also perhaps, in the question most relevant to ourselves, have pressed for him to tell us who it was who had carried out our own kidnapping. Who was the commander with the hard hands who had held a pistol to my head for an hour, who was he exchanging coded messages with through the radio on the dashboard, and who were the others including the man who raised his automatic rifle and convinced me that we were about to be murdered?

Revelations since that night have made it clear that our gentlemanly hosts should have been well-informed on all these matters. As I will relate, the claim of ignorance did not prove to be a viable defence when the Junta's members and supporters were finally brought to book, a process which continues today. In some armedforces units, knowledge of the military's criminal behaviour had been deliberately spread through the ranks as a means of 'blooding' the soldiers. A surprising number of officers and secret-service men had 'adopted' small children whose real parents had been 'disappeared'. Such adoptions were an open secret, with adopters apparently believing that they were performing an honourable role in taking the children of unworthy parents and bringing them up in Catholic, anti-communist households as true citizens of the new, greater Argentina.

As we dined, however, history was moving on. A little like the Soviet missile crews, the Junta officers were the servants of a doomed regime. Defeat at the hands of Britain would start the process that led to the removal of Galtieri and the Junta's fall, leaving a legacy of chaos, bloodshed and failure. That night our hosts were solicitous and apologetic: what had happened to us was an unfortunate incident carried out by a small fringe group of unrepresentative troublemakers. Whoever had done this had been trying to damage the reputation of Argentina in the world. Passions were running high, but there would be a full investigation. The Argentine government would guarantee our future security and we were invited to carry on with our reporting mission. We left the Minister's company at around three in the morning for what turned out to be the last time. The following day for understandable reasons we were instructed by Thames Television in London to leave Buenos Aires and return home. I went on to report on many other crises and live through many other dangers. It would take the best part of 40 years to unlock the frightening mysteries of what had happened to us and to so many others in Argentina.

CHAPTER 6

Secrets

LIKE MANY JOURNALISTS I have always been fascinated by secrets and, in particular, secret documents which give a glimpse of political or military realities that mere mortals who vote or serve in uniform are not privileged to see. Some of the most satisfying hours of my working life took place a few days after the fall of communism in what was then Czechoslovakia when, through the help of a middle-man who established relations with the relevant officials of the Státní Bezpečnost, the StB secret service, I was admitted to a small room in the gatehouse of their baroque office complex, and permitted to photocopy hundreds of pages from their files. I had brought a heavy old manual photocopier, the best portable technology then available, on the plane from London, since such equipment had always been heavily restricted under the communist regime and could not be obtained at that time in Prague. For hour after hour I sat, laboriously copying the pages one by one and finally flew back to London with our prize, which gave the details of an operation that the now-fallen communist authorities had conducted against a group of dissidents and, happily, confirmed the accuracy of a filmed report we had made about them.

In the case of our kidnapping in Buenos Aires the disclosure of vital information, including the identity of the man who led the operation, was rather less melodramatic and involved no journalistic mock heroics. Instead it was the result of the sort of labour that the modern world has made possible and often burdened us with: the sifting of tens of thousands of documents stored in hundreds of computer files. The search was made a little easier by some initial advice from the independent National Security Archive in Washington, which has played a leading role in bringing the contents of these documents to public attention, and made more difficult by my own poor computer skills.

Most of the documents, and our own small corner within them, have been made public as the result of a deliberate shift in US government policy when President Barack Obama set out to improve Washington's frayed relationship with the government and people of Argentina by the mass release of thousands of pages of previously secret emails and reports dealing with the Junta's Dirty War, as well as a carefully sifted and smaller selection dealing with its war with Britain in the Falklands. Some Dirty War files had already been released under President Clinton but Obama's much more extensive 'Declassification Project', which included large numbers of CIA documents, was intended to be a display of openness which would hopefully be welcomed in the now more democratic atmosphere in Argentina.

As so often in that very particular country, emotions about the past were both fierce and contradictory. In 1983 the military Junta had fallen as a direct result of its defeat by Britain and had been replaced by a succession of more or less chaotic civilian governments. The United States was still widely blamed both for propping up the Junta during the worst of its excesses and for betraying

Argentina and its armed forces by siding with Britain during the war for the Malvinas, which remained and remains to this day a cause of aggressive unhappiness for much of the population.

The question of US support for Britain in the war was in the last analysis reasonably clear. After a month-long prelude following Argentina's seizure of the islands, in which Washington's envoys had tried without success to encourage the two sides to find common ground, the US began to make public its support for Britain. The factors by which the Junta had set great store – Argentina's common interests with the US in Latin America and worries, particularly at the US State Department, that she could be pushed into the arms of the Soviet bloc – were in the end decisively outweighed by Britain's longstanding status as key ally and her central role as a nuclear-armed partner in NATO and a member of the United Nations Security Council. The result, following a highly skilful campaign by Britain's diplomats which could not be matched by the less practised Argentinian apparatus, was Reagan's declaration that 'Maggie' should be given what she needed. Thus the US rapidly provided Britain, *inter alia*, with advanced weapons including 200 AIM-9 'Sidewinder' air-to-air missiles which enabled the Harriers to dominate the skies over the Falklands, eight 'Stinger' anti-aircraft systems, thousands of mortar shells and 12.5 million gallons of aviation fuel delivered to the strategically vital facilities at Ascension Island. These crucial deliveries led the US Defense Secretary Caspar Weinberger to refer to himself after the war as Britain's 'advance quartermaster'. He was duly rewarded with an honorary knighthood.

Aid behind the scenes was perhaps even more important. The US government had promised that if either of the British carriers, *Hermes* or *Invincible*, were to be put out of action or sunk the US would lend Britain the 12,000-ton assault ship USS *Guam*, to enable the operation to continue. This had allowed Mrs Thatcher to display complete commitment at key moments, a determination which culminated in her rejection of American suggestions near the end of the war that she stop short of complete victory and allow the Argentines some face-saving way of withdrawing from the islands.

Also highly significant, though least-publicised, was the valuable intelligence the Americans provided. The US took the extraordinary step of relocating a spy satellite to a position over the South Atlantic, where it could provide real-time information on Argentinian military activity. The satellite, codenamed 'Vortex', was designed to intercept signals intelligence and the Americans had the ability to read most of Argentina's coded military communications. In what *The Washington Post* has recently described as 'The Intelligence Coup of the Century',[1] the US government had earlier successfully encouraged more than 100 governments worldwide, including Argentina's, to buy cryptographic machines originally inspired by the German Second World War Enigma system and manufactured by the Swiss company, Crypto AG. One of the recently released CIA documents described this as 'a manual machine system of Swiss origin ... similar in appearance to an old cash register which has numbers, slide handles and a manually operated dial on the side which is turned after each entry.'

The CIA codenamed the operation 'Minerva' and what the purchasers of the machine did not know was that far from being an independent concern, Crypto AG was jointly owned by the BND (the West German intelligence service) and the CIA, and that both agencies had the ability to decrypt its transmissions. Details of decryption during the Falklands conflict are not available but it seems that the American information was of value. In a war against an enemy with a much more limited intelligence capability, it may well have given Britain a key advantage.

In the years since, most Argentines have been prepared to believe the words of their wartime Foreign Minister, Nicanor Costa Méndez, who said after his country's surrender, 'we were not defeated by Great Britain. We were defeated because they had US support.'[2]

While victory in the Falklands provided a great boost for Britain and in particular for Prime Minister Margaret Thatcher, the United States paid a diplomatic price. The loss of Argentina's covert assistance in Nicaragua had complicated American efforts to halt the leftist Sandinista movement and had even, according to US officials, led to the 'Irangate' affair, the tangled series of covert transactions involving Israel and Iran that was intended to provide secret and illegal funding for the anti-communist Contras and which, when revealed, greatly damaged Ronald Reagan's second term as President. More publicly, Reagan's decision to side with Britain had provided anti-American groups in Latin America with ready ammunition and convinced many that the US was, in essence, a pro-colonial power that did not have Latin American interests at heart.

Perhaps the darkest cloud hanging over any attempt to recast relations with Buenos Aires was Washington's perceived role in supporting the military Junta in their seizure of power on March 24th, 1976. The Argentine Nobel Peace Prize winner, Adolfo Pérez Esquivel, had described the United States as 'an accomplice of coups d'état', and when the White House announced that President Barack Obama would visit Argentina on the 40th anniversary of the military takeover the result was uproar. Human-rights groups announced plans for massive demonstrations and the Mothers and Grandmothers of the Plaza de Mayo called on the US President to release intelligence records that might help them to establish the fate of their missing loved ones. After consultations with the Argentine

President Mauricio Macri, who fifteen years earlier had himself survived the ordeal of being kidnapped and held to ransom by a gang of rogue policemen, Obama agreed to an anniversary visit to the Parque de la Memoria, the park beside the great estuary of the River Plate commemorating the brutal excesses of the Dirty War with thousands of small plaques that record the names of identified victims, and there he announced what would become the Declassification initiative.

'Today,' declared the US President, 'in response to a request from President Macri, and to continue helping the families of the victims find some of the truth and justice they deserve, I can announce that the United States government will declassify even more documents from that period, including, for the first time, military and intelligence records. I believe we have a responsibility to confront the past with honesty and transparency.'

The White House then issued a directive to national security agencies, telling them 'to prioritize support for this effort'. In response some 400 officials are said to have spent 30,000 hours trawling through previously secret files. In the end, the disclosure was completed by Obama's successor, President Donald Trump, in 2019, just over a year before his election defeat and spectacular fall from power. Typically, Trump boasted that his handover of 47,000 files to the Argentine government was the largest-ever release of classified information in US history. This was undeniably a remarkable exercise – the rewriting of a country's history by the spies, military officers and diplomats of another nation in the often voluminous reports they had filed from Buenos Aires or compiled in Washington and Virginia.

Some of the material is heavily redacted and entire pages are sometimes blacked out or marked 'Denied'. In possible deference to the concerns of the British government, much material relating to the Falklands conflict and the vital assistance which the United States provided to Britain, seems to have been excluded. But two points about that war emerge with clarity: that the leader of the military Junta, General Galtieri, had launched and persisted with his operation to seize the islands in the face of warnings from US officials, including the President himself, that the US would in the end support Britain; and that Argentina's ability to wage such a war had been seriously undermined by the international consequences of the human-rights abuses carried out by the Junta against its own population. It could be argued from the new documents that the Junta had sown the seeds of its own destruction.

The thousands of pages to which academics and journalists have since had access, and which I have laboured to read and fully understand, contain a mass of detail and include material which must damage the reputation of the United States.

The documents reveal the pervasive and obsessive depth of Washington's anti-communist crusade in Latin America and Argentina's place within it. They reveal at least part of Washington's contemporaneous knowledge of the murder and torture being carried out by a regime which was its principal ally in the region. They show that when CIA officers paused to analyse what was taking place, the result was sometimes little more than an apologia:

The military-controlled governments ... all consider themselves targets of international Marxism. Having endured real and perceived threats from leftist terrorists these governments believe that the very foundations of their societies are threatened. In most cases government leaders seek to be selective in the pursuit and apprehension of suspected subversives but control over

security forces generally is not tight enough to prevent inno-
cents from being harmed or mistreated.[3]

The power of the released material is in the wealth of detail. It shows
the extensive structure of repression which was put in place with
tacit American approval and it names some of the men who emerged
as the Argentine Junta's most skilled killers and torturers. One of
the most important documents now released by the CIA is the
entire secret text of the 1976 agreement between six Latin American
nations for Operation Condor, designed as a joint security-service
project to exchange information on, and eliminate, extreme leftist
movements throughout much of the Latin American continent. It
concerns the organisation of kidnap and assassination squads to deal
with subversive elements and it sets out the methods to be used:

> IDENTIFICATION OF THE TARGET: This is the responsibil-
> ity of the intelligence team which should identify him, locate
> him, monitor him, communicate with the operations centre,
> withdraw (all except one who will make contact with the oper-
> ational team), and withdrawal of the contact man once the
> target has been identified to the operational team ...

> EXECUTION OF THE TARGET: This is the responsibil-
> ity of the operational team which will A) Intercept the target,
> B) Carry out the operation, and C) Escape.[4]

In this system Argentina was named as Condor 1. An operational
base for Condor was set up on its territory and, as I learned piecing
the many fragments of information together, a key role was assigned
to the man who would later, according to the CIA, carry out our
kidnapping in the heart of Buenos Aires.

CHAPTER 7

Executioners

A STRIKING FEATURE OF the Argentina Declassification Project launched by President Obama is that along with naming many of the victims of kidnap, torture and murder, the documents also identify some of the perpetrators. A CIA report, dated nine days after our kidnapping, states unambiguously that it was carried out by a team working with the Argentine Army's 601st Intelligence Battalion and names its leader as a secret-service killer called Aníbal Gordon, a man on whose murders the CIA had reported before and who was to become infamous for his blood-stained ruthlessness as the history of the Argentinian Junta's war against its own people became better known. Gordon, and the crimes he committed, are now seen as central in what are called the 'Years of Lead'.

This CIA document, which is the most informative report about our kidnapping, was in the form of a cable identified as CIA 231283 and sent to Langley, Virginia on May 21st, 1982. It states that the operation was 'executed by an Argentine paramilitary group under the command of "Aníbal" ... The journalists had been under heavy surveillance by personnel from the Argentine Army 601st Intelligence Battalion before being selected by Gordon's group as specific targets for kidnapping.'[1] The following two paragraphs had been deleted by the CIA as still too sensitive to release but the name was there in full: Aníbal Gordon. As I was to discover, it was a name already notorious in Argentina's murderous secret world.

The CIA report was to some extent corroborated by an anonymous letter apparently written by a group of serving policemen who sent it to an Argentinian judge the following year, as the Junta disintegrated following the Falklands defeat.[2] The letter, which produced little action at the time but has since commanded attention, accused the same Aníbal Gordon of responsibility for a string of murders, including that of Argentina's first woman diplomat, Elena Holmberg, who was suspected of having learned damaging information about one of the Junta's most senior figures while she served in Paris, and whose body was found in the Luján river near Buenos Aires. It also accused him of carrying out the attack on us: 'the kidnapping, stripping and robbery of three British journalists during the Malvinas War.' The letter said that the police could not do anything about these crimes because they were under the orders of the military.

The identification of Gordon is in one of five CIA documents which refer directly to our case. I read them and then read them again, scarcely believing that these almost 40 year-old files contained the answer to one of the nagging mysteries of my life. I examined photographs of the man they identified and found myself propelled straight back to the horrifying moments in the back of the Ford Falcon and in the field near Pilar. Looking at Aníbal Gordon's image I felt a stab of recognition and fear. Through the mists of the years it seemed that I was looking at the face of the man I had last seen apparently preparing to kill me. I set out to cross-reference the American documents that mentioned him in connection with a series of crimes, with Argentinian judicial records and with 40 years'-worth of newspaper articles from publications large and small across the country. The picture that emerged was of a professional killer, both cruel and charismatic, valued by his superiors in the military secret services for the ruthless efficiency that he displayed in seizing victims, extracting information by torture and disposing of the finally valueless corpse. He was admired for leading his paramilitary unit in shoot-outs, in several of which he was apparently wounded, and having no qualms about whom he killed. 'Gordon has no enemies', it was said of him approvingly, 'The ones he had are all dead.'[3] Even today investigations into his murderous activities are still taking place and he is believed to have been personally responsible for dozens of killings and to have organised and supervised many more. Gordon himself boasted to friends that he was responsible for the deaths of hundreds of *subversivos*.[4]

In Argentina's melting pot, Aníbal Gordon carried the surname of his Scottish ancestry along with a forename, in English Hannibal, remembering the Carthaginian general who brought Rome to its knees and who is still a celebrated figure in Latin lore. He was a career criminal turned Dirty War assassin. Born in 1932 in the small town of Colón north of Buenos Aires, he started out as a businessman selling metals and plastics before embarking on a dramatically different career as Argentina began its descent into disintegration and political violence.

After a number of smaller-scale crimes including extortion and acts of violence, during which time he also learned to fly a light aircraft used to bring contraband cigarettes into the country, Gordon came to public notice in February 1971 as the man who planned and led Argentina's most spectacular bank robbery of modern times. The target was the Provincial Bank of Río Negro, a large province in the centre of the country, and Gordon's gang made off with 88 million pesos which even allowing for the rapidly weakening Argentine currency was the equivalent at the time of more than £7 million.[5]

Gordon's planning was meticulous, and the well-executed robbery has since entered Argentine criminal legend. Members of the gang, armed with pistols and submachine guns, went late at night to the home addresses of two executives of the bank. They bound and gagged them along with a neighbour who tried to investigate, pausing only in Latin style to kiss the small daughter of one of the bank employees while also warning their captives that they would be killed if they tried to escape their bonds. Learning from the prisoners that the bank's assistant manager was staying at a nearby hotel, they drove there and seized him, his wife, and crucially the keys to the bank itself. At four in the morning Gordon and his accomplices managed to get into the bank's vault and loaded the vast haul, which was in bundles of 5,000- and 10,000-peso notes, into a Ford van. Then they drove to an open area outside the town, boarded a light aircraft which Gordon later claimed to have piloted himself, and made their escape. The almost military nature of the operation and the daring use of a light plane led to speculation that the robbery had been carried out with the assistance of members of the security services profiting from the growing anarchy gripping the country. What happened to the money – hundreds of bundles of rapidly devaluing Argentinian banknotes – and how large Gordon's share of it was, is not in the public record, though he did in that period purchase a property in a wealthy district of Colón, which then served as his *aguantadero* (hide-out). What is known is that a few months later Gordon and his gang carried out another bank robbery near Buenos Aires, this time shooting at least one bank guard in broad daylight and making off with another 1.5 million pesos. Gordon was later arrested after a failed attempt to rob a jewellery business in the centre of the capital.

The story of what took place in the next two years indicates that Gordon was already connected to the dark recesses of Argentina's secret world. He was jailed in the forbidding, barracks-like Villa Devoto prison near the capital and then, surprisingly, released two years later as part of a general amnesty before his multiple charges of bank robbery and violent assault had come to trial as the Dirty War began to intensify.[6] It appears that while in prison he collaborated with the secret police who arranged for him to be placed in the same area as prisoners from the leftist ERP, the 'Ejército Revolucionario del Pueblo', which was then attempting to ignite a Cuban-style armed revolt in the province of Tucumán where Argentina's original declaration of independence from Spain had taken place and which was regarded as the birthplace of the nation. Some of the leftists are said to have asked Gordon why he, a criminal, had been put with them in the political wing of the prison. Gordon apparently told them that he was regarded as particularly dangerous because of his use of military-style automatic weapons during his last bank robbery.

A vivid picture of Gordon has been provided by one of the 'politicals', Luís Lea Place, then a 23 year-old Marxist revolutionary held in the same cell block as the gangster. Place seems to have been completely taken in: 'He was very kind, gentlemanly, talkative, a good cook and, by his own account, could fly a plane. He joined in our political discussions and what he said seemed to fit in.'

Another surviving leftist prisoner, Eduardo Menajovsky, who slept in a bunk next to Gordon, remembers him talking about escape plans and reacting with what seemed exaggerated fury to news of a failed escape bid by leftists held at another prison in the south of the country which had resulted in the deaths of nineteen escapees including Place's sister. Gordon, he said, had seized a cooking pot, climbed a fence and, banging the pot on the wire, started shouting 'Assassins, sons of bitches' at the guards.

'I always thought he was up to something,' says Menajovsky, 'I was suspicious of the guy.' Menajovsky describes Gordon as 'very contradictory', capable of speaking with pride of the violence he had used in carrying out his robberies, but also to be discovered in the middle of the night sitting, clutching his head and grieving for his own family. 'He was crying,' he says.

Then the leftists were moved to another prison and Gordon was released under the partial government amnesty. Outside the prison walls, the Dirty War had been growing in intensity, with the ERP ordering bloody reprisals for their slain comrades. Their victims soon included a three year-old girl shot down with her policeman father as he walked with her in the street.

Out of prison Aníbal Gordon embarked upon the career which would eventually make him one of the most feared and reviled figures of the Dirty War, described by the author Carlos Juvenal as 'a sinister shadow over the memory of the Argentinian people'.[7] He was quickly recruited by the military secret service, SIDE, under the man who would become his mentor and then his partner in terrible crimes, General Otto Paladino. Remarkably, Paladino deployed him as a bodyguard for Juan Perón during the dictator's brief return to power, a period marked by violent confrontations between rival political forces. We next see Gordon in a photograph attached to a surviving police file from 1974, a year after he was released from prison. He is wearing an Army uniform with the badges of the SIDE intelligence service and showing something of the powerful presence he was later to display.[8] The file relates that Captain Aníbal

Gordon presented himself to the police in the town of Quilmes near the capital at the head of a group of eleven men in civilian clothes armed with submachine guns, rifles and grenades and sent on the authority of the Presidential administration with the mission of confronting leftist elements that might be trying to 'take advantage' of the unstable situation. Notable in the report is its description of Gordon's unit as irregular and heavily armed, a style of operation that would become all too frequent as the Dirty War progressed. Another police report from Mar del Plata sees Gordon, again equipped with secret-police credentials issued by the presidency, carrying out a raid on a metal workshop, 'where it was believed that the repair of weapons and other work linked to extremist elements was being carried out'. The raid found metal hooks enabling gunmen to conceal pistols in their clothing, communist literature and a portrait of Che Guevara. Gordon apparently arrested suspects but the report does not provide details of their fate.

The new champion of law and order also joined a secret organisation that worked closely with the security forces but was becoming notorious in its own right, the Argentine Anti-communist Alliance, known as the 'Triple A'. Formed under the dictatorship of Juan Perón, apparently with his full support, it was for a time based with macabre irony in the Ministry for Social Welfare. Its membership grew into a motley cocktail of army officers, secret service agents, professional sportsmen and career criminals, given an ideology by such extreme right-wing academics as the then Rector of Buenos Aires University, Alberto Ottalagano, who made no secret of his Nazi sympathies and declared that 'History now needs a new Christianised Hitler'.[9] Similar loyalties were openly expressed by leading figures in the armed forces including General Roberto Viola, who in the year before the Falklands War would briefly become

President of Argentina. He brushed off criticism of murderous repression by opining on a visit to Washington that: 'If the troops of the Third Reich had won the last world war the [war crimes] trial would not have been held in Nuremberg but in Virginia.'[10] After the fall of the Junta, Viola would be found guilty of ordering kidnapping, torture and theft, but in the 1970s the policies he and other key figures authorised enabled Triple A to pioneer a killing machine designed to crush what they saw as subversion that would otherwise destroy their state.

Members of the Triple A saw murder as their sacred Christian duty and Aníbal Gordon quickly proved his value to the cause. He is today held responsible for a series of high-profile assassinations. In August 1974 he is said to have led a team of gunmen in an attack on left-wing leaders in the city of La Plata. Gordon was apparently attempting to kill a man called Gonzalo 'El Negro' Chávez but, failing to find him, murdered his father and brother instead.[11] Before withdrawing, Gordon and his men killed another five known activists whose deaths are still commemorated today. A month later Gordon was one of a team of gunmen who shot down the well-known leftist parliamentary deputy and sympathiser with the Argentine revolutionaries of the ERP, Rodolfo Ortega Peña. Peña was riddled with fifteen bullets as he got into a taxi outside his home. Hundreds turned out for his funeral and clashes with the police prefigured the greater violence still to come. Eight weeks on, Gordon struck again, taking part in the murder of the leftist law professor and brother of a former President of Argentina, Silvio Frondizi. Frondizi had expressed support for the Cuban leader Fidel Castro, and had advised the ERP. On September 27th, 1974, gunmen including Aníbal Gordon broke into Frondizi's house in Buenos Aires, killing his son-in-law who tried to defend him and kidnapping the professor himself. Hours later the

Triple A claimed responsibility for his murder and announced the location of Frondizi's corpse, which showed that he had been brutally beaten and then, according to the autopsy, riddled with about 50 bullets. In a statement which rang with triumph, the Triple A said that they had executed 'a traitor of traitors, a communist, a Bolshevik and founder of the ERP ... he polluted our youth with communist ideas. He died as traitors die, shot in the back.'

Once again thousands thronged the funeral. 'Militants [of the left] mourned while the jackals celebrated', wrote one supporter of the victims, but Aníbal Gordon was building himself a career. He had access to an arsenal of weapons held in the basement of the Ministry of Social Welfare and to a network of paid informers that the Triple A was creating. Investigations after the fall of the Junta indicated that the Triple A had carried out nineteen murders in 1973, 50 in 1974 and 359 in 1975; the question, still unanswered, is how many more of those was Gordon personally involved in.

What is clear is that he had become the faithful servant of a particularly Argentine version of fascism, with roots stretching back to well before the Germany of Hitler and the Italy of Mussolini – and outliving both of them. In the last year of the Second World War the US President Franklin D. Roosevelt declared his puzzlement that an ideology which was being painfully and comprehensively defeated in Europe should continue to exercise a powerful influence in America's ally Argentina. There, a number of German war criminals who escaped justice, including, most notoriously, Adolf Eichmann, were quietly welcomed and assisted and the Nazi Stuka ace Hans-Ulrich Rudel was appointed instructor to the Argentine Air Force.

As ever, outsiders struggled to understand the looking-glass nature of Argentinian political thought, as this vast country with the potential to be an agricultural and natural resources superpower fell under the spell of the populist General Juan Perón. With his support anchored in the low-income and working-class Argentines referred to as *descamisados* (shirtless ones), with the oratorical talent to enrapture vast crowds, and with a First Lady, Eva or 'Evita' Perón who until her early death was glamorous, dynamic and the object of international fascination, the General was even lauded with a hymn, the 'Marcha Peronista':

> Perón, Perón, how great you are!
> My General, how great your worth!
> Perón, Perón, great leader!
> You are the first of our workers!

Existing alongside and sometimes in partnership with this populist phenomenon were the forces that would give birth to the Triple A and then to the Junta which eventually confronted Britain. They were the spawn of extreme right-wing movements which had burgeoned in the 1920s and 30s and which, in many but not all ways, resembled their European counterparts in Italy and Germany. Certainly identification with Mussolini was strong. The Italian dictator had won favour in Argentina by declaring his support for its sovereignty over the Malvinas, while he was lionised as the hero of a popular children's book by a fascist author, in which the brave farmer 'Benedicto Mulosini' deals with a plague of locusts in his field by setting fire to it and incinerating them.[12]

Argentine fascists called for 'virility' in cleansing the country of communist ideas and declared that the 'hour of the sword' had arrived. Historic acts of genocide against the Amerindian population were applauded even though, as historian Federico Finchelstein points out, they had been carried out by modern Argentines, not pre-modern conquistadors. In what was then a rising Argentina, such ideas came under the broad umbrella of *nacionalismo* which, for its followers, was a pure and sacred doctrine where the 'Führer' was Jesus Christ and the aim was not just support for the European Axis powers but the creation of a 'Greater Argentina' dominant in Latin America.

The Army included many fervent believers in these ideas and it had a taste of power when the Generals staged a coup in 1943 even as the Second World War still raged. Juan Perón had been one of their number but won the presidency with a broader labour-supporting platform when elections were permitted in 1946. Charting a personal and mercurial political path, Perón permitted and sometimes even encouraged fascist ideology but its full flowering and even implementation would have to await the war between leftist terrorists and the Generals in the 1970s which, according to an ideologist of the right, offered the simple choice of 'either the red flag with its hammer and sickle, or the blue and white [Argentine] flag under Christ's cross'.

Marxist and revolutionary ideas had gradually taken root in intellectual circles and in part of the younger generation in Argentina. Che Guevara had studied at Buenos Aires University before helping Fidel Castro to take power in Cuba and becoming a revolutionary icon. Cuba itself, not yet derided as an authoritarian economic basket-case, held a romantic allure for Argentinian would-be revolutionaries, who were relatively small in number but committed and well organised. The revolutionary left was not united – one of the first armed groups to emerge, the ERP, took its inspiration from Leon Trotsky and was therefore suspect in the eyes of Fidel Castro who followed the line of his Soviet backers. The other principal group, the Montoneros, took its name from the gaucho riders who helped to defeat Spain in the Independence War of the 19th century. A number of its members were both Marxists and followers of Juan Perón and it was the Montoneros who were generally seen as having fired the opening shots of the Dirty War in 1970, with the kidnapping and murder of the former President, General Pedro Aramburu. As was to be the case many times in the following years, neither the motives for the killing nor the identity of the killers was entirely clear but a fatal chain of events had been set in motion.

It was a shocking series of attacks by Marxist groups which gave the far right renewed vigour and led in turn to the growth of the Triple A and the recruitment of men such as Aníbal Gordon. In the six years before the Junta's coup in 1976, leftist guerrillas killed almost 700 people including more than 500 policemen and soldiers. Victims included the head of the national gendarmerie, shot down in his house, and the General commanding the Second Army Corps, machine-gunned in his car along with his driver and a newspaper-seller who happened to be standing nearby. Along with the killings there were high-profile kidnappings of business owners and executives, often foreigners, which were designed both to extract ransoms to fund the terrorist groups and to damage the performance and reputation of the Argentine economy. The Coca-Cola company paid out $1 million in ransoms, Kodak $1.5 million and British-American Tobacco almost $2 million. Esso (Exxon) paid the ERP $12 million for the release of their executive Victor Samuelson and it was eventually claimed that the ERP had raided more than 50 towns, robbed 160 banks and taken US $76 million in ransoms from more than 180 kidnappings. The Montoneros hit a criminal jackpot with their kidnapping of the enormously wealthy Born brothers, heirs to a food-processing conglomerate which in the end paid some $60 million in ransoms. An attempt by the ERP to score a populist victory by kidnapping the chief executive of the Argentine branch of the Fiat car company and demanding that a billion pesos be distributed to poor families living near the car plant ended in futile bloodshed when police identified the building where the car boss was being held. After a gun battle the body of the Fiat man was found inside with two bullets in his chest and one in his head. It was, as chroniclers of this period have described, a time of extreme and mounting tension driven by an upward spiral of terror and counterterror. Above all, the revolutionary groups had provided themselves with large war chests to fund their military and terrorist campaigns. The ERP even set up its own arms industry manufacturing bombs and submachine guns, and brought in supplies by air from nearby countries.

As something close to paranoia gripped the leaders of Argentina's security forces, fuelled by an understandable fear of themselves becoming targets, their perception of events and the threat facing them was also strongly influenced by dramatic developments taking place on the other side of the Pacific Ocean in Vietnam. There on April 30th, 1975 the United States had suffered the final defeat of its struggle against communist forces, with the collapse of the South Vietnamese Army and the fall of Saigon to North Vietnamese and Viet Cong troops.

I witnessed these events at first hand, having reported on the last weeks of the war and remained behind to witness the communist takeover. The images were indelible: American helicopters flying desperate people out to the aircraft carriers where the now valueless machines were unceremoniously pushed overboard, increasingly desperate crowds jammed around the US Embassy compound and my own failure to force a way through them to try to evacuate the young daughter of Vietnamese friends, left behind in the chaos when the rest of her family fled by boat. I had to return her to her home to await whatever would take place. A day later in the streets there was the historic but chilling sight of long lines of communist infantrymen walking into the city, clad in simple uniforms and sandals, with rifles in their hands or rocket launchers balanced on their shoulders.[13] It was the final extinction of the Kennedy-era belief that the United States could defend democracy in the paddy fields of Indochina, an idea that had, in reality, died many years before.

For me, behind the exhilaration of covering the story, emotions were mixed. Like many others I felt admiration for the disciplined communist troops and the extraordinary casualties and sacrifices they had endured to achieve their victory. There was a sense of relief that the terrible sufferings of this small country were finally coming to some sort of end and on the other hand there was apprehension at the dark curtain that was now falling on South Vietnam, a place where many city-dwellers in particular had no desire to live under communist rulers, no matter how determined and heroic.

In Argentina, as I was to discover, responses to Vietnam were vivid and often clear-cut. For the small bands of guerrillas and urban terrorists of the ERP, there was inspiration to be found in the triumph of the 'people' and above all the defeat of the imperial ambitions of the United States. ERP leader Roberto Santucho spoke of creating 'many Vietnams', a call that was echoed in Marxist circles across Latin America. The ERP had fewer than 100 armed fighters staging hit-and-run attacks in the mountains of Tucumán but, briefly, it seemed that they could challenge the Argentine Army. Their propaganda sheet, *El Combatiente*, proclaimed: 'We are living a situation of mass uprising in all the Latin American countries ... the concrete possibility of liberated zones is beginning to be seen.'

For the Army and the cruel crusaders of the Triple A, the American defeat by communist guerrillas was a dire and chilling warning of what could take place in their own country unless the most extreme measures were taken. What they found particularly shocking was America's decision to abandon its ally, and in some senses its creation: the South Vietnamese military regime which it had propped up for so long. In Washington a mildly worded but penetrating analysis of sentiment in Latin America prepared for Secretary of State Henry Kissinger spoke of 'A suspicion that even the U.S. has "lost its will" to stand firm against communism because of Viet-Nam, détente, and social decay.' Many Argentinian Army officers saw it in even more simple terms: what had happened to the Generals in Saigon could also happen to them. The American diplomat 'Tex' Harris remembered the explanations given by the military officers with whom it was his job to liaise and who some-times seemed determined to convert him to their cause:

They would discuss with me the need to rid Argentina of the cancer of communism and that the unfortunate thing is that, when you cut out a cancer, sometimes as you're cutting out the bad tissue, you have to take out some of the good tissue in order to protect it. These were the kinds of analogies. Tracing it back, you began to see the roots of these medical analogies to a professor at the Army Military College who so thoroughly indoctrinated each generation of each succeeding class of offi-cers going through the military school. Military school in Argentina takes people who at a young age go to military high schools, then go to military college, and then go to military where they live on a base. They generally marry the daugh-ters of senior officers. They live in this little insular world, and their values and ideas, like a hothouse gone weird, produced a doctrine of killing people who had bad thoughts. It was done knowledgeably. They realized that the people that they were disappearing, interrogating, torturing, and then killing were not people who were going to shoot someone, but they were people who were infected with the bad ideas, and they thought that they were fighting World War III against communism and that the United States one day would wake up and realize that this was the first skirmishes of World War III and these were the battles that were being fought and they were being fought for the West, and that the United States, instead of censuring them for human-rights violations, should in fact be applauding their bravery and their action.[14]

Amid the turmoil Aníbal Gordon was finding his blood-stained destiny. It was a central objective of the authorities' strategy to break the left's hold on trades unionism in key industries. In March 1975 Gordon took part in the violent suppression of industrial action by workers in the city of Villa Constitución. The strikers had taken effective control of the Acindar steelworks whose major shareholder was Eton-educated 'Joe' Martínez de Hoz, soon to become Minister for the Economy under the military Junta and whose austerity policies would reduce wages by 40%, producing chaos. Gordon arrived at the plant as part of a squad of heavily armed paramilitaries, some hooded and wearing dark glasses, in a fleet of the unmarked Ford Falcon cars that would rapidly become the trademark of the *represores*. They set up an interrogation centre in the lodges normally used by the company's executives and, with no pause for niceties such as negotiation with the strikers, proceeded to arrest and torture a number of the workers in order to identify the ringleaders.[15] At least nine supporters of the strike, including a lawyer trying to advise them, were murdered. The industrial 'insurrection' was put down.

At a national level, it was increasingly clear that the more or less civilian government of Juan Perón's widow Isabel was coming apart at the seams. A former nightclub dancer who had comforted the famously charismatic but ageing dictator in his final years, 'Isabelita', as she had been known professionally, had tied the knot with Perón when, during a period in exile in Spain, he came under pressure from the Spanish government to regularise their relationship on proper Catholic lines. Now she was helpless in the face of economic collapse and mounting political violence. In February 1976 the CIA predicted a military takeover:

> [T]he most probable course of events is for the spiral of increasing political violence and economic breakdown to lead to an indefinite takeover of the government by the army. This time the rule of the army would likely be much harsher and more authoritarian than at any time in the past because:
> – The Argentine society will be much closer to anarchy than on any previous occasion of army intervention and, hence the measures to restore order and stimulate economic recovery will have to be much more severe in order to succeed.
> – The limits on using violence will have largely disappeared, so that the army will be less inhibited by cultural constraints from forcibly suppressing any political opposition.[16]

Put at its simplest, this was a prediction of a military coup and an officially authorised campaign of bloodshed which proved all too accurate. The coup duly took place a month later when shortly after midnight on March 24th, the helicopter crew which normally flew President Isabel Perón from the Casa Rosada to her home informed her instead that she was under arrest. 'Isabelita' was taken to the military airport and flown to a base in the south from where she eventually found her way into exile in Spain. Naval officers took control of the Casa Rosada, cutting all telex and telephone communications, while Army soldiers occupied the headquarters of the powerful trades union confederation, the CGT, and the offices of the metalworkers union, whose chief was a principal supporter of the ousted President. Meanwhile armoured vehicles roared up and down the main avenues of the capital in a show of strength. In fact there was little resistance and the takeover of power in this modern society had been surprisingly simple. The question now was how would the Generals, Admirals and Air Commodores who made up the new tripartite military Junta tackle the country's problems?

Almost immediately the crackdown on leftist groups and sympathisers went into high gear. Some leaders of the armed forces had made no secret of their intentions. General Luciano Benjamín Menéndez, Commander of the Third Army Corps in embattled Tucumán province, gave a grim, mathematically-framed, prediction: 'We are going to have to kill 50,000 people: 25,000 subversives, 20,000 sympathisers and we will make 5,000 mistakes,' he said.[17] The Junta's newly appointed Governor of Buenos Aires province, General Ibérico Saint-Jean, was just as brutally explicit: 'First we will kill all the subversives; then we will kill all their collaborators; then their sympathisers; then those who remained indifferent; and finally we'll kill the undecided.'[18]

The chiefs of the Army had decided that subversion by leftist groups must be extirpated with, as far as possible, no survivors left to fight another day.

The organisation of the crackdown reflected the structure of the armed forces throughout the country. The Navy took responsibility for part of the capital, which is historically a port city. Its secret units of killers and torturers were headquartered in the architecturally elegant Escuela de Mecánica de la Armada, the Naval Mechanical School, where behind the classical portico some of the most savage cruelties of the repression took place.

The Air Force took control of a couple of the capital's outer suburbs near one of its bases, while the rest of Buenos Aires and most of the rest of the country were placed in the hands of the Army with its network of regional commands. General Luciano Menéndez, he of the mathematical formula for murder and whose nephew General Mario Menéndez would later be the Junta's Army commander in the Falklands during the war with Britain, set out his justification for 'Operation Independence', which he was carrying out to destroy the ERP guerrilla force in Tucumán, once known as the garden of Argentina:

> We have to act drastically. Operación Independencia can't just consist of a roundup of political prisoners, because the army can't risk the lives of its men and lay its prestige on the line simply to act as a kind of police force that ends up by turning over X-number of political prisoners to some timorous judge ... who will apply lenient punishment which, in turn, will be cancelled out by amnesties granted by ambitious politicians courting popularity. We're at war, and war obeys another law: he who wipes out the other side wins.[19]

The US Embassy soon received a dramatic first-hand account of how these words were being put into effect.[20] Just over a month after the coup a 34 year-old woman called Mercedes Naveiro Bender joined the ranks of victims when she was kidnapped from her home in the capital by six men in civilian clothes. Armed with pistols and claiming to be a 'combined police and military command', they forced their way into her flat after threatening to shoot the door down and proceeded to systematically loot her possessions including money, camera and jewellery before pushing her blindfolded into the well of a car and driving her to an unknown destination. What made the case of Mercedes Naveiro Bender different and provoked the interest of the US government was that she was the divorced wife of an American university professor and an American citizen – though this did not at first appear to impress her kidnappers. In the car, they told the helpless woman that it made no difference to them and that if she did not obey their orders, they would shoot her and dump her on the road.

Bender had no idea where she ended up but it is now thought that she may have been taken to a house in Bacacay Street, Buenos Aires, which had been rented by the military intelligence service, SIDE, and was under the control of none other than Aníbal Gordon. In normal circumstances an unremarkable villa screened from the road by sprawling flowering plants, it was now one of the Junta's many secret detention centres. Some of the prisoners were held in a basement accessed by a ladder. Bender heard the voices of people she knew and the screams and cries of victims apparently being tortured with electric cattle prods. She heard a friend, the owner of an advertising firm, begging for medical attention while his wife appeared to be in a state of delirium.

Her captors told Bender that they were a 'Nazi-Fascist and anti-Semitic organisation dedicated to combating subversion, leftist elements, American cooperation and capitalism as well as the Jewish plot to control the world.'

Bender herself was interrogated to the accompaniment of blows in the face and to the back of the head, causing injuries which were later confirmed and detailed by the US Embassy doctor. She was told that she was a friend of leftist activists and was accused of involvement in international subversion. Her interrogators pressed her to sign some sort of confession, saying that they alone would decide if she left alive or 'feet first'.

She nonetheless described her captors as professional and 'totally systematic'. Their leader, whom she identified as an Air Force Colonel, may in fact have been Aníbal Gordon who was now widely known in the secret world as 'El Coronel' (the Colonel) and often made intimidatory remarks of the kind addressed to Bender. The 'Colonel' told her that 'He would have liked to have killed her but she was a member of the [Argentine] oligarchy and Argentina was still dependent upon American help.'

It was, in fact, prompt American action that appears to have saved Bender's life. The Argentine government made no response to repeated Embassy complaints about her disappearance but inside the house on Bacacay Street, her interrogators were showing signs of being under pressure. One told her that the 'American Embassy is driving us crazy trying to find out where she was being held'. After two days Bender was released on a promise to make no public statement about what had happened and no complaint about the theft of her property. She was told that if she did not keep the promise, she would be followed and killed anywhere in the world. Perhaps to drive the point home, she was told that in the two days she had been at the secret address, four people being held there had been executed.

The US Embassy reported the successful release and a degree of frustration:

Under normal circumstances, we would make strong protest to GOA [Government of Argentina] over incident ... We presume

GOA would simply deny any knowledge of incident, however, and Mrs Bender has repeatedly insisted that she does not wish such a protest to be made in any event ... She fears for her life.

She was not alone.

The establishment of a network of as many as 300 secret prisons and interrogation centres, where kidnapped detainees could be tortured to produce the information enabling further arrests, was a crucial component of the Junta's plans. Some of these were operated by the national police, others were part of a new dark world staffed by men such as Aníbal Gordon, whose importance had grown with the need for killers who would carry out their function professionally and without pity or remorse. These teams worked in close liaison with the Army's 601st Intelligence Battalion that played a key and leading role in collecting and coordinating the information which enabled thousands of victims to be targeted.

The terrorist threat was seen as international, with militant groups in different Latin American nations seeking to form a joint command. To try to ensure that the *subversivos* could not create such a cross-border network Operation Condor and its cutting edge of murder squads, codenamed 'Teseo' after the Greek hero Theseus, had now been agreed between the secret services of half a dozen countries. Argentina was now seen as the country at most immediate risk and Aníbal Gordon was given a key role in turning counter-insurgency theory into brutal and effective practice. Following the orders of General Otto Paladino, the chief of the Army secret service, SIDE, with whom he had a strong personal relationship, Gordon took over a dilapidated former car workshop known as the Automotores Orletti, which still sits across the road from a railway track in a suburb of Buenos Aires, and turned it into a secret torture and execution centre much larger than Bacacay Street. The inside of the building was crudely converted to provide cells, offices and a large chamber equipped with numerous electric power points and suitable for torture. Attempts were made to deaden sound by attaching sheets of cardboard and even egg boxes to the walls. Gordon now had his own *patota*, or gang, consisting both of men with criminal records and Army intelligence officers. The centre he established was to become one of the most notorious locations of the Dirty War and is still, some 45 years later, the object of legal investigation with recently concluded trials of some of the men who ran it. For the people of Buenos Aires, the run-down but still sinister building has become a shrine to the many victims who suffered and died while being held there.

CHAPTER 8

'A world so terrible that it is difficult to imagine'

THESE WERE THE WORDS of the Argentine Attorney General, Pablo Ouviña,[1] when surviving members of Aníbal Gordon's team at the Automotores Orletti finally, after years of evasion and delay, faced a series of trials some 40 years after the worst of their crimes. The former car workshop turned secret prison has become one of the poignant and horrifying sites that continue to remind Argentinians of the period of darkness their country went through.

The secret designation of the men at Automotores Orletti was OT18 (Tactical Operations 18), a unit controlled by the SIDE secret police and the 601st Intelligence Battalion. In practice this torture centre was run by a corps of killers that included both secret policemen and paramilitary civilian criminals, led by Gordon himself. He went under a variety of aliases including, most frequently, 'Colonel Silva' and presided in an 'office' adorned with leather armchairs and a large portrait of Adolf Hitler. There was also a dartboard with a picture of Che Guevara. Gordon and several others in the team were or had been members of the Triple A anti-communist alliance and the entire collective was imbued with anti-Semitism. Gordon boasted to some of the prisoners that he was an admirer of Hitler and lamented the fact that there were still Jews on the face of the Earth. With the black humour common to their breed, members of Gordon's gang knew the oil-stained and sordid Orletti premises as 'El Jardín' (The Garden). They used the ground floor of the building to garage the Ford Falcon cars they drove on their deadly missions, accessing it through the large metal roller-door which remains in place to this day, after radioing in the password, 'Open Sesame'. More than 300 captives were brought here during Aníbal Gordon's reign. Most did not emerge alive. Gordon and his men had their own grimly sarcastic way of describing the fate of their murder victims: 'Está tocando el arpa con San Pedro.' ('That one is playing the harp with Saint Peter.')

Automotores Orletti had a key role under Operation Condor and many of the victims were foreigners, often Uruguayans, Chileans or Bolivians seized by the operation's international tentacles. In the words of the Argentine human-rights organisation CELS, the Centre for Legal and Social Studies:

> Automotores Orletti was the most important clandestine detention centre in the country, although not the only one, placed at the service of the Operation Condor Plan. Militaries from other countries such as Uruguay operated there, carrying out the kidnapping, torture and disappearance of compatriots ... Aníbal Gordon's gang headed the Argentine group of Operation Condor.[2]

The victims were subjected to a swift and brutal production line starting with interrogation under torture. As the kidnapped journalist and survivor Enrique Rodríguez Larreta described in a statement to Amnesty International, it was clear from the first moments, despite the sugar bag his captors had placed over his head, that they had been brought to a house of torment:

> Some of the people were immediately taken upstairs for inter-rogation. From the heart-rending screams that could constantly be heard, I gathered that they were being tortured; this was confirmed when I heard them being brought down again to the place where I was being kept. The guards dragged them along, moaning, and flung them on the concrete floor; they were for-bidden any water, as they 'had been in the machine.'[3]

Prisoners were kept for days or weeks, living in fear under appalling conditions. Food was produced rarely and consisted of the slopped-out remnants of their captors' meals, sometimes with cigarette butts, bottle tops or fruit peel floating in it. The victims' ordeal might in a few cases end with release or transfer to another detention centre, but more often with 'final disposal', a euphemism for murder and the erasure of all physical remains. As Pablo Ouviña described it, 'disap-pearance applied to the corpses of the victims.'

Torture was the *raison d'être* of Aníbal Gordon's 'Jardín'. In recent years Argentina's courts have heard terrible descriptions of the sufferings endured by the prisoners as their interrogators sought to extract information in the most brutal fashion. Torture is prohib-ited under international law, not least by the Universal Declaration of Human Rights of 1948, and is also listed as one of the crimes that constitute a 'grave breach' of the 1949 Geneva Conventions on the treatment of victims of war. Among western political leaders, at least in their public statements, torture was generally regarded with revulsion and seen as a problem being dealt with by the basic human-rights standards developed after the Second World War. But much of Latin America, and in particular Argentina, had followed a different path of post-war political development.

The Argentine military and its instruments like the Automotores Orletti were determined to follow what they called the French Model, referring to France's bloody colonial struggles in Vietnam and, above all, in Algeria where police operations had been placed under the direct control of the military, use of torture had been widespread and, according to its practitioners, highly effective. In the battle for control of Algiers in 1957, the French Army under the command of General Jacques Massu had divided the city into blocks with informants, often hooded when they worked openly with the French troops, reporting suspicious individuals. These were then arrested and frequently tortured to reveal and cripple resistance networks. Historians now believe that about a third of all males living in the Algiers Casbah, which at the time had a total population of some 80,000 inhabitants, were subjected to this treatment. The French Generals claimed complete success, with the destruction of the FLN (Front de Libération Nationale) in Algiers in just seven months. The soldier-historian Bernard Fall, who wrote two influential studies of the French war in Vietnam and who was himself killed by a Viet Cong landmine at the start of the American war, wrote of what he believed was the inescapable role of torture in counter-insurgency warfare: 'Torture is the particular bane of the terrorist, just as anti-aircraft artillery is that of the airman or machine-gun fire that of the foot soldier.'[4]

For Bernard Fall, torture of prisoners was the only way to break up terrorist networks, and commanders in the field had to be authorised to make use of it. From the start of its Dirty War, the Argentine military accepted the truth of this doctrine and based its efforts on it. A new generation of French officers, some of whom were now helping to train the Argentine forces, advised them not to take this course as it would lead to human-rights abuses and great damage to the country's reputation. Their advice was ignored. Commanders, many of whom had been trained at the US School of the Americas in Panama, which Washington has always maintained did not teach methods of physical torture, set up a series of clandestine detention centres like Automotores Orletti – more than 30 in Buenos Aires alone. They did not accept the public mantra of most European security forces, including the British, that information extracted under torture is unreliable, and had no time for more supposedly sophisticated methods such as sensory deprivation or even the waterboarding known to have been used later by the CIA on Islamist terrorists. At Orletti pressure was applied with medieval savagery and some very basic modern skills. A key objective was speed. An informant told the American Defense Intelligence Agency that 'information "literally flies" from one HQ to another. Then, operations are mounted, sometimes in a matter of hours to exploit leads before the terrorists have time to react.'

At Automotores Orletti the surviving victims recall being brought blindfolded by car to an unknown address and then placed in a sort of holding cell. What they remember are the sounds: the loud metallic grinding of the large roller-door leading into what had been the car repair workshop. They recall the sound of trains, which passed in front of the building. They can still hear the voices and laughter of children who played in the yard of a school not far away. Above all they remember the screams of other victims. Some who managed to see past their blindfold or had it taken off remember a man they identified as Aníbal Gordon giving orders as he presided over his personal version of hell.

One of the torturers' favourites was the *colgada* or 'hanging'. People were taken to a large room 'where there was a steel frame with a hook from which the victims were suspended, making them dangle with their arms placed behind them.' They were then lowered, causing them to touch the floor, which had been flooded with water and coarse salt, with the tips of their feet while electric shocks were applied, often with the cattle prods long favoured by Argentine interrogators. Buckets of water were thrown over the prisoners to intensify the effects of the electricity. 'In this way the victims suffered multiple injuries and humiliations (such as the inability to control their bodily functions).'

Further torture techniques recounted by survivors included 'brutal beatings'; the 'telephone', which consisted of blows to the ears; the 'dry submarine' in which bags were placed over the head to produce asphyxiation, or 'wet submarine', where victims were lowered from the hook into a vat of water until they were close to drowning. There was also the *plantón* – being forced to remain standing for long periods; mock executions; and being forced to watch loved ones themselves being tortured.

Sometimes the torturers would seek to display the depth of their knowledge about the victims' activities and the subversive organisations to which they were said to belong. One man recalled attempting to deny any contact with a fellow activist only for his interrogators to play sound recordings of telephone conversations between the two of them. This was then used as a cue for further torture and, possibly, further arrests or, more accurately, kidnappings, outside.

Today the grim, roughly constructed building in which these events took place is a 'Sitio Recuperado Para la Memoria', a site preserved as a memorial. The large metal garage door is covered in crude painted inscriptions proclaiming that this is where more than 300 of the 'disappeared' met their end. In the age of Covid, internet tours enable inspection of chambers that in the days of Aníbal Gordon would have been for many a final destination. Inside, the crude bare brick interiors have been whitewashed and small printed cards telling the stories of individual victims placed at different points on the walls. In converting the former car-repair workshop into a prison Gordon's men had knocked down walls to create larger, easy-to-control spaces where the prisoners would be held or taken to be tortured. Victims sat or slept on the concrete floors under orders to remain silent. Holes had been made in the walls of their cells by the simple expedient of knocking out individual bricks so that any noise they made was audible to the armed men next door.

In the centre of the upper floor was the large double-height chamber where the hook was fastened to the ceiling and the *colgada* took place. All around the walls was electric cabling punctuated at regular intervals with power sockets enabling the electric shocks which were an essential part of the torture to be administered. The room believed to have been Aníbal Gordon's office with the image of his hero on the wall was next door. In another chamber the walls are pockmarked with bullet holes, some of them covered with render by the building's owner when he took back possession after renting it to the secret police.

Next to the building is the small yard where children used to play. It is said that some of the youngsters reported to their parents that they had heard terrible sounds coming from inside. The parents apparently told them that they must be imagining it or that they should simply keep quiet. The era of Aníbal Gordon was not a time to report such happenings, least of all to the police.

Even as Gordon's gang were launching into their grisly business, terrorists of the People's Revolutionary Army (ERP) threw down the gauntlet in June 1976 with the carefully prepared murder of the Federal Police chief, Brigadier General Cesáreo Cardozo, a killing that illustrated all the chilling horror of the conflict. A bombing was carried out by an eighteen year-old girl, Ana María González, who was a classmate of the police chief's daughter and had set out to befriend her in order to gain access to their home. She had earlier been arrested herself on suspicion of involvement in terrorism, but the police chief's daughter had persuaded her father to secure her release. On the night of the murder González came to dinner at Cardozo's house carrying a concealed time bomb which, on the excuse of going to the bathroom, she managed to place under his bed. It exploded later that night, killing both the Brigadier General and his wife. González went into hiding but later gave an interview about her exploit in which she complained about having had to make 'one of the militant's worst sacrifices', 'namely socialising with the detested enemy in order to win their confidence'.

A fortnight later the ERP's competitors, the Montoneros, carried out their own deadly attack on the police by detonating a powerful bomb in the dining room of the police intelligence department in the capital. The bomb went off at lunchtime, blowing part of the building into the street and killing at least eighteen people, mainly police officials. Another 66 were injured. That this was a blow at the heart of the Junta that had seized power only four months before was shown by the appearance of the new unelected President, General Jorge Videla, among the mourners at the mass funeral that was attended by thousands and escorted by troops in historic parade-ground dress.

Aníbal Gordon himself was soon exploring new realms of horror as he strove to do his masters' bidding and penetrate the terrorist networks. The arrest of a young Argentine woman emerging from the Cuban Embassy in Buenos Aires had proved a fruitful line of inquiry and provides a vivid insight into part of the secret struggle of the Cold War as carried out in the unrestrained environment of Argentina. The woman was found to be in possession of a large amount of currency and under 'interrogation' by Gordon's team she confessed that the Cubans had given her the money to support the subversive activities of the Marxist ERP. Some intelligence services would have regarded this as a considerable opportunity to be exploited with care to extract maximum advantage. But it seems that Argentina's military men saw the event as dramatic confirmation of the belief which they hoped their US allies would share – that they were at the front line of a new world war unfolding in Latin America. The affair was placed in the hands of Aníbal Gordon who organised a savage response aimed at kidnapping members of the Cuban Embassy. According to a US Embassy report on the event, he placed an ambulance in the street near the Cuban Embassy and used it and a number of other vehicles to ambush two Cuban security men when they left the building. Gordon's gang were apparently under orders not to fire their weapons and a brutal physical struggle ensued. In the end the two Cubans, Jesús Cejas Arias and Crescencio Galañena, who had allegedly been involved in providing material support to Argentine armed groups, were overpowered and driven to Automotores Orletti, where they were subjected to severe torture.[5] A leading anti-communist Cuban exile, Luis Posada Carriles, who dedicated his life to the overthrow of Fidel Castro and his regime, later boasted in his memoirs, *The Paths of the Warrior*, that he had flown to Buenos Aires to take part in the torture of his fellow countrymen in Aníbal Gordon's secret prison. All useful information extracted, Gordon and his team are then said to have finished off the two Cubans with bursts of fire from submachine guns fitted with silencers and cemented the bodies inside a pair of 55-gallon oil drums which were dumped in the Paraná River. The US Embassy reported some of the details a few weeks later and the Cuban Ambassador seems to have been informed in the same time frame. He made a formal request to the Argentine Junta that the disappearance of the two men, both accredited as diplomats, be investigated. But it was not until 2013 that a forensic team assigned by the now civilian Argentine government used earth-moving equipment to try to find the oil drums and the human remains inside them. They located more than twenty drums containing human body parts, two of which, they believe, held the Cubans. Partly disintegrated and stranded above the waterline, one of the drums had become home to a colony of bees.

At the 'Jardín', a number of witnesses whose veracity has been accepted by the courts of the post-Junta era have described how Gordon and his gang enjoyed their licence to torture and kill. Gordon himself was in operational command as the most senior civilian working for the SIDE intelligence service under the orders of its chief, General Otto Paladino. Their relationship was reinforced by the General's ownership of a private security company named 'Magister', which employed Gordon's sister.

Gordon's qualifications, and his value to the Junta, were in violence and he and his men appeared to celebrate that. They gave each other familiar nicknames reflecting their position in the team or some particular attribute. As well as 'El Coronel', Gordon was known as 'El Viejo' (the Old Man). Another gang member, Osvaldo Forese, who was notable for his size and strength, as well as his brutal and bloodthirsty nature, was known as 'Paqui' after *paquidermo*, the Spanish word for elephant, because of his talent for breaking down doors during raids. Others, for reasons that can only be guessed at, were known as 'Puma', 'kric-kric', or 'Chino'. Like Gordon, these men made no secret of their Nazi sympathies. According to survivor Raúl Luis Altuna Facal, 'several times I heard them talking about the "final solution" and "the best enemy is the dead enemy".' Enrique Rodríguez Larreta said he was asked by Gordon if he spelt Rodríguez with an S or with a Z, because if it was with an S it could be of Jewish origin and in that case 'it would be worse for him'.

In their role as a core team of Operation Condor – which was headquartered in Argentina – the Gordon Gang, as it came to be known, worked closely with their opposite numbers from Uruguay, Chile and several other Latin American nations, frequently arresting and torturing citizens of those countries before sometimes flying them back to face the tender mercies of their own secret services. Formulae by which the nations involved would pay the expenses of these operations were even then being negotiated in detail. They were recorded in the Condor agreement now made public by US declassification and provide yet another lesson in the banality of evil:

1. The administration of expenses incurred by the operations centre will be the responsibility of the headquarters country (Argentina).

2. A common fund composed of $10,000 donations from each member country is established for the purpose of offsetting operational expenses. This fund will be replenished in equal parts at the end of each operation during a period not to exceed 15 days ...

To ensure that the travelling killers could present a respectable appearance – they tended to favour light grey suits – there was even a clothing allowance:

4. Operational costs abroad are estimated at $3,500 per person for ten days, with an additional $1,000 the first time out for clothing allowance.

In the ghastly reality of Automotores Orletti, Gordon's team and their cross-border collaborators had seized on their role as a means of self-enrichment considerably in excess of any pettifogging allowances. A common recollection of those who for one reason or another survived the process of kidnap and torture is of the systematic looting of their homes and personal possessions by the men who sometimes, like Gordon, had graduated to the security services from a career in crime. Items of value were frequently brought back to the Automotores Orletti along with their owners and the potential resale value openly discussed in front of them. Some Uruguayan prisoners recall that when, after repeated bouts of torture, they were flown to the Uruguayan capital Montevideo, a number of their possessions, which had now become the 'war booty' of their guards, were loaded with them on the plane that carried them.

Amid the profiteering, Aníbal Gordon and his masters in the intelligence service and the Army enjoyed a major triumph in their war against the left. A principal objective had always been to seize or kill the leader of the ERP, Mario Roberto Santucho, the guerrilla leader some compared to Che Guevara. At the end of March 1976 Federal Police had raided a property in Buenos Aires province where the ERP leadership was holding a top-level conference with Chilean, Uruguayan and Bolivian revolutionaries. They were meeting to consolidate the so-called 'Revolutionary Coordinating Junta' or JCR, which was intended to coordinate the activities of left-wing insurgent groups throughout the region. The result of the security forces' attack on this secret meeting was a running battle in which a number of the leftists were killed or captured but Santucho himself managed to escape. Soon afterwards Aníbal Gordon seized the guerrilla leader's brother Carlos and sister Manuela, and subjected Carlos in particular to savage torture to the point where a surviving witness describes him as crawling in delirium on the floor.

In one of the now-declassified American reports filed soon after the event, the FBI representative at the US Embassy, Robert Scherrer, implied that crucial information leading to the ERP leader's final hiding place was extracted by torture from a captured terrorist named Mena: 'Mena, after initial resistance, cooperated ... in providing locations of ERP safe houses and the identities of ERP support personnel.'[6]

A team of agents from the SIE, the operational branch of the SIDE intelligence service, then burst into one of the safe houses where a chaotic battle ensued.

Immediately after entering the apartment, two unidentified male individuals were observed sitting in an extremely small kitchen ... The SIE Captain, armed with a 9mm machine gun, commanded the two unidentified male individuals to stand up from the table and put themselves on the floor of the kitchen. In the process of placing themselves on the floor, an individual, subsequently identified as ERP leader JORGE BENITO URTEAGA, managed to execute an abrupt manoeuvre, kicking the machine gun out of the Army Captain's hands. After clattering to the floor, the machine gun was recovered by the other male individual subsequently identified as MARIO ROBERTO SANTUCHO. SANTUCHO fired the machine gun at point blank range at the Army Captain and two rounds were discharged striking the Captain in the chest and arm before the machine gun jammed. URTEAGA and SANTUCHO had no other weapons available to them and were gunned down by two SIE Agents. The SIE Army Captain died on route to a hospital.

The FBI officer drew his own moral from the story. He was concerned by the poor organisation of the security forces' operation, in particular the way that information extracted from captured terrorists was being used.

> The entire episode as narrated above demonstrates the general modus operandi of Argentine security forces in running down leads secured from ... ERP prisoners and/or documentation without first conducting basic checks of the information.

However, when the shooting was over the leader of the People's Revolutionary Army, revered by his followers and still mourned by some to this day, was dead. At the Automotores Orletti, Aníbal Gordon celebrated in his own cruel fashion. Roberto Santucho's sister Manuela was forced to read out newspaper reports announcing her brother's death to the other prisoners while his brother Carlos was goaded by being told he must eat something to mark the event. According to the witness who survived, a Uruguayan named Alicia Cadenas who was picked up under Operation Condor and still does not understand how she emerged alive, Carlos Santucho told his captors: '... kill me whenever you want, you have already taken the lives of my children and my entire family, I am not interested in living ...'

Gordon's gang was quick to oblige. Turning on the engines of their cars to hide Santucho's cries, they repeatedly lowered him into a tank of water until he lost consciousness. His body was later found dumped in a vacant lot some distance away. Soon afterwards

Manuela Santucho was also murdered and joined the ranks of the 'disappeared'. A now released document from the US Department of Defense remarked clinically that 'security forces have engaged in additional neutralization operations and have reportedly wiped out most of the ERP organization.'[7]

Reading the files of evidence assembled by the new Argentine judicial authorities of what took place under Operation Condor – and in particular in the Orletti building which was for a time its operational base – is a chilling experience, especially for those who can claim to have had a taste of Aníbal Gordon's methods. Examining the details of one kidnapping carried out by Gordon and his men, I suddenly found myself living again what happened to us in the streets of Buenos Aires a few years later. The victims in this case were three Argentinian actors, including Adalberto Luis Brandoni, the General Secretary of the Argentine Actors' Association, and his wife Marta Raquel Bianchi. The couple, who both had strong left-wing sympathies, had earlier been threatened by the far-right Triple A for which, as I have related, Gordon had already carried out a series of killings, and had taken the warning sufficiently seriously to leave the country and spend a year abroad. Now back in Buenos Aires, the couple left the theatre where they were performing and got into a car belonging to friends. They were immediately intercepted by a group of heavily armed men dressed in civilian clothes led by someone they later identified as Aníbal Gordon. Brandoni was forced into Gordon's car at gunpoint and quickly blindfolded – 'walled in'. His wife and a female friend were forced into a second vehicle. Bianchi described being forced to lie in the rear well of the car and having a cloth placed over her head. As he did in my case, Gordon used the radio in his car to exchange messages with his base. According to later prosecutions, the purpose of such messages was to clear the transit of these armed convoys through different security zones in the capital, in this case an area for which the Argentine Navy was responsible. This is said to demonstrate that these kidnappings were officially sanctioned operations.

On this night in 1976, the destination was the Automotores Orletti and the statements the actors later made in court after the fall of the Junta give a unique and terrifying first-hand glimpse of what many victims went through, never to re-emerge. The actors described Orletti as a frightening, noisy place with men shouting, car doors banging and martial music playing through loudspeakers. They were interrogated by Gordon in his upstairs office beneath his portrait of Adolf Hitler and with men armed with automatic weapons standing beside him. He asked them why they had left the country the year before.

Brandoni replied, 'Because I was threatened by the Triple A.'

'And why did you come back?'

Brandoni recalled saying something like, 'Because I am Argentine and I have the right to be in my country.'

According to his account, Gordon then said: 'Well, we are the Triple A. You came back to sh*t on us and now we are going to sh*t on you ...' He told them that the two women would be raped and then they would all be killed. However, after this 'interrogation' Gordon received another radio message and his tone changed from violent threats to gallows humour. From now on, he told them, they should celebrate their birthdays on that date, July 9th, because they had been 'born again'.

This was Aníbal Gordon's way of saying that his orders had changed and he was going to release them. 'You must have your very own God,' the actors remember him saying, 'because no one gets out of here alive.'[8]

After a final warning not to do what Gordon called 'Bolshy' (Bolshevik) work or associate with Jews, they were loaded back into Ford Falcon cars and deposited in the frightening streets of the capital.

Outside the walls of the oil- and blood-stained torture centre the vicious cycle of violence and reprisal was again taking hold. On August 19th, 1976, a month after the publicly announced killing of Roberto Santucho and the private murder by Aníbal Gordon's team of the guerrilla leader's brother and sister, a terrorist group gunned down the retired General Omar Actis, whom the Junta had placed in charge of preparations for the forthcoming 1978 football World Cup, an appointment of enormous significance in Argentine eyes. On the day of his murder he had been due to introduce the committee appointed to organise the event. Instead he was cut down in a hail of gunfire while driving his Chevrolet near his home in a well-to-do district of the capital. On the same day other terrorists murdered the Italian deputy manager of Fiat's largest railroad equipment plant in Latin America, in the town of Córdoba. The Junta leader, General Videla, attended the funeral of General Actis and then appointed his replacement, a Navy Admiral who promptly declared that he had a habit of keeping a loaded pistol with him at all times.

The terrible reprisals taken by the security forces for the Actis murder have been described in Chapter 2. The mangled remains of the dead Montoneros from what is now known as 'the Fatima Massacre' were duly picked up by a truck from the Municipality of Pilar.

Throughout this entire period in 1976, Gordon himself was engaged in a detailed hunt with a very precise objective. His leading role in Operation Condor's international network opened the door to collaboration with the secret police of neighbouring Uruguay which was then battling another Marxist group, the 'Partido por la Victoria del Pueblo' (the People's Victory Party) or PVP. Following a crackdown in Uruguay a number of the PVP's leaders and sympathisers had taken refuge on the other side of the River Plate in Buenos Aires, but the reason for Gordon's increasingly obsessive interest in them appears to have been less ideological than mercenary. Two years earlier the PVP had succeeded in taking possession of a substantial 'war chest' of $10 million by kidnapping and ransoming a Dutch businessman who had made his fortune in the wool trade between Latin America and Europe. The question that Gordon was determined to answer was: where had the PVP hidden the money?

To try to solve this lucrative riddle Gordon and his Uruguayan opposite number, Major José Gavazzo, carried out a series of kidnap operations, seizing and then torturing Uruguayan leftists in the Argentine capital with Uruguayan secret-service officers apparently playing a leading role in the torments being applied in this Argentine dungeon. The targets kept in shackles at the Automotores Orletti included Gerardo Gatti, the leader of the PVP, and León Duarte, a trades unionist who was also a key figure in the revolutionary group, but in spite of the terrible pressure applied to them the two would not, or could not, provide the required information. Gordon then permitted a blindfolded intermediary from the PVP to be brought under guard to the Automotores Orletti and offered to release Gatti in exchange for $2 million. A series of such meetings took place, Gordon assisting with the production of a photograph of Gatti holding a newspaper in the Orletti prison to prove that he was still alive. But the ghastly bargaining produced no results. Gordon then claimed that Gatti had been moved; Duarte was last seen by the intermediary who later described what he witnessed:

He said that Duarte appeared in a half-sleeved shirt and a scarf wrapped around him, that he looked like a mummy, totally white, that his feet were bare, that when he saw him he asked him how he was and Duarte answered, 'How am I going to be? It has been four or five days since they barely gave me a piece of bread and some water.' Gordon then gave orders to bring him food and some shoes, but the person who was supposed to look for Duarte's shoes asked how he was going to find them since there were 80 pairs of shoes downstairs.

According to the intermediary, Gordon told the Uruguayan Major Gavazzo: 'These guys are bullshitting. We are going to have to kill 20 or 30 of them so that they stop screwing around and trying to take us for a ride.' Duarte whispered to the intermediary: 'Leave now. They are going to kill you.'[9]

The intermediary was able to depart and immediately fled to Sweden. Neither of the two PVP leaders was ever seen again.

Gordon and Gavazzo pressed on with a further round-up of Uruguayans in September. This time the hiding place of much of the money was identified and a large search party equipped with pickaxes took over a building in Buenos Aires and apparently recovered as much as $6 million from inside a wall where the money had been concealed. With no further use for them, Gordon's men seem to have simply killed a number of the people they had seized. Others were flown back to Uruguay with their guards telling them, apparently truthfully, that they were being saved from the Argentinian 'murderers'.

To Aníbal Gordon's gang and their Uruguayan cohorts, it might have seemed like a job well done but there were loose ends that would come back to haunt them. What had happened to the millions of dollars? The Uruguayan Major Gavazzo is known to have flown some of it to Montevideo stuffed in a briefcase with bundles of notes visible under the flap. The question of what became of the rest is still being argued over today. More important was the human cost: How many had died at Automotores Orletti and in the other clandestine centres, and could anything have been done to halt the murders?

CHAPTER 9

Americans Divided

ASSEMBLING A PICTURE of how the US government reacted to the crimes committed by its leading ally in Latin America has been a complex process. It began with the release of some State Department documents in the early 2000s and was greatly amplified by President Obama's decision which opened many CIA and Department of Defense files. Though much material is still denied, the declassification of so many previously secret US documents amounts to an at least partial admission of complicity in the horrors that were taking place in Argentina. It is also a display of openness and internal debate in which no other major country has yet engaged on such an issue. It has provided evidence of disquiet and disagreements in Washington and at the US Embassy in Buenos Aires over what were seen as the excesses of the Junta's 'anti-terrorist campaign' and Operation Condor.

Initially the US Ambassador to Buenos Aires, Robert Hill, had described the Junta's leader, General Jorge Videla, as a 'moderate' and awarded the coup the dubious accolade of 'probably the best executed and most civilised coup in Argentine history'. Three months later as the evidence of 'disappearances' piled up he reported to Washington that the numbers of illegal arrests being carried out 'run into the thousands and many have been tortured and murdered', but he attributed these 'excesses' to paramilitaries and elements of the armed forces and police on whom President Videla was forced to depend. Meanwhile the Assistant Secretary of State, Harry Shlaudeman, had told his boss Henry Kissinger that the Argentine 'security forces are totally out of control'.[1]

It was, however, Operation Condor and its threat of cross-border murder missions organised by Latin American nations collaborating independently that seemed to provoke the greatest concern. In August 1976, while Aníbal Gordon's blood-stained activities at Automotores Orletti were gathering pace, the US State Department held an internal meeting to discuss Condor and what was described as the 'assassination problem'. A cable in the name of the Secretary of State Henry Kissinger was then sent to US Embassies in the countries that had signed up to Operation Condor. It expressed approval of the information exchanges that were taking place as a result of the operation but concern at 'rumours' that the assassination of 'subversives, politicians and prominent figures' was being planned on an international scale. The cable went on:

> While we cannot substantiate the assassination rumors, we feel impelled to bring to your attention our deep concern. If these rumors were to have any shred of truth they would create a most serious moral and political problem ... Counter-terrorist activity of this type would further exacerbate public world criticism of governments involved.[2]

The cable instructed Ambassadors to make representations to the highest appropriate officials, preferably to the heads of state of the

Condor countries. But, in the case of Argentina, it also appeared to suggest that what the Junta did to its own citizens was its own business:

> We are fully aware of security threats created by terrorist activities within Argentina. It is not the intention of the U.S. Government to attempt to advise the Government of Argentina on how best to get its internal security problem under control.

In fact there is no evidence that any 'representations' were made to the Condor countries at that stage. Soon afterwards, however, Kissinger himself met the Argentine Junta's Foreign Minister, Admiral César Guzzetti, in Santiago, Chile, and gave him some crisp advice. 'If there are things that have to be done, you should do them quickly,' Kissinger told him, though he also urged Guzzetti to 'get back quickly to normal procedures.'[3] He told Guzzetti that he wanted to see the Argentine government 'succeed'. In what appears to have been an attempted witticism, Kissinger told the Argentine that they could give their spare terrorists to the Palestine Liberation Organisation: 'They need more terrorists.'

It is known that Kissinger's remarks horrified Ambassador Robert Hill, from whose eyes scales were gradually falling. Hill met Guzzetti on his return to Buenos Aires from a further trip to Washington and described him as 'euphoric' and 'almost ecstatic'.[4] According to the Ambassador, Guzzetti had been 'fully expecting to hear some strong, firm, direct warnings on his government's human-rights practices. Rather than that, he has returned in a state of jubilation, convinced that there is no real problem with the United States over this issue.'

In a rare display of open dissent by an Ambassador, Hill expressed his disappointment with the impression of US support which

Guzzetti had received: 'While this conviction exists, it will be unrealistic and ineffective for this Embassy to press representations to the GOA [Government of Argentina] over human-rights violations.' Ambassador Hill was later replaced; meanwhile Kissinger himself came to be revered by the Junta as a sort of patron saint. Even after his departure from government with the victory of Democrat Jimmy Carter in the Presidential election of 1976, he was introduced as guest of honour to fervent crowds at the 1978 football World Cup in Argentina. In a bizarre episode still debated by football historians, Kissinger accompanied the leader of the Junta, President Jorge Videla, on a visit to the dressing room of the Peruvian team shortly before their all-important match with the host nation, in which the Argentinian team needed an overwhelming victory to get through to the final. In front of Kissinger and surrounded by armed guards, the Junta leader told the Peruvian team that this was a match between brothers which he hoped would go well. On the pitch Argentina duly secured the win by the four goals they needed to go through and then, as predicted by Kissinger, won the cup. Only sceptics claimed that the Peruvian team had been bribed to lose the vital match and that Videla had brokered a secret deal with Peru's leader, General Morales-Bermúdez, to arrest and imprison more than a dozen Peruvian dissidents in Argentina and make secret payments totalling US $50 million to high officials in Peru in exchange for the needed triumph on the pitch.

As the Dirty War continued some of the US diplomats inside their Embassy feared that they themselves might become targets of terrorism. An American honorary consul in a provincial town was shot in what appeared to be a terrorist attack and an Embassy security officer warned that staff should try to make their routines unpredictable, even when they played golf. According to diplomat

'Tex' Harris he said: 'If you do play golf, then don't play the holes in order. Play one and then play six and then play seven and eight, and then play two and four and whatever, but change it around.' US Marines armed with heavy machine guns were stationed at the Ambassador's residence. At the Embassy itself, 'They even had automatic shotguns with not just three or four shells in them but had big magazines of fifteen or twenty shotgun shells, and enough tear gas to quell a hundred riots, just absolute over-reaction.'

The most severe tensions were over how to report the 'repression' that the Argentine Junta was engaged in. 'Tex' Harris was the Embassy's Human Rights Officer. Known as a friendly giant whose all-American name and manner belied his East European Jewish descent, he was appalled by undeniable evidence of the Junta's widespread use of torture and murder and, for a time, found a receptive audience in Washington under the new presidency of Jimmy Carter, who was determined to put human rights at the centre of policy-making. But most of the Embassy saw these concerns as a dangerous distraction from its central mission of cementing a key political and military alliance and assisting the sale of valuable military equipment to Argentina.

'I had many fights at the Embassy,' Harris said later. Though the participants were not to know it, these 'fights' would have a significant impact on the Argentine Junta's performance in the Falklands War just a few years later.

The now-released State Department documents include the transcript of a remarkable voice message sent in 1978 by Harris to Patricia 'Patt' Derian, the Under Secretary of State for Human Rights in Washington, who was sympathetic to Harris's concerns. The lengthy statement sent over a secure line spelt out the difficulties the diplomat was experiencing in reporting the Junta's criminal behaviour through the normal Embassy channels and the misleading picture that resulted.

> We are polishing up the good news – delaying and homogenizing the bad news – and we have now come to a point where we're just not reporting certain things at all. I had hoped that my constant pecking away at the conscience of the country team would over time produce some results. I am now convinced that to a man everyone in the embassy feels that the implementation of the President's human rights policy towards Argentina is wrong. They, of course, to a man would agree human rights is a terribly important part of our foreign policy and our national heritage however we should not refuse to sell sophisticated communications systems, tear gas or helicopters as an expression of our concerns with the Argentine human rights situation.

'Tex' Harris himself had become a lightning rod. Determined to compile some sort of record of the mounting numbers of 'disappeared', he printed up business cards and went to Buenos Aires' central square, Plaza de Mayo, where he handed them out, particularly to the victims' mothers who demonstrated there once a week. He encouraged families of the disappeared to visit him at the US Embassy. 'I opened the door to the embassy, and people started coming. Then we worked the operation like a high turn-over doctor's or dentist's office,' Harris recalled in an interview shortly before his death in 2020,[5] describing how each disappearance was recorded by his assistant on a file card:

> [T]his was before computers – their name, their address, their telephone number, the name of their child or relative that had

disappeared or friend who had disappeared, the date of the disappearance ... and I would interview the person, generally in Spanish, for ten minutes maximum, maybe five, getting the facts, writing the information down on the card ... We did literally thousands of interviews.

Harris was another who experienced the looking-glass world of dealings with the Argentine military with whom he was supposed to preserve friendly relations. 'So I'd be sitting and having a lunch with generals and captains who were actually running the squads that were killing the people whose parents I interviewed that afternoon. It was really crazy.'

From 1977 to 1979 Harris filed 13,500 complaints about human-rights violations with the Argentine authorities, reporting to the State Department that Argentina's military leaders had 'a clear intention to exterminate' anyone who opposed them.

'There was no due process,' Harris said. 'There were no trials. There were no appeals.'

Even Harris and his family came under threat from Argentine authorities and militia groups but he did not allow this to affect his reporting.

Despite the Carter administration's proclaimed emphasis on human rights, Harris found only limited support in the upper echelons of the State Department. However, Patricia Derian, Carter's human-rights chief, acted on Harris's reporting by flying to Argentina in 1977 to confront the Junta's leaders including Admiral Emilio Massera, commander of the Navy and, according to subsequent evidence, one of the most blood-stained figures in the Dirty War.

According to Derian's own account she told Massera at his Naval headquarters: 'You and I both know that as we speak, people are being tortured right here under this roof. In fact somebody's probably being tortured under our feet right now.'[6] After that meeting, an aide to the President of Argentina employed an increasingly familiar mantra, declaring that Derian had failed to understand the central issue: 'what we are having to do here to fight World War III.'

But as the Americans would soon discover, the claim made by the Argentines and their Latin American allies that they were pursuing an essential global mission, would rapidly produce some very uncomfortable results.

CHAPTER 10

Flight of the Condor

Aníbal Gordon was emerging as a key figure in the area which was causing real concern in Washington – the development of Operation Condor into an international strike-force carrying out its killings and kidnappings almost anywhere in the world. An important document written by the US Department of Defense Intelligence in late 1976 had signalled this new phase in the operation:

> A special team has apparently been organised in Argentina for use in 'Operation Condor'. They are members of the Argentine Army Intelligence Service and the State Secretariat for Information. They are reportedly structured much like a US Special Forces Team with a medic, (doctor), demolition expert, etc. They are apparently being prepared for action in Phase Three.[1]

Another report from the CIA spelled out the objectives of Phase Three even more clearly:

> A third and most secret phase of 'Operation Condor' involves the formation of special teams from member countries who

are to travel anywhere in the world to non-member countries
to carry out sanctions up to assassination against terrorists or
supporters of terrorist organisations from 'Operation Condor'
member countries.[2]

Gordon himself was apparently a key member of a Phase Three special
team. He was now in possession of a Uruguayan diplomatic passport
in a false name and, grimly amusing for me at least, a fake press card
naming him as a correspondent of the Argentina News Agency. A
detailed CIA report, the first mentioning him by name, states that he
had been given the job of organising an operation to kill Montonero
leaders who had taken refuge in Europe: 'Aníbal Gordon was the person who was to direct and personally take part in the operation.'[3]

A series of US documents, some of them heavily redacted,
explains that France and Portugal were regarded as principal areas of
operation, and that the 'terrorists' would be hunted down and killed
in or near their homes.

> The basic mission of the teams being sent to operate in France
> as part of Operation Condor will be to liquidate top-level ter-
> rorist leaders. The teams' intelligence collection effort will be
> primarily tactical with the objective of locating where the ter-
> rorist leaders reside.[4]

The CIA quoted its unnamed sources as saying that there would be
a joint target list agreed between the Condor countries and joint
teams to carry out the killings. Once the required intelligence on
targets and locations had been collected, 'the forward command and
coordinating unit in Buenos Aires' would dispatch the assassination
squad. False documentation for these teams would be provided by
the various Condor countries.

It was not explained how differences of opinion on who should be liquidated would be resolved. Chile, under the dictatorship of Augusto Pinochet, was said to be an enthusiastic partner in these efforts, while the secret service of Uruguay was also fully committed and was apparently considering expanding the target list in France to include Uruguayan opposition politicians who might be visiting there. The Uruguayans were, however, complaining that the cost of sending a two-man team to Paris, set at $50,000, was not in their budget. Brazil was said to be unwilling to take part in European operations and would limit its contribution to providing communications equipment for 'Condortel', the supposedly secure communications network which would be established to link the secret services of the different member countries.

In late 1976 the CIA reported that training courses for the teams being sent to France were now being planned, while the scope of operations had been broadened to include potential targets anywhere in the world. Shockingly, the CIA reported that some leaders of Amnesty International, which had infuriated the Junta by repeatedly turning the spotlight on incidents of murder and torture, might be included in the target list.[5]

In December the first operation against three individuals in France took place. It is not known if this was the action directed by Aníbal Gordon but it ended in fiasco with the first target – whose name is redacted from the CIA report but who may have been the Montonero leader Mario Firmenich, then staying in Paris – fleeing before the assassins could locate him. According to the CIA:

One day before the Condor team located his house [REDACTED] suddenly left his residence. The Condor team is convinced there was a leak of information about their

123

operational plan to the terrorists who in turn alerted [REDACTED].[6]

The CIA document naming Gordon says his operation in Europe was 'suspended' and the Argentine leadership of the Condor assassination project apparently complained about the problems of maintaining operational secrecy in teams of mixed nationality. In fact, they had been as lax as anyone. Missions abroad became the subject of gossip, with intelligence officers joking that colleagues sent on one were 'flying like a Condor'.

It is not known to what extent the US government alerted European leaders and security services about the plans of the Condor nations and the target lists they had been drawing up. What is clear is that US officials were increasingly concerned that the wilder elements in Condor were even happy to attack enemies in the United States itself.

What suddenly made Condor a major issue in Washington was a terrorist atrocity carried out in the heart of the US capital. On September 21st, 1976 a powerful explosion ripped through Embassy Row in the centre of the city. The target was a car driven by Orlando Letelier, an increasingly effective exiled opponent of Chile's strongman, General Pinochet. Letelier was killed almost instantly, his legs blown off. His assistant, Ronni Moffitt, also died. As the investigation into the background and organisation of the bombing developed, links began to emerge to the Chilean intelligence service, DINA, and through them to Operation Condor.

Soon afterwards the Director of the CIA, George H.W. Bush, made a telephone call to a US Congressman to warn him that he was on a Latin American hit list. The man he called was Ed Koch, later to become Mayor of New York, who had angered the dictatorship in

Uruguay across the River Plate from Argentina by strong criticism of its human-rights record. The Uruguayan regime had jailed about one in 50 of its citizens and Koch had called for the $3 million in military aid which the US provided annually to be cancelled. Koch apparently hoped that defunding Uruguay would lead to measures against the more powerful military regimes in Chile and Argentina. Bush said he should be very careful.

The warning to Ed Koch was based on a report from Frederick Latrash, the CIA Station Chief in the Uruguayan capital Montevideo, on what he had heard at a party also attended by Uruguayan officers including Major José Gavazzo, collaborator of Aníbal Gordon and enthusiastic torturer. As the drink flowed the CIA man found himself under attack for what the Latin Americans claimed were damaging inconsistencies in US policy. Wasn't it odd that the United States would spend millions of dollars training and equipping Latin American militaries in the war against communism only to criticise the manner in which they pursued their enemies? To the Uruguayan officers it seemed hypocritical and one of them then came out with the remark that set alarm bells ringing: 'Maybe,' he said, according to Latrash's report, 'Maybe [NAME REDACTED] would have to send someone to the U.S. to get Congressman Koch.'[7]

The quote flashed round the American intelligence and diplomatic circuit. Some communications, such as a message to Washington from the US Ambassador to Argentina, sought to play it down as 'nothing more than bravado ... induced by the alcohol he had consumed'. However, the uncomfortable reality could not be ignored: a military official from what was in reality a client state had issued a threat against the life of an elected political leader of the United States. Condor was in danger of getting out of control.

US officials rapidly made it clear to the Condor partners that violent actions inside the United States would not be tolerated. A CIA document sent out from the Directorate of Operations stated that actions such as the Letelier assassination would have 'definite detrimental effects on Condor countries'.[8] The author expressed the view that the Latin Americans had been reined in: 'Activity of this kind would result in retaliatory measures by the US against the country that had been blamed, and [REDACTED] not believe that the Condor countries would take the risk.' The document also stated, in a paragraph that hinted at an American guiding hand in this Latin version of *Murder Incorporated*, that the international activities of Condor outside the Condor countries were 'confined to collection of information on extremists'. The dispatch of a Condor team abroad did not mean that it had automatic authorisation to liquidate the target. Instead Condor should request 'a security service of the country where the extremist resides to carry out the measures.'

In this context it is intriguing to find among the US documents another CIA report stating that in 1977, the period in which the United States attempted to set these guidelines, representatives of the British intelligence service, along with security officials from France and West Germany, visited Argentina 'to discuss methods for the establishment of an anti-subversive organisation similar to "Condor"'.[9] According to the CIA report: 'The intelligence service representatives had explained that ... the terrorist/subversive threat had reached such dangerous levels in Europe that they believed it best if they pooled their intelligence resources in a cooperative organisation such as Condor.' In this age which now seems distant the threat of ideological terrorism was all too real, as the French secret service, in particular, knew well. Not long before this mission two of their officers had been killed blundering into a Paris apartment which sheltered not the Argentinian militant they had been tipped off about, but Carlos the Jackal, the Venezuelan-born Ilich Ramírez Sánchez, who was beginning to achieve fame for a series of terrorist outrages. Carlos seized a weapon and shot his way out, leaving the two policemen in pools of blood. The Jackal remained at liberty for over twenty more years, carrying out such atrocities as the kidnapping of the OPEC oil ministers and the hijacking of an Air France jet that led to the dramatic and bloody Israeli rescue operation at Entebbe airport. Now an almost forgotten relic of that era, Carlos is presently serving three concurrent life terms in the French prison of Clairvaux.

There is no suggestion in the documents that the French, British or other European intelligence services had any intention of setting up their own murder networks and it is not known if the British and European secret service men met the hardened Condor linchpin Aníbal Gordon. What emerges clearly, however, is that senior levels of the US government were fully aware of the original purposes and methods of Condor and of the international opprobrium which could result from its exposure. The CIA's description of what might be termed the revised Condor guidelines makes clear that the individual Condor countries could continue to fight their own extremists in whichever way they chose. Its summary smacks of pious hope rather than the reality of what was taking place in Argentina:

> While the killing of extremists is possible in some Condor countries, it would probably not be the standing order since the human rights issue is now too much in international news and thus serves as a deterrent to such action.

Aníbal Gordon's activities at the Automotores Orletti had been central to Operation Condor but his rule over that charnel house came to a sudden end in a blaze of gunfire in the early hours of November 3rd, 1976, a date that is still commemorated by the survivors and by visitors who tour the grim site. It was ended by the dramatic escape of a married couple, José Ramón Morales and Graciela Vidaillac, who had been seized the day before in one of the Gordon Gang's round-ups of militants in Buenos Aires.[10]

Morales, who was a member of a revolutionary armed group, had suffered a bullet wound in the leg during his arrest. On arrival at Orletti, he received some basic medical treatment and was left tied up in a room on the first floor. Vidaillac was hung by her arms from a hook on the ceiling in a nearby room and, by her own account, was tortured before her captors retired to bed. During the night she gradually managed to free herself and found and freed her husband, who then seized an automatic rifle from one of their sleeping guards. In exchanges of fire Vidaillac was herself hit, but the two of them managed to escape through a door on the ground floor and got across the railway line in front of the building, with Morales firing a burst through the metal roller-door which left bullet holes that can still be seen today. The couple then commandeered a passing pickup truck and made their getaway.

The effect at the torture centre was immediate. Gordon had apparently been concerned for some time that one of the militant groups on which he was inflicting so much damage would identify the Automotores Orletti's location and stage an attack on them. Now he and his boss, the Commander of the SIDE intelligence service, General Otto Paladino, took the decision to close it down and move operations elsewhere.

It seems that Paladino was held responsible for what had

happened and also, perhaps, for the failure of the operation in France. A few days after the escape his retirement as head of SIDE was announced and Gordon organised what was remembered as a splendid farewell dinner at the torturer's favourite watering hole, none other than 'Los Años Locos', the very same establishment where we were later to be wined and dined by the Argentine Interior Minister after our kidnapping by the Gordon Gang during the Falklands War. The Paladino dinner took place in mid-December 1976 and under the strong lighting of the sleek, modern restaurant by the river, it was a glittering affair. It was attended by some 80 people, many in full uniform, including senior Argentine intelligence officers, commanders of the Federal Police and a number of key figures in Operation Condor from the armed forces of Uruguay and Chile. There were also several of the professional criminals that Gordon had known throughout his career and had recruited to do the dirty work at Automotores Orletti. It is certain that, in true Argentine fashion, the roistering went on well into the night. It can only be speculated what the torturers and murderers talked about, and what anecdotes they exchanged, as tender steaks were wolfed down and bottles of fine Argentinian Malbec replaced each other on the white-draped tables.

What is known is what General Paladino himself said about their 'achievements' in a later statement which made no mention of atrocities and was, instead, devoted to valedictory remarks: 'We had to carry the whole weight of SIDE's work in gathering information and producing intelligence to support the fight against subversion.'

Many of the men at this dinner would later be arrested after the defeat in the Falklands led to the fall of the Junta and a series of new democratic governments in Argentina. Today some of them, including Paladino, are dead, others are still in prison for their crimes, but the fate of the two escapees from Orletti was also less than happy.

They managed to get out of Argentina and José Ramón Morales then followed his revolutionary beliefs by joining the Sandinistas fighting the Somoza dictatorship in Nicaragua. Shortly before the fall of Somoza in 1979, Morales was captured by the right-wing Contras who, realising that he was actually from Buenos Aires, handed him over to the Argentinian military advisors from the Junta's Overseas Task Force that was assisting them. By chance these men included one of Gordon's team from Orletti, and Morales was executed by the Argentine soldiers. When his body was recovered it showed signs of savage torture. Graciela Vidaillac, at least, remained at liberty. She lived quietly in Argentina, not wishing to be reminded of what took place at the Automotores Orletti, until her death, reportedly from Covid-19, in 2021.

What was clear at the Paladino dinner was that the campaign against 'subversion' would continue and even grow in intensity. One of the Junta's most bloodily determined figures, General Carlos Suárez Mason, was in command of the First Army Corps which included Buenos Aires and he now issued voluminous and detailed orders on how the campaign against leftist subversion must be pursued. Suárez Mason, who would later be extradited from the United States and who died in prison facing charges of 200 kidnappings and 30 murders, declared that: 'The Police of the province of Buenos Aires will intensify their operations against the subversive criminals by carrying out military operations in the entire area of the Province with the objective of contributing to the annihilation of subversion.' And in what appears to be a reference to teams like Gordon's he ordered the Federal Police to 'maintain the integration of the intelligence working groups'.[11] The police were seeking to make their contribution more 'effective' by constructing their own 'detention and interrogation centre' on Paseo Colón Avenue in a central area of the capital. The unit being based here would not be shown in the organisational structure of the Federal Police but would carry out its own surveillance and quick-reaction operations. This would be a base for what were called in the jargon of the anti-terrorist trade 'left-handed' or 'ultra left-handed' operations, i.e. actions that were outside any legal framework. The idea of a police force with a duty to uphold the law was a vanishing concept in Argentina.

Aníbal Gordon and his gang now had other secret bases of operation in Buenos Aires to replace the compromised Automotores Orletti, along with a further safe house in the town of Córdoba. It is clear that Gordon was now working according to a different set of rules. In these frightening times in Buenos Aires, he was emerging as someone who truly had a licence to murder or carry out almost any crime as long as it targeted opponents of his mysterious backers and, if possible, enriched them and himself. In 1977 he surfaces by name in the CIA documents in an account of the kidnapping and execution of the Argentinian Ambassador to Venezuela, Hidalgo Solá, who was snatched off the street and killed while in Buenos Aires for his daughter's wedding.[12] This crime, which is still debated in Argentina today, provoked a wide range of speculation over its motives and an international response. *The New York Times* reported that Ambassador Solá was a prominent member of the Radical Party, a supporter of a return to democratic institutions, and a personal choice of President Jorge Videla for the post in Venezuela. The paper stated that: 'Members of the Radical Party leadership, and military backers of General Videla ... feel sure that the kidnapping was carried out by right-wing elements opposed to any movement toward political dialogue with the existing parties.'[13]

A secret US intelligence report filed a week after the Ambassador's disappearance, and before his death was confirmed, said that suspicion would fall on 'military hardliners who were upset last year when Hidalgo Solá received at his embassy a labor leader ousted after the March 24, 1976 coup.'[14] While FBI sources believed that he had been eliminated because the military suspected him of providing passports to exiled opponents of the regime who had fled to Venezuela, others suggested that his political ambitions, including his reported hope that he might emerge as a civilian president, may have made him a target.

According to Emilio Mignone, a lawyer and human-rights campaigner whose daughter was one of the victims of the repression, Hidalgo Solá's humanity in opening his Embassy's doors to relatives of the disappeared seeking answers on the fate of their loved ones had put his life under threat. When Mignone met Solá in the Venezuelan capital, Caracas, the Ambassador apparently told him that he would go to Buenos Aires to persuade the military government to change its repressive policies. If he tried that, Mignone is said to have warned, they would kill him.

For her part, when the Ambassador's widow was asked who she thought was responsible for the crime, she replied simply that the leaders of the Junta knew the answer.

It may be that Solá's mounting difficulties with the military regime had given carte blanche to their favoured assassin, Aníbal Gordon. In a secret report on the killing, the CIA identified Gordon as the murderer and explored a mixed set of possible motives. Gordon, it said, had kidnapped the Ambassador and taken him to the safe house at Bacacay Street, earlier used in the case of Mercedes Naveiro Bender, where he was kept hooded to hide his identity. 'Hidalgo Solá was kidnapped and assassinated by a special group which has worked for the State Intelligence Secretariat (SIDE), acting under the direction of one Aníbal "Gordon".'

The report quoted an Army intelligence source as linking the assassination to Solá's issuance of 'false documentation to Argentine terrorists', a fact which was apparently widely known in intelligence circles, but part of the somewhat confused document also claimed that Gordon did not have orders from SIDE to carry out the killing, and that it was done without the knowledge of the intelligence service and simply to make money: 'The group undertook the kidnapping with the sole motive of demanding ransom from the family, thinking that ... the family would pay a large sum of money.'

The CIA report, even now controversial in an Argentina convinced that such a crime could only be authorised at the highest level, claims that when security forces began an intensive search for the Ambassador, Gordon's group changed its plans: 'Instead they killed him and hid his body.'

According to the CIA, this was only the latest such operation by Gordon, who had just secured another ransom by kidnapping a child, presumably from a wealthy family. It said he was now operating with virtual impunity because of the 'numerous and extremely sensitive black operations' he had carried out against terrorist targets which, if made public, would be 'extremely embarrassing to the incumbent military government'. The example which the CIA gave was the failed murder plot in Europe and for this reason, the Agency stated, 'no official action has been taken against Gordon or his group.' The CIA report suggested that 'Aníbal' was now lying low in neighbouring Uruguay or Paraguay, but it is clear that, if true, this was only a temporary expedient, for Gordon was soon once again operating with impunity in Argentina.

With the Ambassador's body barely cold, his assassin was apparently close to untouchable as the man who knew too much. Within his circle of policemen, intelligence officers and criminals he now enjoyed a reputation that blended mystery and deadly threat. In the atmosphere of fear that now prevailed, no one outside the Junta's inner circle could say with certainty why or by whom Hidalgo Solá had been killed – or even dared to ask. And meanwhile the debate inside the US government about how to handle relations with the Argentine Junta and its murderous servants continued.

CHAPTER 11

Weapons for Lives?

I N AUGUST 1977, while President Carter sought to establish his human-rights agenda, the US Congress enacted legislation which would have an important effect on American policy towards Argentina and, eventually, on the Junta's ability to wage war against Britain. The Kennedy-Humphrey Amendment, which took effect the following year, prohibited weapons sales and military assistance to the Junta while human-rights problems persisted, but the disappearances and killings did not stop. Indeed a CIA memorandum reported a defiant response from Buenos Aires: 'The Argentines ... insist that they will not deviate from the practices they deem indispensable in their continuing war with leftist terrorists no matter what outside criticism they incur.'[1]

Argentina's allies in the US military establishment were quick to protest at what they regarded as a misguided policy. In May 1978, shortly before Kennedy-Humphrey came into full effect, the Commander-in-Chief of US Southern Command, General Dennis P. McAuliffe, voiced his protest to the Pentagon:

I am extremely disappointed at our failure to provide at least a partial response to Argentina's requests to purchase training (at their expense) and spare parts. As I noted following my recent visit there, the Argentine Government under General Videla has made some progress in human rights (obviously there have been some negative steps along with the positive) and our approval of at least the training request would have been far more useful than the continuation of our pattern of turndowns.[2]

And a lengthy report to Washington, prepared by a diplomat at the US Embassy dealing with arms sales who had repeatedly clashed with 'Tex' Harris, and signed by the Ambassador, lamented the economic losses which the United States had suffered in the first eighteen months of the ban:

> US firms lost, or were prevented from effectively competing for, sales to Argentina amounting to between $3.5 and $4 billion. The largest share of this total is represented by Argentine arms purchases from third countries ($2.6 billion) for which the US could not compete under existing arms sales policy.[3]

The winners from this policy were said to be France (sales of combat aircraft and Exocet missiles), West Germany (tanks and warships) and Israel (jet fighters). Britain's sales were small not because of any unwillingness to deal with the Junta but possibly, it was said in another document, because of a reluctance to bribe the relevant Argentine officials.

The author of the report on US losses commented sourly that there was 'no evidence that these disincentives have had any effect in furthering the US policy objective of an improvement in the actual observance of human rights.'

'Tex' Harris was transferred out of Argentina in 1979 and the country's military elite reportedly toasted his departure. Harris himself suffered lasting damage to his career: 'I was penalized for not being a "team player" ... my career was paralyzed.'

Argentina's later defeat in the Falklands War and its aftermath vindicated the stand Harris had taken, and in 1984 he received a special award from the American Foreign Service Association. He accepted it with characteristic humour: 'When I got the award I said, "This is a very special award the Foreign Service gives. It's a Purple Heart for self-inflicted wounds."'

Until his death in 2020 Harris was proud of his contribution to restricting US arms exports to Buenos Aires at a key time which undoubtedly weakened Argentina's military effectiveness in the subsequent war with Britain.

We had enormous, mostly military and commercial, relationships with Argentina. Commercial wasn't that significant ... because the Argentine economy's trade links were more towards Europe and the United Kingdom. They'd been a commercial colony of the United Kingdom for many, many years. But the Argentines came to us and they needed parts for their navy aircraft, they needed helmets for their pilots, they needed spare parts for their ships ... In each of these cases the Human Rights Bureau became very adept in terms of understanding the network of relationships between the United States and human rights violators, in this case Argentina ... Military exchanges were cancelled, like the ability to send Argentine soldiers to the United States for training. Of course, everybody in the embassy,

I think correctly, blamed my reporting as being the culprit. 'This never happened before Harris was here.'

The work of Harris, Derian and like-minded officials did help to ensure that when the Junta took its disastrous gamble of going to war with Britain, many of its pilots were still flying the now-obsolete Skyhawk jet wearing dated helmets and seated in ejector seats which were often unreliable for lack of spare parts. The Skyhawks were not carrying advanced missiles but the iron bombs of a previous era, many of which, fortunately for the British task force, were incorrectly fused and failed to explode.

But amid all the friction with Washington the Junta managed to obtain two pieces of American-made equipment without which it could not have prosecuted the Falklands War at all. These were KC-130 aerial refuelling tankers, manufactured by Lockheed, and an essential element in the long-range air strikes mounted by Argentine Air Force and Naval pilots from their bases on the mainland, which inflicted such damage on the British ships. Those ships were deep in the South Atlantic, often deliberately stationed to the east of the Falklands to maximise the range. Attacking aircraft had to fly at low level as they tried to evade British anti-aircraft missiles and this greatly increased fuel consumption. The result was that almost every effective Argentine air strike, from the sinking of the *Sheffield* to the final shocking attacks on the troop transports *Sir Lancelot* and *Sir Galahad* in San Carlos Water, began with air-to-air refuelling shortly after take-off by one or other of the two KC-130s. Only two of the types of aircraft flown by the Argentines – the Skyhawks and the Exocet-carrying Super Étendards – were even capable of such refuelling. The much-vaunted Mirage-based combat jets bought from Israel and which, in theory, should have cleared Britain's slower

Harriers from the skies, lacked refuelling equipment and thus could spend only a few minutes in the combat zone, rendering them much less effective than they would otherwise have been. In the end the KC-130s enabled Argentine jets to carry out 113 missions against the British task force. So important were the airborne tankers to Argentina that during the US attempts to mediate a settlement early in the conflict, General Galtieri asked the American envoy General Vernon Walters if the United States had sold any to Britain. Walters assured him that the RAF had its own capability and did not need them. The question in fact demonstrated Galtieri's lack of understanding of a key factor in the conflict. The British aircraft carriers were too far from any British land base for KC-130s to assist their operations. The task force and the Harriers which provided its air cover were largely on their own. But for Argentina the tankers were the essential element which enabled its pilots to remain a potent threat until the last stages of the war.

The Junta had taken delivery of these aircraft in May 1979 and had conducted its first exercise with them a couple of months later. But how had it managed to obtain them in the face of a US arms embargo made law by the Kennedy-Humphrey Congressional amendment? Though clearly incomplete on this subject, the US documents that have been released suggest that the aircraft and other material may have been part of highly secret negotiations in which the Junta attempted to barter the lives of its own citizens for the American technology and financing it wanted. The 'Tex' Harris recorded message to Washington refers to the Junta's release of a number of so-called 'PEN' prisoners – people who had been arrested and held under the Poder Ejecutivo Nacional (National Executive Powers) in the Argentine constitution and of whom there was some sort of record, unlike the thousands who simply 'disappeared':

Most importantly the government is beginning to ask us for recognition of the things they have done with respect to the PEN prisoners. They are playing their trumps and they want something back for it. Both the Navy and the Foreign Ministry called me in in the week before the IFI [International Financial Institution] loan decision was made ... and pleaded that if there was to be further liberation in Argentina they had to be able to show that their previous moves had been recognized by the United States Government.

Unsurprisingly such possible trade-offs were not referred to in the official record of the meeting between President Carter and the then Junta leader General Videla, in Washington in September 1977. Carter is shown handling the Argentine dictator with the softest of kid gloves, expressing the hope that the 'strength, stability and influence' achieved by the Junta would lead to the 'alleviation of concerns expressed by many' about human rights. Videla is recorded as expressing his hope that the 'problems' of the detainees would be resolved by Christmas that year.[4] In the event, releases were few and reports of kidnap and torture continued to emerge.

The following year Carter's Secretary of State, Cyrus Vance, set out the administration's policy on arms sales in a cable to the Department of Defense which expressed in clear terms the relationship between weapons and lives:

Because of human rights abuses in Argentina we are not in a position to act favourably on either the large number of arms transfer cases that has accumulated or the Argentine request to purchase training, and ... only substantial, authentic human rights improvements in Argentina would permit us to change our position on these matters.[5]

But behind closed doors in Washington, there was mounting criticism of the President's human-rights policy and how it was being applied.

At the Defense Department an official argued that the US should relax its policy on arms sales and that the idea of trading them for human-rights improvements was misconceived:

> In pushing for a more rapid return to rule of law, accounting for prisoners, etc., and by using arms sales as a lever, it now appears that US policies have succeeded not only in alienating the Argentine military but also in creating a huge influence vacuum which other countries have been quick to fill.[6]

In this discordant atmosphere the sale of the all-important KC-130s had slipped through the net. Cyrus Vance had been persuaded to issue a favourable advisory opinion for their sale to Argentina by an 'Action Memorandum' from the Bureau of Politico-Military Affairs which was clearly written to try to minimise opposition to the transfer. It claimed that the tankers could not be used for internal repression and were being bought for peaceful purposes: 'These planes would most likely be used to refuel aircraft involved in search and rescue operations and in Antarctic activities.'[7]

On the basis of this disingenuous sentence the Junta would, in due course, be enabled to go to war in the South Atlantic.

CHAPTER 12

Follow the Money

THE GENERALS HAD seized power in 1976 with resounding and high-minded claims. Military rule would put an end to violent anarchy and corruption and restore Argentina's dignity and national destiny. The officer corps had always had an elevated view of their role in society. They were the only ones who could identify threats facing the country and take the right action to protect it. In their own eyes they were immaculate, serving only the national interest.

In reality the Junta had created a killing machine that could not easily be halted even if the damage it was doing to its international reputation and the modernisation of its own armed forces was becoming ever more evident. Immense power had been handed to a small number of people including Army officers, intelligence agents and career criminals, all linked in a fearsome if mutually mistrustful brotherhood that could not be dismantled until the Junta for which they worked fell.

Aníbal Gordon's name would soon be linked with another high-profile murder that showed the Junta as deadly to even its own supporters. While still attempting to project an image of disciplined national purpose the military regime in truth included men who would do almost anything to satisfy their lust for wealth and power and, as ever, Gordon was on hand to render his violent services. The anonymous letter 'by officers of the Buenos Aires Provincial Police Force' which emerged after the Falklands War and which accused Gordon of our kidnapping, also stated that he was responsible for an infamous killing that had shocked even the hardened Argentinian public. The victim was the country's first female diplomat, Elena Holmberg, who was murdered in 1978. This time the target was not a Marxist rebel or a socially concerned intellectual. Holmberg was deeply conservative and a strong supporter of the Junta but while serving in Paris she had gathered information that one of its most powerful and blood-stained leaders, the then Navy chief and member of the Junta triumvirate, Admiral Emilio Massera, was engaged in secret dealings with the enemy.[1] Massera had apparently held meetings at the Intercontinental Hotel with the exiled but still powerful Montonero leader Mario Firmenich. Their plan, Holmberg was apparently told, was to arrange a truce in the Dirty War on the back of which the charismatic Massera, the possessor of film-star good looks, would be installed as a new dictator in the style of Juan Perón, enjoying populist adulation for ending the terrorist conflict. The negotiations were alleged to have involved a down-payment of a million dollars by Massera to Firmenich, and Holmberg made the fatal mistake of making her disgust with Massera all too plain. At a reception at the Paris Embassy she approached Massera's wife, who was wearing a large diamond, and asked loudly if it was a gift from the Montonero leader. Word of the incident rippled through the hothouse world of Argentina's military leadership.

On her return to Buenos Aires Holmberg was kidnapped brazenly near the Foreign Ministry in similar style to our own abduction.

Her body, initially confused with that of someone else, was found in a river near Buenos Aires much used as a dumping ground by Aníbal Gordon and other regime killers. Indeed, in the month when her corpse was discovered, more than twenty other bodies were found in the same location. Suspicion was initially directed at the Naval secret service which was infamous for its extraordinary brutality at the Naval Mechanical School, but rumours also spread that Aníbal Gordon had carried out the killing on behalf of Admiral Massera in order to silence his accuser. Neither Gordon nor anyone else was ever charged with the murder.

The anonymous police letter also accused Gordon of carrying out numerous other crimes in this period, including extortion and kidnappings for ransom, and it is clear that his special role in the Dirty War enabled him to pursue some extremely lucrative targets. Gordon was the personification of the old journalistic adage much used by a veteran American journalist with whom I became friends in Vietnam, the Saigon correspondent of the *New York Daily News*, Joe Fried: 'Follow the money.' Pursuit of the dollar is the linking thread in most of Gordon's activities. It was no coincidence that he had for a time been placed in charge of hunting down the exiled leaders of the Montonero terrorist organisation which mingled Marxist ideology with nostalgia for the dead dictator, Juan Perón. They had been responsible for the terrorist attack seen by many as the start of the Dirty War, the murder in June 1970 of the former President, General Pedro Aramburu. But they had achieved both fame and strength in 1974 with the elaborate and ruthless kidnapping of two of Argentina's wealthiest businessmen, the brothers Jorge and Juan Born, who controlled the Bunge & Born company, said to be the largest conglomerate in the southern hemisphere and a powerful force in the Argentine economy. The brothers had been taken in a carefully planned operation that saw their driver deceived by fake street signs and cars disguised as public-service vehicles. Some 40 armed Montoneros then killed the driver and one of the Borns' managers before driving the brothers to a windowless basement prison with two separate cells, each with basin, toilet and air-conditioning. The Montoneros had constructed it beneath a paint shop which they had earlier set up in Buenos Aires.

The terms for the brothers' eventual release some six months later were the most spectacular any terrorist group had yet achieved and dwarfed those won by Aníbal Gordon's other opponents, the ERP and the Uruguayan PVP. The Montoneros forced Bunge & Born to pay for a large notice in *The Washington Post* in which the company was made to announce that the brothers had been tried and found guilty of a series of crimes including exploitation of the working class at a time when inflation of 10% a month was destroying the economy, monopolistic practices and 'aggression against national interests'. This notice was to be displayed in all Bunge & Born's premises where, in an attempt to associate the Montoneros with the still potent cult of Juan Perón, busts of the late dictator and his second wife, the famed Evita, were to be installed. A million dollars'-worth of food and other supplies was to be distributed 'to the people' and a 'very large sum in dollars' paid directly to the Montoneros. Bunge & Born never revealed what they had paid for the brothers' freedom but the Montoneros themselves announced triumphantly that the ransom was exactly what they had demanded: $60 million, an immense fortune in the Argentina of that era.[2] The anarchy then gripping the country was amply illustrated by the press conference at which the Montonero leadership declared victory and released the second of the two captive brothers. At a house in Calle Libertad (Liberty Street), invited journalists were offered *empanadas*, tasty Argentinian snacks, given press kits containing details of the tactics used in the kidnapping, and heard Montonero leaders claim that: 'We are now a force to be reckoned with, a political organisation which cannot be ignored.'

As in the case of the smaller but still substantial PVP ransom, the fate of the money came to obsess the Argentinian secret services and featured heavily in the choice of arrest victims and the interrogations overseen by Aníbal Gordon and his associates. Repeated questioning about it was described by one of the surviving victims of the Automotores Orletti at the eventual trial of one of Gordon's close associates, the secret service officer Eduardo Ruffo, who was finally imprisoned for life for his record of kidnap, torture and murder. 'That's all they asked me about,' the former victim said.

It quickly became clear that the massive sum now at the Montoneros' disposal had been secreted in several different destinations, much of it in Europe and some still in Argentina. It is known that, in the same period that he seized and murdered Ambassador Solá, Gordon and his gang also kidnapped a leading Buenos Aires stockbroker, Pedro Zavalia, and held him for a month in another secret prison in the town of Córdoba. When this expert in finance had the good fortune to return in one piece it emerged that, along with trying to secure a ransom from his family, his captors' main concern had been to extract all possible information about the financial network which, reputedly, had already laundered a large part of the Montoneros' massive haul of cash.

The central figure in this network had been the sort of rogue financier who occasionally graces the City of London but is almost a fixture in the shady dealings of Latin America, the sharply suited, rakishly bearded shooting star of Argentina's banking world, a man by the name of David Graiver. By the age of 30, Graiver had managed to acquire controlling interests in two banks in New York and another in Israel. Five years before the military coup, Graiver also acquired the Argentinian Banco de Hurlingham, an institution with a prestigious Anglo name and sufficiently respectable to have had its inauguration blessed by a bishop. Leading figures in the Junta rapidly became convinced that Hurlingham had taken in some $17 million of the Montoneros' ransom funds, promising to pay them a generous 9.5% in annual interest, and moved it into Graiver's banking network in Argentina and abroad. Graiver himself soon took what must have seemed the sensible step of moving his base of operations to a fifteen-room suite on Fifth Avenue in New York; however, fate's finger pursued him. In August 1976, as the torturers in Orletti and other such establishments went into high gear hunting for any trail that would lead them to the cash, Graiver boarded a private jet for a flight between New York and Acapulco on which he was the only passenger. Mysteriously the plane crashed into a Mexican hillside, killing all on board. Soon afterwards, one of the dead tycoon's New York banks collapsed and in Argentina Graiver's inheritors attempted to sell his banking interests there, but the sale was frozen by Argentina's Central Bank on the orders of the Junta. A deep and lengthy investigation with all the brutal hallmarks of the Junta's secret police would now take place.

The main targets of course included the Montonero leadership itself, and the secret services had scored a significant triumph when the organisation's second-in-command, a lawyer called Roberto Quieto, fell into their hands almost by accident. Quieto had planned and led the kidnapping of the Born brothers but now he was spotted on a Buenos Aires beach by a policeman who happened to know him from years before. The policeman called in reinforcements and Quieto was marched to their vehicle in his swimming trunks and driven off while his captors fired triumphantly in the air in front of startled beach-goers. The importance of his arrest was rapidly demonstrated by security forces' raids on hitherto-secure weapons stores and safe houses, which included another newly constructed but unoccupied 'people's prison', seemingly awaiting more kidnap victims, and by instructions from the Montonero leadership to their members that they must use cyanide capsules if about to be captured. Quieto is said to have cracked after just 24 hours of torture and it may well be from him that the secret police learned that millions of the Born ransom dollars had found their way to David Graiver. It has since been reported that it was, in fact, Quieto who had personally negotiated the 'investment' and its lucrative interest rate with the banker in a series of secret meetings before his arrest. It seems that Quieto now became a collaborator, known in chilling jargon as a *quebrado* (broken one). A short-lived campaign for his release that had attracted the support of such socialist luminaries as François Mitterrand and Jean-Paul Sartre was abandoned when reports of his collaboration began to circulate. Quieto had become one of the many unfortunates suspended between life and death while the Junta and its servants decided if there was any value to be had in allowing him to remain alive, a terrible plight that was well understood by a diplomat at the US Embassy reporting to Washington:

> Disappearance is still the standard tactic for the Argentine security forces in dealing with captured terrorists ... Disappeared prisoners yield up information under torture. Disappeared prisoners can be turned against their former comrades. Disappeared prisoners are believed to be a frightening example that inhibits the Montoneros' ability to recruit new personnel.[3]

The Montonero leader, Mario Firmenich, made public his own account of the event in which he described Quieto as a 'snitch' and analysed the consequences in language strikingly similar to that of the historian Bernard Fall years before:

> Betrayal is not a reasonable response even if the torture applied
> is terrible. Because snitching is the real rust that destroys a clan-
> destine organization. If the possibility of informing did not exist,
> it would not be possible to destroy a clandestine organization.

The contents of Quieto's interrogations and even the exact details of his fate are still unknown but, according to the American documents, he told his captors that the Montoneros maintained a Swiss bank account containing the impressive sum of $150 million, and other funds in various locations in Argentina. The security forces were soon on the trail of another man described as the Montoneros' 'financial officer' and the US Embassy described what happened next as a 'spectacular coup'.

> [T]he Argentines had captured the financial officer of the
> Montonero guerrilla forces, taken him to Europe and had
> cleaned out all the bank accounts held by the Montoneros in
> Europe, a sum of millions of dollars.[4]

Another document put the sum taken from banks in Geneva and Madrid at $65 million. The fate of the 'financial officer' was not revealed, though other documents suggest that he was murdered in 1983 shortly before the fall of the Junta after the Falklands War. As for Quieto, the US Embassy reported in 1977 that his life was being 'spared' because of his cooperation. However, it is now believed

Interviewing President Leopoldo Galtieri only hours after our kidnapping. The General claimed that it had been carried out by 'a very small group' that did not want peace.

Thames Television/Fremantle Media

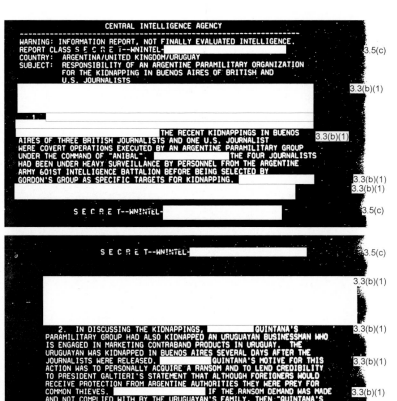

CENTRAL INTELLIGENCE AGENCY

WARNING: INFORMATION REPORT, NOT FINALLY EVALUATED INTELLIGENCE.
REPORT CLASS S E C R E T--WNINTEL-   3.5(c)
COUNTRY: ARGENTINA/UNITED KINGDOM/URUGUAY
SUBJECT: RESPONSIBILITY OF AN ARGENTINE PARAMILITARY ORGANIZATION
          FOR THE KIDNAPPING IN BUENOS AIRES OF BRITISH AND
          U.S. JOURNALISTS
                                                                     3.3(b)(1)

                              THE RECENT KIDNAPPINGS IN BUENOS
AIRES OF THREE BRITISH JOURNALISTS AND ONE U.S. JOURNALIST   3.3(b)(1)
WERE COVERT OPERATIONS EXECUTED BY AN ARGENTINE PARAMILITARY GROUP
UNDER THE COMMAND OF "ANIBAL".   THE FOUR JOURNALISTS
HAD BEEN UNDER HEAVY SURVEILLANCE BY PERSONNEL FROM THE ARGENTINE
ARMY 601ST INTELLIGENCE BATTALION BEFORE BEING SELECTED BY
GORDON'S GROUP AS SPECIFIC TARGETS FOR KIDNAPPING.   3.3(b)(1)
                                                                   3.3(b)(1)

        S E C R E T--WNINTEL-   -   3.5(c)

        S E C R E T--WNINTEL-   3.5(c)

                                                                   3.3(b)(1)

2. IN DISCUSSING THE KIDNAPPINGS,   QUINTANA'S   3.3(b)(1)
PARAMILITARY GROUP HAD ALSO KIDNAPPED AN URUGUAYAN BUSINESSMAN WHO
IS ENGAGED IN MARKETING CONTRABAND PRODUCTS IN URUGUAY. THE
URUGUAYAN WAS KIDNAPPED IN BUENOS AIRES SEVERAL DAYS AFTER THE
JOURNALISTS WERE RELEASED.   QUINTANA'S MOTIVE FOR THIS   3.3(b)(1)
ACTION WAS TO PERSONALLY ACQUIRE A RANSOM AND TO LEND CREDIBILITY
TO PRESIDENT GALTIERI'S STATEMENT THAT ALTHOUGH FOREIGNERS WOULD
RECEIVE PROTECTION FROM ARGENTINE AUTHORITIES THEY WERE PREY FOR
COMMON THIEVES.   IF THE RANSOM DEMAND WAS MADE   3.3(b)(1)
AND NOT COMPLIED WITH BY THE URUGUAYAN'S FAMILY, THEN "QUINTANA'S
ORGANIZATION WOULD HAVE TO SOLVE A POTENTIALLY EMBARRASSING PROBLEM.-
                                                                   3.3(b)(1)

REPORT CLASS S E C R E T--WARNING NOTICE--INTELLIGENCE SOURCES
AND METHODS INVOLVED-

A secret report by the US Central Intelligence Agency stating that we had been kidnapped by 'a paramilitary group' working with the Argentinian Army secret service under the command of Aníbal Gordon.

US government

The first military Junta which seized power in March 1976 and launched the 'repression' in which thousands died. Centre: Lieutenant General Jorge Videla; left: Admiral Emilio Massera, the ruthless Navy chief. Both were later convicted of human rights crimes.

AFP/Stringer/Getty Images

The Junta which lost its war with Britain. President General Leopoldo Galtieri (C), Admiral Jorge Anaya (L) and Air Force Commander Basilio Lami Dozo (R) at their trial for 'negligence' in the Falklands conflict in 1985.

Reuters/Alamy

The Junta used uniformed troops and police to suppress dissent in the streets. Behind the scenes were thousands of secret police and paramilitaries who controlled networks of clandestine prisons and torture chambers.

Eduardo Di Baia/AP/Shutterstock

A massive demonstration in support of the Junta's seizure of the Falkland Islands. Only eleven days earlier the same square had been filled with people protesting against military rule and the Junta's failed economic policies.

AP/Shutterstock

Mothers of the 'disappeared' protested every week in the Plaza de Mayo. They were joined by Grandmothers accusing the regime of stealing the small children of murdered victims.
Eduardo Di Baia/AP/Shutterstock

Aníbal Gordon (L), the man identified as our kidnapper. He was known as 'Colonel', ran two of the regime's torture and murder centres and boasted of having killed hundreds of people. Seen here soon after his arrest in 1984.

La Nación

Allen 'Tex' Harris, the American diplomat who was appalled by the military regime's use of torture and murder and reported his findings to Washington. 'I had many fights at the Embassy', he said.
US State Department

Mario Firmenich, leader of the Montoneros revolutionary group. He organised the training of combat teams in Palestinian camps in Lebanon and sent them back to Argentina in a 'counter offensive'. It was a disastrous failure.
Keystone Press/Alamy

The price of Britain's victory. The frigate HMS *Antelope* sinks after the detonation of two unexploded bombs. An EOD expert was killed. The crew had already abandoned ship.
Shutterstock

Surrender – a British Royal Marines Commando guards Argentinian soldiers captured in the battle of Goose Green.
PA Images/Alamy

Automotores Orletti. The former motor repair shop where Aníbal Gordon ran a secret torture and murder centre. It is now preserved as a memorial.
Public domain: Ginés90

The cellar at 3570 Bacacay Street where victims are said to have been held and tortured.
Public domain

The intelligence officer Miguel Ángel Furci who worked under Aníbal Gordon awaits sentencing in a Federal Court. He was found guilty of multiple cases of torture and sentenced to life imprisonment.
Natacha Pisarenko/ AP/Shutterstock

that he was murdered the following year. It seems that his usefulness had expired.

It is not known if Aníbal Gordon played any part in the torture and killing of Quieto or in the operation in Europe to empty the Montoneros' bank accounts, but around this time there was the first sign of official disquiet at the activities that he and the former head of the SIDE intelligence service, General Paladino, were undertaking with the clear intention of enriching themselves. However, the case only served to demonstrate Gordon's links with the Army and secret service and the brazen impunity with which he was able to carry out his operations.

Following what appears to have been his normal practice Gordon had kidnapped the stockbroker, Pedro Zavalia, after establishing close relations with the commander of an Army unit, the IV Army Brigade in Córdoba. Gordon's rented 'safe house' where the victim was held was apparently behind the Brigade's headquarters and subsequent investigation showed that phone calls to Zavalia's family to demand the ransom, which was set at a million dollars, had been made from a telephone inside the Army base. The men helping Gordon to guard Zavalia included several serving officers of SIDE.[5]

On this occasion, however, the stockbroker had high connections and when the ransom was supposed to be paid troops and police arrived at the house where Zavalia was being held. Immediately, however, they received orders to withdraw. Zavalia was released 24 hours later and a military inquiry officially opened, but this rapidly became what an Argentinian newspaper later described as a 'farce'.[6] Gordon was never arrested or even questioned. Several SIDE officers who were part of Gordon's gang were discharged from the security service but then immediately rehired by the 601st Intelligence Battalion. An Army Major, whose alibi for his part in assisting the kidnappers was that he had only come to the safe house to wish Gordon a happy birthday, was initially charged but the case against him was dropped. The entire case was finally dismissed by the Supreme Council of the Armed Forces despite the fact that the victim, Zavalia, was able to identify his captors and several of them confessed to their role. The anonymous letter written after the Falklands War by a group of serving policemen appears to refer to this case. It states that a police officer who had tried to interfere with a Gordon kidnapping had been summarily fired and that the police were powerless in the face of orders from the Army. It appears that Gordon's role was simply too important for a Junta increasingly riddled with corruption to put a stop to his personal pursuit of wealth.

Despite the loss of the Zavalia ransom, there is no doubt that Gordon and his gang had already made substantial sums of money, and even today legal action is still taking place to identify where it went and what happened to it. Since the fall of the Junta it has been alleged that the principal function of the security company Magister, which was owned by General Paladino and in which Gordon's daughter was an administrator, was to channel the 'spoils of war' – jewellery, cash and even property – from the victims to their torturers and killers. It seems that Gordon, the man whose business was kidnap and murder, dreamed of owning a luxurious boating club in a fashionable area near the capital. Soon after he and his team had seized what was supposedly several million dollars from the Uruguayan People's Victory Party, much of the money was apparently used to purchase a thousand acres of prime lakeside real estate, but the planned development never took place. The impending dramas of Argentine history and the Junta's destiny would get in the way.

CHAPTER 13

Children of the Disappeared

A T AUTOMOTORES ORLETTI Aníbal Gordon had experienced
what in any other field of work would have been called a personnel problem. Contrary to appearances the death squad leader,
along with many of the other 'dirty warriors', also saw himself
as something of a family man. Married to his second wife, Juana
Antonia Herrador, he was raising two sons and two daughters to
observe what he would have regarded as Christian values, a philosophy that did not prevent him from blooding his eldest son Marcelo
with visits to the Automotores Orletti and eventually inducting him
into his kidnap gang. Gordon was therefore less than pleased when
it emerged that one of his team was having an affair that threatened
to disrupt its unity.

The offender was Miguel Ángel Furci, a full-time employee of
the SIDE secret police normally engaged in the collection of intelligence who was eventually found guilty of the use of torture on at
least 127 occasions on 67 victims. According to surviving witnesses
he took part in the killing of Carlos Santucho, described in an earlier chapter and a particularly horrific event. In the words of a victim
who survived, Furci assisted in the murder by dragging the inert

body of the almost unconscious Santucho to the hoist which was used to lower him repeatedly into a vat of water. Santucho was later finished off with gunfire.

Furci's superiors at SIDE saw things differently. While a close colleague doing similar work was recorded as suffering from severe stress and, later, a heart attack, Furci's performance was described as 'excellent'. A superior wrote that he had 'worked in the department which is in charge of front-line combat in the fight against enemy subversives. He had no failures showing courage in the face of danger and serenity and moderation in his conduct.' In the jargon of the secret service designed to obscure the appalling reality in official records, he was described as carrying out 'special intelligence activities', and received a 15% bonus for working in hazardous conditions.[1]

In his private life, however, the married Furci was causing trouble by consorting with the spouse of an official at SIDE headquarters who had reacted with fury. One of the issues in Furci's own marriage was that he and his wife could not have children. It seems that Aníbal Gordon's response to this situation was to shield Furci from the SIDE official's anger – 'he decided to spare my life' was how Furci put it in what was presumably a figurative expression – and to present him with a child.[2] This was the eighteen month-old baby daughter of a pair of Uruguayan militants, Jorge Zaffaroni and María Emilia Islas Zaffaroni, who had been kidnapped as part of Operation Condor and were now being held and 'interrogated' at Automotores Orletti. The docket recording the operation to seize them is one of the few such documents to survive the mass destruction of secret-service records that took place after the Falklands War. In appearance it bears more resemblance to an old-fashioned left-luggage receipt than to the death warrant it actually was. From SIDE to the commander of the First Army Corps, General Carlos Suárez Mason, it records the couple as Uruguayan students and 'active agents' of the Tupamaros terrorist group, the exploits of which had included the kidnapping and eventual release of the British Ambassador to Uruguay, Sir Geoffrey Jackson. The Zaffaronis were to be picked up on September 27th, 1976 with the danger of the operation rated 'maximum', and the docket records that the two were armed when they were arrested. Their destination was given simply as SIDE which, in this case, was the torture and murder centre run by Aníbal Gordon.[3]

The baby, Mariana, was not recorded on the docket and seems to have been an unwanted encumbrance as far as SIDE was concerned. She 'was handed over to me by Aníbal Gordon', Furci told a court in 2013, describing how Gordon had brought the child to his address in a Ford Falcon car and given her to him in a manner he described as 'contemptuous'.[4] Subsequently Mariana's parents 'disappeared', murdered by SIDE in one account, handed over to the Uruguayan secret police for disposal in another. Too small to be aware of anything that had happened, Mariana began a new life as Daniela Furci. Later, while still young, she was to give a heart-rending account of what had happened: 'My dad [she meant Furci] fought on the other side. One day I was brought to him, and he had to choose between shooting me in the head, or taking me and raising me as the daughter he couldn't have.'[5]

The story of how the young Mariana Zaffaroni, to use the birth name that she now carries once again, was brought up by the man who was part of the gang that killed her parents, and how she developed a lasting affection for Furci, which for some time stood in the way of her assumption of her real identity, only came to light after the Falklands War and the collapse of the Junta. As I will describe in a later chapter, the story of Mariana came to grip Argentina. Her identification is one of the great successes of the *Abuelas* or Grandmothers of the Plaza de Mayo, who joined ranks with the Mothers shortly after their foundation when it was realised that the *represores* like Aníbal Gordon were solving the administrative problem of the surviving children of their victims by redistributing them among members of the security services or the Army who for one reason or another were willing to take them.

By the standards of that appalling time, Mariana could perhaps count herself as fortunate. By her own account, the Furcis treated her lovingly. However, that was not the experience of a young girl taken by another one of Gordon's men, Eduardo Ruffo, whom subsequent trials have shown to be one of the most prolific and sadistic torturers at the Automotores Orletti, and a killer credited with at least 30 murders. He took a baby girl whose real name was Carla Rutila, the daughter of Graciela Rutila Artés, a left-wing militant. Mother and daughter had been seized in Bolivia, another Condor country, where baby Carla had apparently been mistreated in front of her mother by the security police to force a confession. The two of them were then transferred to Argentinian security at the land bridge between the two countries and handed into Aníbal Gordon's care at Automotores Orletti. Ruffo, who was a close friend of Gordon and would take part with him in many later crimes, was given Carla shortly before her mother disappeared for ever. He was also given an even younger baby boy, named Alejandro by the Ruffos, whose real parentage has never been established. What is known is that Ruffo was an exceptionally brutal man and a heavy drinker. As she grew up Carla recalled a childhood of surprising luxury, living in the care of a nanny in a succession of houses with large gardens and swimming pools. But it was also a childhood where firearms were openly on display, where televisions, watches and other items taken from victims would mysteriously arrive, and where the violence of the man she believed to be her father was an ever-present threat.[6]

These children – like dozens or perhaps hundreds more in the same dreadful predicament – were now at the mercy of the people who had stolen them. They were helpless not only because of their tender age but also because under the military regime they had been stripped of their real identities, with new names and birth details recorded in false documents issued with the complicity of the authorities. Under the Junta, the police had no interest in their plight, as the Buenos Aires police commander, General Ramón Camps, would demonstrate with his later attempt to justify the appropriations, 'because', he said, 'subversive parents will raise subversive children'. The children of the 'disappeared' were without any kind of legal rights, but ironically they would later prove to be the Achilles heel of the Junta. Their cases and others like them would be the key to breaking down legal impediments and, in the end, putting a number of Junta leaders and their subordinates on trial.

CHAPTER 14

Hubris and Fear

WHEN MARIANA AND CARLA began their new lives they were doing so in an Argentina where the Junta was hoping that its savage methods would now lead to a kind of stability. By the late 1970s the battle against subversion inside the country had effectively been won. The urban-guerrilla structure of the ERP was the first to be destroyed. This was followed by increasingly effective attacks on the Montoneros that drove hundreds of their fighters and activists into exile, leaving only a few at what was supposed to be the front line. According to a memorandum from US Secretary of State Cyrus Vance to President Carter in March 1979, the Argentine Ambassador to Washington had informed him that 'abductions' had been halted and despite his scepticism about such promises, the numbers did appear to have diminished.

The problem of the remaining Montoneros and their ability to mount terrorist attacks would soon be largely resolved. In late 1979, while Argentina celebrated the budding genius of Diego Maradona in their victory at the football World Youth Championship, and some other Argentines scoffed at the musical *Evita* by Tim Rice and Andrew Lloyd Webber, premiering in New York, which they saw as parodying their country, the Montoneros committed a bizarre and still much debated form of organisational suicide. From his command post outside the country their leader, Mario Firmenich, ordered what he described as a strategic counter-offensive. Hundreds of Montoneros, some now based in Cuba, some undergoing training in Palestinian camps in the Middle East, and others scattered around Europe were ordered to find their way back into Argentina and launch concerted attacks against the military regime. The revolutionaries responded with the emotional fervour that Latin America seems particularly able to produce. In Cuba young couples left their children in state nurseries and obeyed the call, in Europe they took flights to Brazil or Chile, thought to be the best points of transit to the battle ground.

The 'counter-offensive' began at 7.30am on September 27th, 1979 with a hallmark machine gun and bomb attack by a team of about a dozen Montoneros dressed as policemen on the home of Guillermo Klein, the government's Secretary for Economic Planning. Klein was seen as the man behind the Junta's economic policies. Two of his bodyguards were killed and the house dynamited, leaving Klein and his family buried under the rubble. Argentines turning on their televisions were startled to see live pictures of the family being dug out alive with only minor injuries, as the commander of the Federal Police personally organised their rescue. It was a spectacular coup but from that moment the Montonero operation went badly wrong. Promised demonstrations by trades union supporters failed to materialise and numbers of Montonero fighters were arrested before they could even go into action. Some were seized immediately after crossing the border into Argentina, leading to suspicions that their identities and movements had been given away. In fact, the security forces had captured a key figure in the movement's military wing, normally the chief of their training operation in Colonel Gaddafi's Libya. He was described as 'cooperating' with his captors, which led in turn to the arrest of more militants trying to come in through various bus stations in Buenos Aires. Those arrested were quickly fed into the intelligence apparatus organised by Aníbal Gordon and his cohorts, where the immediate use of torture produced what was described as information in real time. More than half of the 200 Montoneros who attempted to take part in the 'counter-offensive' were killed and ever since then, as recriminations persist, rumours have circulated that the entire operation was compromised from the start. Once again the ruthless figure of Admiral Emilio Massera is said to have played a characteristically murderous part. No longer one of the Junta's leading trio but still hungry for power and closely connected to the regime's killing machine, he is said to have negotiated a secret deal with elements of the Montoneros' exiled leadership with whom he had maintained clandestine contact: militants returning to Argentina would be arrested and jailed but not killed and would later be able to take part in non-violent political activities. Instead, to quote the highly respected Buenos Aires journalist, the late Andrew Graham-Yooll, describing these claims shortly before his death in 2019, 'They were slaughtered.'[1]

It is at this point in the Junta's progress that the differences within America's political and diplomatic establishment become most apparent. The US Deputy Secretary of State Patricia Derian repeatedly drew attention to shocking reports from Argentina, as in this memorandum of January 1979 to Secretary Vance:

> 38 bodies, many of them without heads or hands, were recently washed ashore on one of Argentina's Atlantic beaches ... Our Embassy estimates that about 55 disappearances a month take

KIDNAPPED BY THE JUNTA

place in Argentina. The International Red Cross representative in Buenos Aires recently characterized the disappearances as 'a calculated policy' of the Argentine authorities.[2]

There were, however, American officials and business leaders prepared to regard that as the price of halting Marxism in this pivotal country in Latin America. President Carter himself began to show signs that he was shifting in his chair. One concern was that Argentina might agree to sell massive quantities of grain to the Soviet Union, undermining the American grain embargo, a crucial pressure point in the Cold War. In his inaugural address Carter had promised that his commitment to human rights was 'absolute', a word later modified to 'very strong'. Arms manufacturers were infuriated by the block on sales to Argentina, citing, in particular, the refusal to approve the sale of battlefield radar only to see a French manufacturer step in and sell similar equipment without difficulty. The influential *Washington Post* columnists Rowland Evans and Robert Novak praised the Argentine Junta for having squashed an impending communist takeover and claimed that Carter's human-rights policy had inflicted severe damage on the US economy to the tune of $1.4 billion in lost business. Concerned about the political and economic impact, Carter sought to smooth the way for 'non-lethal' exports to Argentina and these rose sharply, to the horror of human-rights advocates. They pointed to the fact that the Junta was flatly refusing to disclose figures for the numbers of dead and disappeared. President Videla continued to claim that the issue of the disappeared was beyond the government's control and stated, in remarks that were presumably intended to be placatory but only succeeded in incriminating his regime, that nothing could be done for them because they were 'neither dead nor alive'.[3]

It is clear from the released American documents that the US Embassy in Buenos Aires had a full understanding of the methods still being used. A detailed breakdown sent to the Secretary of State in Washington in September 1980 reported that 'Disappearance is still the standard tactic for the Argentine Security Services in dealing with captured terrorists'. The author went on: 'Based on everything we know, we believe that detainees are usually tortured as part of interrogation and eventually executed without any semblance of due process.' The report stated that the numbers of such murders had declined but that they were still being carried out 'because it worked', and persuading the Argentine authorities to moderate their tactics would be 'an uphill battle'.[4]

Five years later, under the very different American presidency of Ronald Reagan, the Central Intelligence Agency produced a secret historical study for internal circulation of the methods which had been used by the Argentine Junta in its successful elimination of armed subversion. Drawing on earlier reports, it used clear, cold language to set out the reasons for the military regime's effectiveness against the ERP and the Montoneros:

> Paramilitary terror was effective in decimating the insurgent support network and intimidating the population to dissociate themselves from the insurgents. This type of terror was effective in Argentina because a large portion of the population, while having grievances, had a standard of living high enough to prevent them risking their lives and well-being for the dubious goals of the insurgents.[5]

Thus 'paramilitary terror' aimed at 'decimating' the insurgency's supporters – and which was Aníbal Gordon's stock-in-trade – was regarded by the CIA as a legitimate and effective government measure. This followed years in which the Junta had claimed that the worst excesses of the Dirty War were the work of rogue elements that could not be controlled and many, though not all, US officials had chosen to believe them. In fact the truth was far more uncomfortable. The Junta, for all its professed desire to restore order and stability to Argentina, had based its authority on the exercise of wide-ranging violence which had undeniably proved extremely effective in its core aim of eliminating armed resistance.

The death squads and secret detention centres had killed thousands of people, both armed revolutionaries and what Aníbal Gordon called 'typewriter terrorists' – writers and in particular journalists whose work appeared to feed subversion. The definition was broad. At least 84 Argentinian journalists were murdered in the period prior to the Falklands War and one of the country's leading novelists, Haroldo Conti, joined the tally of the disappeared at the Automotores Orletti. As far as the executioners were concerned, the novelist and teacher of Latin had made his sympathies all too clear by visiting Cuba.

There were at least twenty more clandestine detention centres in Buenos Aires alone, including, most notoriously, the Naval Mechanical School known as ESMA, which did its business behind a splendidly columned portico. It was here that the executioners believed they had solved the problem of the disposal of victims by injecting them with a powerful anaesthetic of a kind often used on horses before throwing them from aircraft into the South Atlantic. It was a method that soon came to the ears of the US Embassy, which had reported it to Washington in a communication dated July 21st, 1978:

A human rights source contact in the medical profession whose reporting has been reliable in the past informed the Embassy in late June that terrorists and subversives selected for elimination were now being administered injections of 'Ketalar', which sources described as powerful anaesthetic ... According to source, Ketalar is administered in an intramuscular injection to the prisoner as a preventive health measure, the subject rapidly loses consciousness and vital functions cease. Source alleges that subjects are then disposed of in rivers or the ocean.[6]

A year later the US Embassy would report information that it had evidently received on the diplomatic circuit. It quoted the General in command of Zone 1, which included much of the capital, Carlos Suárez Mason, as telling another country's ambassador that for long periods he had been signing between 50 and 100 death warrants each day. The American report continued: 'Asked whether this was not an overwhelming responsibility, Suárez Mason replied that no, it was not, since in all cases persons had confessed to some association with terrorism.'[7]

The confessions were, of course, of the sort extracted by Aníbal Gordon who then, as one of his subordinates was to testify, issued his own written orders for the kidnapping of victims with whom he did not deal himself. All this was confirmation both of the centralised bureaucratic process that underpinned the murder machine and of the complete, officially endorsed, abandonment of any concept of justice. It was put even more simply by Gordon, the officially authorised assassin and torturer, when he boasted that he was responsible for the deaths of hundreds of subversives.

With its own guerrilla movements defeated or at least suppressed, the Junta came to believe that it was part of its sacred mission to export these successful Argentinian tactics to other countries, particularly those in Central America that were in deep turmoil and where the advance of communism was of profound concern to the United States. At the forefront of these were Nicaragua, where Sandinista revolutionaries had just toppled the Somoza dictatorship and celebrated with a revolutionary carnival attended by Che Guevara and Mario Firmenich, and El Salvador, where a savage civil war was under way. Some members of the Junta, in characteristically hubristic fashion, even saw themselves as inheriting leadership of the Christian anti-communist crusade to which President Carter was not, they believed, sufficiently committed. Others, more realistic, hoped that assisting American objectives in this important region would help to defuse the human-rights issue at home. Argentinian policy, responding to the US desire to keep its involvement as low-profile as possible, was to send teams of military and paramilitary advisors, now supposedly expert in counter-insurgency warfare, to school right-wing elements in the dark arts of 'Dirty War'. These efforts received strong American backing when the Republican Ronald Reagan became US President in January 1981 and debate in Washington was for a time dominated by talk of Central America falling victim to a revolutionary 'domino effect'. The small Argentinian expeditionary force was organised by the 601st Intelligence Battalion, which created a special 'Overseas Task Force'. One of those placed in command of it was a close collaborator of Aníbal Gordon and veteran of the Automotores Orletti, Raúl Guglielminetti.

Aníbal Gordon would later tell an Argentinian judge that in this period he held a senior position in the SIDE intelligence service and that he had worked in Nicaragua where Argentinian military aid was being funnelled to the right-wing Contra rebels launching raids across the Honduran border.[8] Other reports also placed him in Honduras where both the Argentinian and US teams were based, and in El Salvador where the military-dominated junta was hanging on to power by the assassination of opponents in the towns while the army battled guerrillas in the countryside. This was what was becoming known as the 'Argentinian Method' and I witnessed it at first hand when I reported from El Salvador in 1981 as the pace of killing reached its height.

Our report[9] was one that today, in an age when the slightest impropriety or pictorial evidence of bloodshed has to be pixelated or otherwise obscured, could probably never be shown on television in its original form. In El Salvador in 1981, however, we were able to film and days later show pictures of the 'Argentinian Method' being practised in a rocky gorge just outside the capital. Here every night the bodies of murder victims were thrown from the cliff tops, sometimes landing on the remains of those thrown down before. Those with families courageous enough to associate themselves with the victims were with difficulty collected for a Christian burial. Occasionally the corpses would be accompanied by a piece of paper denouncing them as communists. In other cases the murderers did not bother to transport the dead that far, let alone give even the most basic explanation. In the city we saw motorists driving impassively past the body of what we were told was a *subversivo* who had simply been left there or thrown out of a passing vehicle. The drivers sounding their horns as they tried to get to work in the morning traffic did not let their eyes linger on him for even a moment.

An official at the US Embassy, presumably well informed, told us that some 10,000 people had been murdered in the previous year, though he maintained that it was difficult to establish if they were the victims of right or left. In fact the right was responsible for about four-fifths of the killings. Looking at the pictures we shot, I am reminded of the risks that our cameraman and sound recordist took to film them, and of the particular scene where a human-rights worker, Armando Paz, acted out for me the mock execution that he had suffered from a death squad before, miraculously, they let him live with nothing worse than bruising from a blow to his head. His re-enactment and the emotions he described are chillingly similar to what I and our team were to suffer at the hands of Aníbal Gordon little more than a year later.

The influence of the Argentine secret service on events in Central America was marked by their particular brand of violence and by accusations that the officers involved were both helping to fund the operation and making substantial profits from smuggling cocaine into the United States. There were also allegations that some of the Argentine 'volunteers' had kidnapped wealthy Salvadorans for ransom. What became clear, not least from the evidence of an Argentinian officer who had the misfortune of falling into the hands of Sandinista forces in Nicaragua, is that the advisors from Buenos Aires applied all the brutal skills they had learned at home to the Central American conflicts, where they sometimes found themselves pitted against Argentinian revolutionaries who had elected to continue the revolutionary struggle in exile.

Under their agreement with Washington – which evolved into Operation Charly, a name perhaps chosen because it sounded less menacing than Condor – the Argentinians provided manpower and training while the United States secretly paid many of the bills. The training given to Contra units and elements of the Salvadoran security forces included conventional military skills such as the use of rifles, machine guns, mortars and light artillery as well as the particular expertise the Argentinians had developed in the torture of prisoners and suspects, and the use of the information gained to quickly carry out more arrests. In the words of one Salvadoran paramilitary who worked with the Argentines: 'You capture one [guerrilla] and he hands over three, with three you get ten. You get ten, you get fifty.'

Even some who opposed the communist insurgency were horrified by the Argentine method of arresting and often torturing a suspect's entire family. 'For example,' said Alicia Llovera, a supporter of the ruling regime, 'I have a cousin who is a communist but does that mean they can kill me? No, this country is very small. Everyone is family. We would all end up dead.'[10]

As at Automotores Orletti and the other clandestine detention centres in Argentina, the methods used included electric shock torture with the effects enhanced by drenching the victim with water. Some Salvadoran trainees are said to have admired the irresistible agonies produced by this system. Groups of trainees are said to have been flown to Buenos Aires to be lectured on the decisive successes that the Argentine security forces had achieved against communist subversion.[11] A Salvadoran torturer who later thought it prudent to move to the United States described his work in terms that Aníbal Gordon would have recognised:

> In general, you will kill the prisoners because there's an assumption they shouldn't live. If we pass them to the judge, they'll go free and we'll maybe have to pick them up again. If there's lots of pressure – like from Amnesty International or some foreign countries – then we might pass them on to a judge, but if there's no pressure, then they're dead.

The effects of these joint US–Argentinian efforts were rapidly visible. In El Salvador, Argentina passed on military aid worth some

$20 million and the regime succeeded in halting the advance of the revolutionary forces, while in Nicaragua the disparate groups that had originally made up the right-wing Contra rebels were consolidated, became more effective and able to carry out raids deeper inside the country. Meanwhile in Honduras, the nation that had come to serve as a base for these efforts and where Marxist subversion did not represent a serious threat, the government was nonetheless encouraged to form an 'intelligence battalion' on Argentinian lines. According to the man who later became Commissioner of Human Rights in Honduras, Leo Valladares, the phenomenon of forced disappearance of people in his country was put into practice with the arrival of the Argentine military in Honduran territory. He accused them of the creation of death squads that kidnapped and murdered more than 100 people in his country. The Charly agreement with the governments of Honduras and El Salvador also allowed the Argentine military to assassinate and disappear former militants from their own country now exiled in these other nations. For the US administration, the arrangement enabled Washington to funnel weapons, training and funds to the Nicaraguan Contra rebels in clandestine fashion without Congressional interference. However, it was to set the pattern for the Iran–Contra or 'Irangate' scandal that would eventually come close to wrecking the Reagan presidency.

The real significance of the Argentinian effort in Central America was not in its local military results or even in the trail of murder that accompanied it, but in the confidence it gave to the Junta's leadership in Buenos Aires and in particular to General Leopoldo Galtieri, who was to take over as President late in 1981. Shortly before that, with Ronald Reagan now installed in the White House, Galtieri had used a speech in Miami to declare his country an unconditional ally of the US in the struggle against communism. He pledged that

Argentina and the United States would 'march together in the ideological war which is starting in the world'. Plans were even discussed for the creation of a large Latin American military force, to be commanded by an Argentinian officer, which would land in El Salvador, drive the revolutionaries into Honduras where they would be wiped out, and then invade Nicaragua to topple the Sandinista regime. At the same time the new men in Washington made it clear that the Carter 'obsession' with human rights was no longer an obstacle to close ties with Buenos Aires. According to Reagan's Secretary of State Alexander Haig, writing in his memoirs: 'We told Argentina that it had heard its last public lecture from the United States in human rights.'[12] Galtieri himself became convinced that the alliance with Washington which he was constructing would be indissoluble. It was a conviction that would soon lead to the catastrophic misjudgement which he would inflict on his country. For the Junta was winning battles prior to losing a war.

A victorious exercise of military power was something that the Junta craved both in order to distract from economic crisis and to justify its savagery during the 'repression'. Some of its members also nourished the belief that war would forge a new breed of Argentine 'supermen'. The Malvinas had always been high on the list of possible objectives, with the cause kept alive in the 1960s with the hijacking by nationalists of a civilian passenger aircraft belonging to Aerolíneas Argentinas. The hijackers forced the pilot to fly to the Falklands and land on the racecourse near Port Stanley. There they raised Argentine flags and claimed sovereignty before giving themselves up and being shipped back to the mainland. However, some key figures in the military regime had their eyes on a different prize. In the belief that they had the right to expand Argentina's borders by force if they deemed it necessary, the Junta's leaders had devoted some energy to planning a short, sharp war against their Condor ally Chile, to gain control of the Beagle Channel and associated islands near the southern tip of the country. The issue had earlier gone to the International Court of Justice at The Hague, where the justices found unanimously for Chile, whereupon the Argentine Junta repudiated both the judgement and the treaty which lay behind it, under which Britain was supposed to adjudicate in disputes, and prepared for military action. The plan that was to be put into effect around Christmas 1978 was to seize the islands and then negotiate on Argentina's terms, 'ocupar para negociar', very much the same formula which three years later it hoped would produce success against Britain. The Junta's forces would certainly have been more formidable in such a regional conflict and the plan perhaps makes sense of Argentina's decision to equip itself with Dagger combat jets, built by Israel from a French Mirage design. These were effective as air superiority fighters but less successful at long range over the Falklands because of their lack of any air-to-air refuelling capability, as we have seen. In fact on this occasion the Junta was denied its prey. Pope John Paul II intervened and a Papal envoy succeeded in negotiating a settlement. The believers in the cleansing and fortifying effects of war would have to wait.

Argentina's forces may have looked relatively impressive on paper and the Junta's leadership doubtless took comfort from its acquisitions of modern equipment, including two decommissioned British destroyers and French-manufactured aircraft and missiles, but there was rot inside the system. The Junta was to prove itself incapable of developing and pursuing a long-term strategy to deal with what was viewed as the running sore of the Falkland Islands. Above all the regime did not possess the resources to fully assess the diplomatic and military consequences of pursuing a confrontation with Britain.

The regime's intelligence services had proved themselves highly skilled in electric shock and various other kinds of torture. They were world-beaters in tracking, kidnapping and murdering suspects and looting their possessions, Aníbal Gordon being a past master of this sort of expertise, but there is little evidence of the analytical and technical depth which is now a required precursor to modern warfare. Indeed the Argentine author Horacio Verbitsky has made the claim, which would have been dismissed were it not from such a well-informed source, that the Junta's plans for military confrontations with both Chile and Britain were drawn up by a 'think-tank' of captured Montoneros. These men, some of whom benefited from both higher education and military training abroad, apparently attempted to save their lives by working on detailed military assessments and plans for the Junta. It should be mentioned that Verbitsky himself had been a member of the Montonero movement at an earlier stage of the insurgency though, he said, he had never taken part in acts of violence. He was later the author who famously persuaded the former Naval officer Adolfo Scilingo to confess to throwing drugged victims out of aircraft into the sea (see Chapter 19).

In fact under the Junta's rule the secret services were large and unwieldy, obsessed with pursuing a dwindling number of subversives who no longer posed any real threat, and fearful of the personal consequences of their crimes should the Junta ever lose power. Prior to the conflict with Britain, Argentina's secret world consisted of at least nine separate services, all of them controlled by the military. Principal among these were the State Intelligence Secretariat (SIDE), supposedly the main collector of internal and external intelligence and responsible directly to the President. Aníbal Gordon would later state that he held a rank equivalent to Colonel in this organisation and claimed that the radio in his specially equipped vehicle was linked directly to the switchboard at the Presidential Palace.

Working with SIDE and, under the Junta, closely integrated with it, was the Army Intelligence Service, confusingly named SIE, and generally known by the designation of its most active unit in the Dirty War, the 601st Intelligence Battalion. This officially reported to the Ministry of Defence but, according to the organisational chart described in Chapter 3, had a chain of command leading again to the President.

Working in parallel to and sometimes in competition with these organisations were the separate intelligence services of the Navy (SIN), notorious for the torture and murders at its Mechanical School. There was also the Air Force Intelligence Service (SIFA), the Police Federal Security Department and the Gendarmerie Intelligence Directorate, reporting to the Ministry of the Interior. Recruitment was often based on perceived loyalty to the regime and rather less on knowledge or intellectual achievement. In all, these services employed some 12,000 agents and officials and ran at least 30,000 informers in different areas of Argentine society. Their efforts were, in theory, linked and given direction by the Central Nacional de Inteligencia (CNI) but this body had no coordinating powers and was to prove ineffective before and during the Falklands conflict. Instead Argentina's security services remained mired in what they continued to see as their principal mission: the destruction of 'terrorist elements' inside the country.

Just over eighteen months before the Falklands invasion, a political officer at the US Embassy in Buenos Aires, Townsend B. Friedman, composed a highly perceptive memorandum entitled 'Hypothesis – The GOA [Government of Argentina] As Prisoner of Army Intelligence'. He wrote: 'It is possible to conclude that the policy-making levels of the GOA are prisoners and victims of intelligence services here, particularly the Army's 601 Battalion.' Friedman went on to list a series of recent murderous and internationally embarrassing operations, including kidnappings in Peru and the 'suspicious discovery of one of the kidnapping victims dead in Madrid ... disappearance is 601 work.' Friedman went on: 'On the basis of my contacts, there is little reason to have much confidence that these services have either the smarts or the political skills to match their tremendous influence on this government ... I think we all have serious cause for concern that these men will be telling the government what to see and what to do about what they see.'[13]

The US Embassy was receiving its information from a number of well-placed, though understandably anonymous, military figures. One of these had already given Friedman his own assessment of where Argentina was going wrong, above all the relentless focus on the fast-dwindling threat of subversion:

My source minimized the current real threat against Argentines posed by terrorists. He claims they were eliminated. Their capabilities, he said, were restricted to an occasional clandestine radio broadcast or perhaps 'a bomb or two'. In any case, he said, there was nothing ... to justify the current siege mentality and activity of the military.

The source went on to explain the secret concerns that were influencing decision-making inside the military regime:

[S]ome of those most deeply involved in the 'Dirty War' are terribly frightened that as the climate returns to normality they are being moved closer to the time when they must account for their acts and suffer retribution. On the other hand, if the 'Dirty War' can be kept going they are protected – and besides, he said, in some cases doing what they like best.[14]

As if to prove the accuracy of this US Embassy report, the newly installed commander of the Air Force and member of the ruling Junta, General Omar Graffigna, made clear that the war of terror against terror would continue: 'The enemy will change his tactics and terrain,' the General declared, 'He will appear to be in retreat ... only to reappear in the most remote places, in classrooms, universities, in all the areas of the nation's life that can be used as a base.'[15]

The Junta sought to reassure its dirty warriors by passing a new law preventing judicial investigation of the *desaparecidos*. It stated that anyone who had disappeared between November 1974 and September 1979 could be declared legally dead; however, the Junta's leaders knew that more would be needed to try to protect itself and its followers. Thus a populist campaign and even a military operation to 'recover' the Falklands, which the military correctly judged would be extremely popular, came to be seen as a possible way out. And the rigidly hierarchical structure of what passed for an intelligence community – where no individual could prosper by introducing discordant opinions or facts – ensured that decisions would not be taken on a reasoned basis.

After the disaster of the Falklands War a panel of military men chaired by retired General Benjamín Rattenbach was commissioned to report on the reasons for Argentina's defeat. Rattenbach, it is worth recording, had his early training in 1930s Germany, where he had been an unabashed admirer of Adolf Hitler, and clearly did not accept such failure with equanimity. He castigated the Junta's leadership and, in particular, the inadequacy of its intelligence services, denouncing them for a failure to coordinate with each other, the production of low-quality information, an inability to appreciate Britain's capabilities and even a lack of knowledge of the geography of the Falkland Islands themselves.[16]

The Junta would launch its confrontation with Britain intoxicated by a cocktail of inadequate information and wishful thinking. In particular they drew confidence from the deep cuts that Mrs Thatcher's government was having to impose in the 1981 Defence Review, and which included the decision to withdraw HMS *Endurance*, the lightly armed guard ship normally posted to the islands. They also failed to analyse properly the limitations of Argentina's newly acquired military strength when pitted against the technology and professionalism of what was still a leading NATO power. And, perhaps most importantly of all, they wholly misjudged the position of the United States, where the limits of her friendship lay and where her loyalties would finally rest.

Most of the information that the Junta received about developments in other countries came from SIDE agents posted inside Argentine embassies abroad, but their principal mission was normally to track the activities of potentially dangerous political exiles. When the military attaché in Washington was asked to give an opinion he apparently reassured his superiors that the new Reagan administration put a high value on Argentina's collaborative effort in Central America and that 'in a crunch it would tilt towards Buenos Aires, not London'.

It was this sort of assurance that fed the overweening self-confidence of Argentina's new President, General Leopoldo Galtieri who, somewhat eccentrically, had taken to referring to himself as the 'North Americans' pampered child'.[17] He would soon discover that such sentimentality, if it existed, played little part in the decision-making process.

CHAPTER 15

Murderer Turns Art Lover

C HRISTMAS 1980 WAS not a joyful one for many Argentines. The Junta's promise to bring stability was looking increasingly forlorn as the country plunged into yet another economic crisis. Inflation was running at more than 100%, production and exports were falling, unemployment and poverty rising. The defeat of terrorism had brought no cure for fundamental ills and the nation which had appeared to promise so much when it was hailed early in the 20th century as the tenth most prosperous in the world, on the basis of per capita income, was now headed yet again for the rocks.

The trigger for this latest setback was a sudden and spectacular banking crisis. In March 1980, one of the largest private banks in Argentina, the Banco de Intercambio Regional (BIR), failed. Over the next week the Central Bank had to intervene to try to save three other major banks, two of which subsequently collapsed. Thus began a period of serious turmoil in the Argentine system, which resulted in the liquidation of 71 financial institutions over the next two years in the run-up to the Falklands War. Argentina has always been a favourite stamping ground for experts in economic theory because problems are so stark and consequences so dramatic. In this case a cascade of failures appears to have been set off by a growing number of companies running into difficulty or simply going bankrupt and defaulting on their bank loans. A key cause was that the Junta's attempts at rigour had actually led to a situation where interest and exchange rates were increasingly unpredictable. A particularly Argentine feature of the crisis was that some of the banks that went bust did so at a time when they were enjoying spectacular rates of growth, a phenomenon which experts have put down to 'speculation'.

The Junta's Minster of the Economy, Martínez de Hoz, the scion of an established and wealthy cattle-ranching family whose education had taken place far away on the playing fields of Eton, took urgent action to try and arrest the meltdown but the measures he chose inflicted great damage on what was already a discredited economic policy. Martínez de Hoz, one of the few civilians at a senior level in the government, had attempted to restore some faith in the peso by a system of scheduled and predictable devaluations. Now he was forced to suddenly slash its value by 23%. Business failures jumped, share prices fell, tradeable assets rose in value and consumer prices rocketed. Home-owners and small businesses were faced with loans they could not repay and the Central Bank rapidly found itself the largest owner of real estate in the country. Financial anarchy began to grip Argentina. It was an atmosphere in which the weak went to the wall and the strong, which in practice often meant those protected by some element of the Junta, found their own ways to survive and even prosper.

Despite the economic tensions Christmas 1980 was celebrated in traditional fashion. In common with most Catholic countries, Argentinians eat their Christmas meal late on Christmas Eve, when fireworks are set off and *globos* (paper lanterns) are launched into the night sky. Christmas Day is for church and family visits, as well as recovery from excess.

It was in the midst of these comforting rituals that, in the very early hours of December 25th, a well-organised gang of thieves broke into the National Museum of Fine Arts, a dignified, columned building in the centre of the capital. They were on a mission to steal assets which they clearly believed to be internationally tradeable. The thieves, apparently four in number, gained access through the roof, which was in the process of being repaired. They used the ladders and scaffolding that had been left in place to climb down into the galleries below and went about their business. The small number of guards present in the museum were seemingly unaware of the intrusion.

The operation was impressively systematic. What appears to have been a list of paintings and drawings was targeted, taken down from the walls and loaded into a vehicle waiting outside. A point which later emerged as potentially significant is that the thieves used cutting equipment to open cases containing rare Chinese vases and ivory carvings, which were also stolen. Apparently confident and assured, the gang is said to have paused for refreshments in the midst of their labours.

The haul was impressive: some 23 artworks including sixteen French Impressionist paintings and drawings. There were internationally known works by Renoir ('Tête de Jeune Fille au Ruban'), Gauguin ('Le Cri'), and works by Cézanne and Degas. All the works were part of what was known as the Santamarina Donation, a collection assembled by a wealthy ranching couple, Antonio and Mercedes Santamarina, and donated to the National Museum after a bitter dispute with the state. The value of the stolen items was provisionally set at $25 million.

The question was: who had committed the theft, and where had the artworks gone? The police, in a reflexive gesture, beat up and tortured with electric cattle prods the two security guards who had been in the museum at the time and who had apparently been drugged prior to the robbery. It did not however seem likely that they had been the authors of such an effective scheme. A witness apparently claimed that a green Ford Falcon had been waiting outside the museum and that the haul had been taken away in an Army truck. What seemed clear to many was that only criminals with authorisation from the very top would have dared to loot such a target, let alone do it in such a relaxed fashion.

Various possible names were bandied about but the one that has stuck is, once again, that of Aníbal Gordon. In his book about Argentina's kidnap industry that he titled ironically *Buenos Muchachos* ('Goodfellas'), Carlos Juvenal reports that the Buenos Aires police, who were still expected to carry out some sort of investigation, however formalistic, intercepted a telephone call between Gordon and his son Marcelo, now a fully-fledged member of the gang, in which the two appear to have discussed hiding the artworks.

'Marcelo,' Gordon is claimed to have said, 'Tell Miguelito to keep the paintings in the General's house.' 'Miguelito' was a possible reference to Miguel Ángel Furci, the SIDE agent who was part of Gordon's gang and had taken baby Mariana. 'The General' was believed to be General Otto Paladino, the former head of SIDE who had a close relationship with Gordon and was still a highly influential figure. Gordon was soon to be directly accused of the theft by Guillermo Patricio Kelly, a well-informed but widely distrusted politician who would in due course become one of the kidnapper's victims. Later, under democracy, a judge assigned to the case, Norberto Oyarbide, expressed his belief that the trail led to Gordon, who had demonstrated a taste for art theft if not for the art itself. He would later be linked to another major robbery, the looting of the Museum of Decorative Arts in Rosario, in which works by Goya, El Greco and Murillo were stolen. In the latter case, the connection to Gordon was established by the arrest years later of his former secret service driver and close collaborator, Ernesto Lorenzo, who went by the name of Major Guzmán and was a veteran of many of Gordon's crimes. In 1995 Lorenzo was found in possession of one of the missing Old Masters from the Rosario robbery, a portrait by Goya which, according to newspaper reports, he was carrying in the boot of his car. Gordon had apparently given it to him as a reward for his services. (Lorenzo himself was released after a surprisingly short period and then arrested and jailed again for his leading role in a criminal conspiracy to smuggle a ton of cocaine into Spain.)

Following the dramatic Christmas robbery from the National Museum in Buenos Aires, the stolen artworks quickly made their way out of Argentina and took a roundabout and exotic route via Brazil, Suriname and Hong Kong to Taiwan. There, in that island state, the remains of what was once nationalist China, which because of its limited recognition sits outside many international agreements, the trail appeared to lead to a pair of brothers who had made a fortune in business. It then went cold. It was not until twenty years later that another Taiwanese gentleman claiming to represent the brothers attempted to sell three of the paintings to a Paris art gallery, but could produce no proof of ownership nor any explanation as to how they had come to be in possession of these fine examples of European art, last seen hanging on a museum wall half a world away. A British investigator was given a blunt brush-off by one of the brothers who asked him, 'Why are you coming here when you British pillaged China?', adding opaquely that they had close contacts with the Taiwanese Ministry of Defence and could not discuss the artworks without its authorisation.

The Argentinian Junta, itself an international pariah in the eyes of many, had long seen the advantages of good relations with Taiwan. In the period when President Carter was implementing US efforts to impose an arms embargo, Taiwan, with its own vigorous arms industry, stood out as a possible location for such purchases where no unpleasant questions about human rights might be asked.

All this has led to speculation in newspapers and a recently published book[1] that the robbery at the National Museum of Fine Arts was carried out by the Junta itself to help finance its military plans, specifically the seizure, or as they regarded it the recovery, of the Falkland Islands from Britain. It is suggested that Aníbal Gordon, with his track-record of successful and sometimes complex criminal operations, was assigned the task of stripping key sections of the museum and sending the art treasures on their way out of the country. The funds raised in hard currency were to be used to buy weapons that the Junta's plans required.

It is a relatively neat theory, which draws support from a later statement by the museum's director that such a robbery could only have taken place with high-level approval, and from an earlier reported remark by Aníbal Gordon to one of his kidnap victims – perhaps to make him feel better about the scale of his ransom – that it would be used to help fund the recovery of the Malvinas. However, there are also factors which raise questions about the 'Falklands Theory'. The real-world value of the artworks was actually surprisingly small. Though most were by great artists they tended to be among their lesser works. Sotheby's, which examined the paintings and drawings before realising that they were stolen, put their value at a mere $2 million, very small beer on the international arms market. There is also debate over the timing of the theft. As the Nazi-sympathising General Rattenbach affirmed in his report on the war, the first meeting of the National Intelligence Centre (CNI) to discuss a possible confrontation with Britain over the Falklands took place on September 3rd, 1981, nine months after the robbery at the museum. Given this timing it is even possible that, if the aim was to raise hard currency to assist in weapons purchases, these were actually intended for the Argentine task force in Central America, at that moment pivotal to the Junta's hopes of building strong relations with the new American administration of Ronald Reagan, and whose weapons requirements would have been rather smaller than war in the South Atlantic. Then again, in this period of economic chaos, the robbery could have been intended to achieve an entirely different purpose: the positioning abroad of hard currency for the benefit of key members of the Junta against the day, which did indeed come later, when a rapid flight from Argentina might prove the most sensible option. In the end it is unclear what profit, if any, resulted from the spectacular robbery. No hard evidence has ever been produced linking anyone in Taiwan to the crime itself. The three paintings put on sale in Paris were confiscated by the French authorities, before Judge Oyarbide himself flew to Paris and brought them back to Buenos Aires, rolled up in a package, in the economy-class cabin. The other stolen works of art have never been securely located. If Taiwanese weapons were received and used in the Falklands, they do not appear to have affected the outcome.

What the robbery does illustrate – along, it seems, with Aníbal Gordon's undeniable criminal skills – is the deepening chaos in Argentine society less than sixteen months before the confrontation with Britain began. Crime was being committed by the very forces that were supposed to prevent or punish it, for motives which ranged from self-enrichment to political fanaticism. Only seven months before the Museum of Fine Arts robbery, another spectacular theft had taken place, that of the heavily jewelled gold crown of the Virgin of Guadalupe, the centrepiece of the basilica in Santa Fe. The thieves also took the Bishop's cross encrusted with emeralds, a silver-and-gold chalice and a trove of smaller items.

The Archbishop, Monsignor Vicente Zazpe, responded by excommunicating the thieves, whoever they might be. However, ten days later a statement appeared from the self-styled Argentine Catholic Movement against Communism, declaring that the precious objects were in safe hands, but would not be returned until the communist-sympathising Zazpe was removed. The Archbishop himself then found a written message to him in one of the cathedral's confessionals. It said simply, 'Leftist son of a bitch, we are going to kill you.' This may, however, have been little more than cover for a robbery, which according to later investigation by Argentine journalists was organised by senior policemen in Santa Fe and carried out by their criminal connections, with policemen cordoning off the area to make sure the thieves were not disturbed. The loot is said to have been divided, with the crown going to the senior policemen and the smaller items distributed among the common thieves. The case would remain officially unsolved. A similar crime took place in Córdoba Cathedral, where a syndicate including policemen, antique dealers and churchmen stole precious jewels and replaced them with fakes.

The Argentine author Daniel Schavelzon has written in his book, *The Plunder of Art in Argentina*,[2] of the terrible condition of his country in this dark and lawless period: 'Those were the years when most of the country's museums were looted, when hundreds of statues

were stolen, when thousands of books disappeared from the librar-
ies.' It was, he says, 'a decade of plundering'.

Aníbal Gordon was, of course, a man who lived off such troubles
and for him life appears to have been good. He was operating with
what the late Judge Oyarbide was to call 'total impunity',[3] equipped
with a variety of weapons ranging from pistols and automatic rifles to
explosives, and driving a small fleet of radio-equipped Ford Falcon
cars recognised throughout the country as the feared trademark of
repression. He enjoyed these privileges to perform vital services for
the most hard-line elements in the Junta. Later in 1981 their determination to hold on to power was reflected by an assignment to use
his particular talents in the field of civilian internal politics.

Both the economic crisis and the defeat of armed insurgency
had increased the relevance of formerly mainstream political parties which, though they had no democratic outlet for their activities
under military rule, were still enjoying increased support among the
population, a matter of growing concern to the Junta. Public demonstrations to protest at the dire state of the economy were taking
place, sending the Junta into what the US Embassy described as 'political jitters'. Leading among the political groupings was the Peronist
Justicialist Party, which had been the legendary dictator's political
vehicle and was now once again gaining in importance through its
strong ties to Labour. One of its most important leaders was Julio
Bárbaro, a man who for years had been walking Argentina's political
tightrope and who was later to incur the displeasure of many on his
own wing of politics, by declaring that Peronism was not a political philosophy but simply a memory that won votes. He would also
anger the left by telling them that their resort to armed violence had
been 'a fundamental and fatal mistake'. However, in October 1981
this apparent moderation did not provide protection. He was to

receive what appears to have been a very direct and brutal message from the Junta.

Bárbaro was in his office in Libertad Street in Buenos Aires when Aníbal Gordon entered, showed him Federal Police credentials and took him away in a Ford Falcon car.[4] Two more vehicles joined the convoy and following what appears to have been their established kidnap procedure – which I can say caused tremors when I read an account of it – they turned off the main highway and took a dirt track into a field near Pilar, perhaps the very same spot to which we were taken a few months later. There Bárbaro, if he had not grasped it already, realised the predicament in which he found himself. In his case, this was the point where all his valuables including his watch were taken and he was blindfolded and made to lie down in the rear of one of the vehicles. Aníbal Gordon was in the car and commanded the operation.

Their final destination was another field in a more remote area where Bárbaro was systematically interrogated and tortured for hours. The interrogator was Gordon himself, who repeatedly plunged the politician's head into a bucket of water, coming close to drowning him as he demanded answers to questions about the Justicialist Party and its 'ideology'. After what he said was eight hours of this treatment, Bárbaro was driven back to Buenos Aires and left near a bus station. The message not to challenge or interfere in the Junta's running of the country had been delivered.

The US government expressed its concern over what had happened to Bárbaro and another Peronist leader but the drive to improve relations, and arms sales, was now under way. In October 1981, the Kennedy-Humphrey Congressional Amendment which had blocked most purchases of American weapons by Argentina was lifted. General Galtieri, widely seen as the next Argentine

President, paid a series of visits to the United States including a tour of Disneyland and a splendid formal lunch of Scottish salmon and filet mignon with senior US officials in Washington. Galtieri declared Argentina's willingness to help the US by sending troops to join the peacekeeping force in the Sinai Peninsula, while the Americans indicated that they hoped for a 'more fluid dialogue' with Buenos Aires on the basis that 'disappearances' in Argentina would cease and the military would retain its capacity to control public order while, at the same time, negotiating with the political parties, in pursuit of a gradual 'democratization'.

Galtieri made no secret of his desire to secure the 'return' of the Malvinas, and his rise to power took place as Britain's determination to retain the islands may have appeared to be weakening. The year before, Foreign Minister Nicholas Ridley had flown to the Falklands in a somewhat half-hearted attempt to interest the islanders in a scheme involving the transfer of formal sovereignty to Argentina, which would lease back administrative rights. The mission was covered by some 50 Argentine journalists but Ridley's suggestions were rejected by the islanders themselves. Then in 1981, as Galtieri was courting the US leadership, the Argentine Naval attaché in London, Rear Admiral Gualter Allara, reported that the British government was considering the sale of the 'Harrier-carrier' HMS *Invincible*, a budget-driven move that followed the scrapping two years earlier of Britain's last full-size aircraft carrier, HMS *Ark Royal*.[5] The news must have helped to convince the Junta that the British lion was increasingly toothless, but Argentina's diplomatic efforts to press the Falklands issue nonetheless appeared to be getting nowhere. In September 1981 their then Foreign Minister, Oscar Camilión, reported on his attempt to discuss the matter with Britain's Lord Carrington at the United Nations. He was met, he claimed, with clear signs of boredom and impatience. He told Buenos Aires that the Malvinas appeared to be about item 238 in the British government's list of concerns.[6]

Meanwhile the Minister of Commerce and Maritime Interests, Carlos García Martínez, in what he apparently believed was an off-the-record, not-for-publication interview with accredited journalists, stated that the Argentinian economy was 'on the verge of collapse'. The effect was another damaging run on the peso, which resulted in the flight of more than $400 million from Argentina, and further pressure on the Junta to take some action that might assist its own survival. In December 1981 General Galtieri took over as Argentina's President. In January 1982, the Argentinian newspaper *La Prensa* predicted an invasion of the Malvinas before the 150th anniversary of British rule in 1983. However, the paper had made such predictions before and there were many in Britain and even in Argentina who believed these warnings could safely be disregarded.

Certainly Aníbal Gordon and his gang appear to have been more or less immune to such concerns. In between his operations in the service of the Junta and others for personal profit, he was now spending much of his downtime at a bar called the 'Pucara', a name perhaps derived from the pre-Hispanic word for 'fortress' and also carried by the light propeller-driven combat aircraft that would be used by Argentine forces in the Falklands. Gordon is said to have owned the bar through intermediaries. In Argentine style, it boasted an outdoor swimming pool where secret-service men and gangsters could meet and relax after their labours. Habitués of the bar and other witnesses were to claim that among the regular clientele, they had seen Gordon's right-hand man, Eduardo Ruffo alias 'Zapato' or 'Captain', Gordon's son Marcelo and other members of the gang. They were said to have frequently carried pistols. Here, as the Argentine spring turned into the southern-hemisphere summer, these men drank and made their plans, little knowing that their country was only months away from the military confrontation that would transform Argentina's history and wreck the strange, privileged existence that they enjoyed.

Meanwhile some British politicians and officials were nourishing their own illusions. Over the years Britain had sold the Junta two destroyers and more than 140 surface-to-air missiles. Now, on March 3rd, 1982 on what was in reality the eve of war, David Joy, a Counsellor at the British Embassy in Buenos Aires, penned these thoughts about the Argentine regime:

> Although I am all for human rights ... I am already beginning to have more than a sneaking suspicion that the country is more likely to progress materially under the present regime which re-established order and government, than any government elected by the rabid communist/left-wing Peronist taxi driver who drove me to the office this morning.[7]

The days that followed would provide a harsh awakening.

CHAPTER 16

The Gamble that Failed

THE DECISION WAS TAKEN in January 1982 soon after General Galtieri formally took power. If Britain did not make the required concessions Argentina would 're-establish sovereignty' over the islands by force. Within the Junta's powerful Military Committee a small group was formed to draw up the plans. To try to preserve absolute secrecy the team had the smallest possible staff and wrote its documents by hand.

A key operational plan which they produced was the 'Directiva de Estrategia Militar' (Military Strategy Directive) numbered '1/82 (Caso Malvinas)'. It was laboriously written in a fine, almost copperplate, script and ran to thirteen pages, with annexes filling a further twelve pages. Judging from the contents it was written before February 15th, 1982 and probably earlier, bearing in mind how long the military operations it describes would have taken to prepare. However, it was finally distributed to a shortlist of military officials on March 16th, two weeks before the amphibious assault took place. There was an original document for the Military Committee and seventeen numbered copies. The one I have been able to examine is copy number three, which was intended for the

Commander-in-Chief of the Air Force, General Basilio Lami Dozo. It bears his signature, along with those of his fellow Junta leaders President Galtieri and Admiral Anaya.[1]

The timing of the document's distribution supports the idea that the invasion of the Falklands was brought forward, perhaps because of the deteriorating political situation in Buenos Aires where riots were breaking out, or out of concern that as tension mounted Britain might send a nuclear submarine to the South Atlantic. Three days after the document's distribution a party of Argentinians, officially described as scrap-metal dealers but including military personnel, landed on the island of South Georgia and raised the Argentine flag. This and the sharp British response in sending the ice patrol vessel HMS *Endurance* with two dozen Royal Marines from Port Stanley has often been seen as a trigger for the conflict. However, it is worth noting that the secret hand-written plan had already stated that all units taking part in what would become known as 'Operation Rosario' should be in a state of readiness before April 1st, 1982, though the actual timing of what was called 'D-Day' could be affected by the weather.

For those receiving it, the plan may have appeared as neat as the handwriting. The need for tactical surprise was stressed. Naval units were to give the appearance of being on manoeuvres. There were details of how different units were to be deployed and an exhortation that since Argentina was simply taking back its own territory, bloodshed or material losses to the inhabitants of the islands should be avoided if possible. The plan envisaged the establishment of a military government to administer 'the regained territory', and the early withdrawal of most forces, leaving just a sufficient garrison in place. There is even the suggestion that the new administration could seek to improve the standard of living of the islanders in order to encourage them to accept Argentinian rule. There were, however, no details of any longer-term strategy in this document or in any other that has been released. It was apparently believed that Britain would accept the Argentine takeover as an act of *force majeure*. If not, the Argentine Navy was given the task of 'dissuading and interdicting any military reaction by Great Britain'. This, of course, was rapidly exposed as wishful thinking when the Navy was effectively knocked out of the war by the sinking of the *Belgrano* by HMS *Conqueror*.

In the Argentine heart of government, the Casa Rosada, General Leopoldo Fortunato Galtieri launched his campaign in scenes more evocative of Peter Sellers at his satirical best than of the heroic leadership he wished to display. A startling insight into the Junta's almost comical lack of readiness for the conflict it started with Britain has been chronicled in the book *1982* by Juan Yofre, the well-informed Argentinian writer who was later to become head of the SIDE secret service under democracy. Yofre says that he compiled his version of events from secret official records he was able to examine at SIDE.[2]

All accounts agree that on April 1st, 1982, while Argentine Naval vessels prepared to land troops on the islands, the most powerful leader in the world, US President Ronald Reagan, found himself unable to get through to the Argentinian President on the telephone. As we saw in an earlier chapter, American officials, knowing of Galtieri's fondness for a drink at lunchtime, speculated that this might be the cause. But Yofre paints a picture of tragi-comic chaos at the Presidential Palace.

Initially, it seems, Galtieri did not want to take the call until the troops were ashore and a point of no return had been reached, but by the evening it was realised that Reagan could not be put off any longer. As I was to witness a few weeks later, Galtieri's English was extremely poor and a Foreign Ministry translator had to be brought in but, for reasons that are unclear, the one who normally handled official meetings declined the task and a younger, less experienced official was sent to the Casa Rosada. He found that instead of modern communications equipment Galtieri's office was only furnished with an old Bakelite telephone probably dating from the 1960s, to which a Colonel in the intelligence service had attached a tape recorder to provide a record of the call. Galtieri and the translator were supposed to share the single handset.

When the conversation with Reagan began Galtieri gave a long exposition of the history of the dispute and Argentina's rights. Reagan apparently responded by warning of the consequences of hostilities and cautioning Galtieri that Margaret Thatcher was a 'friend' and that Britain was a 'special ally' of the United States. At this point Galtieri apparently became infuriated and started berating the unfortunate translator as if he were personally to blame for the contents of the message, telling him in a loud voice, 'You cannot say that.'

When the call ended Galtieri claimed that the translation of Reagan's remarks must have been wrong and demanded that the tape recording be played back. According to Yofre, the intelligence officer who had installed the recorder rewound the tape: 'Once the tape was back to the beginning, the Colonel stopped the rewind and pressed play. A "click" was heard and then a long buzzing sound ... and nothing else. The officer had not connected the devices properly and nothing had been recorded.'

'Thus', writes Yofre, 'began an armed confrontation against the third military and technological power on the planet.'[3]

In the world of diplomacy, small details often take on extraordinary significance – and never more so than in a conversation between the two Presidents as hostilities with Britain were about to begin. Galtieri apparently demanded to know if any of the secret services had recorded the call but none had; 'There were no orders to do it,' an official explained. There was then an attempt to reconstruct its contents from the recollections of the unfortunate translator and others who had overheard some of the exchanges in the room. Two differing versions emerged but the central elements were unambiguous. Reagan had told Galtieri that Mrs Thatcher would not back down and that Argentina was heading for a conflict that would damage its relationship with the United States and destabilise Latin America. He had asked Galtieri to halt the disembarkation. Galtieri had replied that it was too late for that and the solution was for Britain to recognise Argentinian sovereignty over the Malvinas without delay. It soon became clear that Reagan had not been impressed by Galtieri's blustering tone, but hubris had now become the central feature of Argentinian policy.

It was hubris against a background of political pandemonium. In preceding days the Junta had made ham-fisted attempts to enlist the support of Argentina's mainstream civilian politicians, most of whose activities were still banned. There was a suggestion that the parties would be recognised, that prisoners not guilty of terrorist offences would be released and that there would be a new national council to chart a fresh economic policy. A key objective, as Yofre writes, was that those who had ordered or carried out the atrocities of the Dirty War should not be the target of reprisals: 'Conditions must be created so that politicians do not call for revenge.' None of this was enough to halt the massive anti-government demonstration under the slogan 'Peace, Bread, Work', which surged to the gates of the Presidential Palace just days before the announcement that Argentine troops had landed on the Malvinas. The growing vehemence of such demonstrations had led the Junta to fear that it might even be toppled. When a senior Air Force officer who had been summoned to Buenos Aires to be briefed on his role in the Falklands operation asked why it was happening, he was told: 'It is necessary to change the mood of society.' That, at least, was briefly achieved.

The first part of the military operation had gone according to plan. Before launching it the Junta had taken the advice of a senior diplomat who had said that if they wished to negotiate with Britain at a later stage, they should at all costs avoid shedding the blood of the small Royal Marine garrison. Orders to that effect were issued and obeyed. The British troops did open fire on the attackers but were forced to surrender without losses to themselves. Total Argentine losses in Port Stanley and the separate operation in South Georgia were four soldiers dead and six wounded, the figures given by General Galtieri to US officials. However, any possible propaganda benefit of this on British public opinion was immediately lost by the decision to photograph the captured Royal Marines in a humiliating posture, lying prone on the ground under the guard of Argentine commandos armed with automatic weapons. But the main difficulty faced by Galtieri and his fellow Junta members was their profound ignorance of political strategy and international relations, which was deepened rather than relieved by misleading advice from their Foreign Minister Nicanor Costa Méndez who, on the day the invasion was publicly announced, declared that the British would not react: '*Nunca van a mandar la flota*', he said – they're never going to send the fleet. A photograph of him smiling triumphantly appeared on the front page of the Argentine newspaper, *La Nación*.

The Minister – who walked with a stick and, as I learned in my first attempt to interview him, was short-tempered with an acute sense of his own dignity – exercised what can only be described as a malign influence on the naive Galtieri who treated him with exaggerated respect.

Some days before the invasion Costa Méndez had summoned senior Foreign Ministry officials to the Green Room of the San Martín Palace, the splendid Beaux Arts building that was then the Ministry's working headquarters. There, after swearing his audience to secrecy, he spoke about the Malvinas plans; he recalled the history of failed negotiations with Britain and emphasised the now-excellent relations with the United States, whose people he described as 'great defenders of new nations against the colonial powers'. He spoke of the decline of the United Kingdom and the difficult economic situation which had forced the government of Mrs Thatcher to sell its aircraft carrier and other warships because it could not afford to maintain them. After speaking, he said: 'Gentlemen, are there any questions?' If there were any, no record of them has survived but clearly not all his officials were convinced.

The head of the West European Department at the Foreign Ministry, Ambassador Keller Sarmiento, had already contributed a memorandum which was soon to look remarkably prescient:

> Taking the conflict to a military confrontation of doubtful outcome for Argentina is our worst option, total isolation, risk of humiliation, serious economic, institutional and political consequences, partial or total destruction of our Air Force, fleet and military personnel, probable fall of the government, diminished capacity to negotiate with the United Kingdom the future status of the Islands ... I believe that this should be avoided.

The memorandum was ignored but almost at once Costa Méndez was outmanoeuvred at the United Nations. Britain succeeded in gaining support for Resolution 502, which expressed concern at Argentina's invasion of the islands and gave the UK the option to invoke Article 51 of the United Nations Charter and claim the right of self-defence. Argentina was thus branded, accurately, as having been the first to use force.

As Argentine troops secured their positions in the Falklands and the British task force began to assemble, Costa Méndez flew to Washington for talks with the American Secretary of State, Alexander Haig and his deputy, Thomas Enders. Reporting to Galtieri by telephone with a recording system now in place, Costa Méndez claimed that Haig had told him that Argentina had 'unquestionable title' to the Malvinas and boasted of how he had ridiculed the prospect of a British task force coming to retake the islands:

> 'I gave them something of a caricature of an invincible fleet of the last century advancing across the Atlantic when they [the British] are living through recession, hardship, unemployment, etc., etc., which is ridiculous. Enders, who was present, supported me and even Haig himself agreed. They say that a formula must be found to save Thatcher's face.'[4]

Over-confidence, diplomatic clumsiness and a nervous bellicosity were the defining characteristics of Galtieri's approach when Alexander Haig flew to Buenos Aires as President Reagan's special representative to try to resolve the crisis. In their first meeting the Argentine President harked back to the victories over Britain in 1806 and 1807 and threatened that countries '*que no son occidentales*' ('who are not westerners'), by which he may have intended Haig to understand the Soviet bloc, were offering him aircraft, pilots and weapons.

For his part Haig stressed the importance of the anti-communist struggle in Central America and Argentina's contribution to it. The only winners in a war between Argentina and Britain would be the Soviet Union. But he attempted to make clear that Mrs Thatcher's statements and actions amounted to an ultimatum: the first step must be the withdrawal of the Argentinian troops. Without that Britain would not engage in negotiations.

Galtieri's reply then and at a second meeting was bombastic. The flag of Argentina would continue to fly over the Malvinas come what may. 'For 150 years they took down our flag. Now that we have put it back, we cannot ask the Argentine people to accept that it is pulled down again.'[5]

In a remark he may have intended to be helpful, Foreign Minister Costa Méndez told Haig that if this caused difficulties for the British inhabitants of the islands, the 'kelpers', Argentina was ready to pay them compensation which they could use to buy land in Australia.

Haig offered the Junta an American peace plan which, while it fell short of immediate sovereignty, would nonetheless have left Argentina in a far better position than the humiliating defeat it finally suffered. The Junta, however, rejected it and after his fruit-less efforts Haig provided President Reagan with an assessment of Galtieri's position which proved to be entirely accurate:

Galtieri's problem is that he has so excited the Argentine people that he has left himself little room for manoeuvre. He must show something for the invasion – which many Argentines, despite their excitement, think was a blunder – or else he will be swept aside in ignominy. But if he is humiliated militarily, the result will be the same.[6]

For Britain, President Reagan and top officials in his administration were the key figures whose sympathy and support had to be preserved at all costs. While Galtieri referred to the lesser known victories of 1806 and 1807, Mrs Thatcher was able to show the US Secretary of State the portraits of Wellington and Nelson that hang in Number 10 Downing Street and to remind him of Britain's continuing important role in the Cold War with Moscow, which was reaching a pivotal moment as communist rule in Poland disintegrated. But there were still worries about the influence of at least two American officials, the US Ambassador to the United Nations, Jeanne Kirkpatrick, and the Assistant Secretary of State for Latin American Affairs, Thomas Enders, both of whose sympathies were believed to lie with Argentina. Kirkpatrick had nailed her colours to the mast in public when she used a television interview to question whether the Argentine invasion really constituted 'aggression': 'The Argentines, of course, have claimed for two hundred years [*sic*] that they own these islands. Now, if the Argentines own the islands, then moving troops into them is not armed aggression.'[7] Kirkpatrick also suggested provocatively: 'Why not disband the State Department and have the British Foreign Office make our policy?'

The British Ambassador to Washington, Sir Nicholas 'Nicko' Henderson, had been alerted to Thomas Enders' possibly pro-Argentine feelings when he visited Alexander Haig on the eve of the invasion to express concern about Argentine troop movements. In that meeting Enders claimed that the US government had received an assurance from the Argentine Foreign Minister that his country was not contemplating confrontation with Britain, an assurance that, if it existed, was shown to be worthless only hours later. In his final ambassadorial dispatch to London, Sir 'Nicko' would later use a wonderfully obscure word from the English lexicon to make clear exactly what he thought of the two American officials: 'Comparing Kirkpatrick with Enders, it is difficult to improve on the apophthegm going the rounds of the State Department that whereas the latter is more fascist than fool, Kirkpatrick is more fool than fascist.'[8]

Set against them was the more senior figure of US Defense Secretary Caspar Weinberger, historically so pro-British that he had actually volunteered to serve in the RAF in the early stages of the Second World War, only to be turned down because his eyesight had inadequate 'depth perception'. He was to play a fundamental role in shaping US policy and the actions that stemmed from it.

Alexander Haig carried out his attempt at mediation dutifully but, in the end, with few results. Neither General Galtieri nor Margaret Thatcher were great believers in the sinuous skills of diplomacy and for both of them, their reputations and political futures were on the line. In the case of Galtieri the stakes were even higher for he knew all too well that if he failed and the Junta fell he might well face trial and imprisonment for its crimes. Haig shuttled back and forth, trying and failing to find forms of words that would paper over the issues of troop withdrawal, interim administration for the islands and long-term sovereignty. Mrs Thatcher and her government stood firm on their insistence that the rights of the Falkland islanders must be paramount. At a meeting of the US National Security Council on April 30th Haig showed his frustration, describing the situation 'as tragic with both sides, similar to a demented man on a ledge ready to jump, reaching for help but unable to grab our hand.'

The Secretary of State may have understood what was happening in Argentina but he underestimated British resolve. In the end, as Reagan and Caspar Weinberger knew well, Britain was part of the nuclear club and still too central to American strategy and vital interests for Mrs Thatcher to be allowed to fail. Reagan himself finally made the US view of the Junta's invasion clear when he declared that 'armed aggression of that kind must not be allowed to succeed'. Behind the scenes a British Foreign Office situation report summed up what appeared to be a satisfactory relationship: 'The President is completely on our side and the Americans are ready to do anything we want.'[9]

The result was assistance for Britain in key areas and on a major scale without which the task force could probably not have carried out its mission.

As a journalist I had been 'parachuted' into this mounting crisis with little knowledge of the area's history and struggling, not unlike many Argentines, to make sense of their politics and the passions that were being aroused. What was immediately perceptible was that many in Buenos Aires, including above all much of their leadership, were psychologically unprepared for what they were now facing. Galtieri himself later confessed to the Italian journalist Oriana Fallaci that he had not expected the British to send their fleet, and even after the sinking of the *Belgrano* and the reciprocal destruction of HMS *Sheffield* there was still a widespread hope – Alexander Haig called it wishful thinking – that matters would be settled by negotiation. Among the problems that ultimately arose were divisions inside the Junta and dwindling respect within its ranks for General Galtieri himself. These made it difficult for the cold light of reality to penetrate the ornate curtained windows of the Casa Rosada.

As might be expected, Harry Shlaudeman, previously Assistant Secretary of State and now US Ambassador to Argentina, had already had personal experience of the deadlock. Before President Reagan's declaration of support for Britain he had, without Washington's direct authority, held a midnight meeting with Galtieri and made a personal appeal to him to withdraw Argentine troops from the Falklands as a gesture of good faith.[10] He later said that he found Galtieri despondent, not, he emphasised tellingly, drunk, but unwilling to make any moves without the approval of the other members of the Junta. This was not forthcoming, with the Commander-in-Chief of the Navy, Admiral Jorge Anaya, who had already made support for Galtieri's presidency conditional on an operation to seize the Falklands, expressing his refusal with particular virulence. 'The Navy is hungry for action,' Galtieri explained, unaware at that stage that the destruction of the *Belgrano* by a British nuclear submarine would consign it to impotent immobility for the rest of the conflict. For his part the US Ambassador was soon to be accused by the increasingly fevered Argentine press of conspiring to bring down the Junta.

The last formal US effort to prevent all-out conflict came on May 11th with a flying visit to Buenos Aires by US Special Envoy General Vernon Walters, who held a two-hour meeting with General Galtieri that evening. He had a particularly American perception of the difficulties he faced, describing the 'silly war' as a 'conflict of two machismos', and then said pointedly with apparent reference to Britain's Margaret Thatcher: 'The machismo of woman is even more sensitive than the machismo of men.' The Walters mission was abortive, with members of the Junta complaining bitterly about the increasingly evident US help for Britain and, in particular, the military intelligence information which they believed the US was already passing to the British government.

In fact, as insiders reported, any decision by the Junta now had to be argued over and approved by some 50 senior officers, including a number taking part in the military operation; and standing behind them in the shadows were the extremist factions in the secret services and the paramilitary units which still served to maintain the Junta's hold on power. The pressure already being applied by the

British task force was producing apprehension, anger and irrationality inside the military regime and it is against this background that our sudden kidnapping should perhaps be seen.

The tensions now reverberating in the Argentine governing structure are revealed in a cable sent by the Director of the FBI to the Director of the CIA on May 7th. The cable warned that what was described as an 'Argentine paramilitary organisation' was planning to select one North American journalist or one Argentine employee of the United States Embassy in Buenos Aires as 'a candidate for assassination'. A follow-up message stated that 'a US newsperson in Buenos Aires may be murdered by the Argentine intelligence service. Based on this information, the above recommends that CIA consider advising the news media of the possible threat.'[11] If any such warning was issued, it did not reach our British team.

On the morning of May 12th, the day we were kidnapped, President Galtieri held a meeting of his military-dominated Cabinet in which he appeared to veer uncertainly between the prospects for war or peace. He was doubtless aware of the views of the Chief of Staff of the Army's Southern Command, General Antonio Vaquero, who said he did not wish to see a bloodbath and called for some sort of compromise; but that opinion, or at least the expression of it, remained very much in the minority. Now Galtieri told his Cabinet that there would be a negotiated settlement after another clash of arms even more serious than those which had happened thus far. He claimed that neither Britain nor Argentina would be able to impose its will on the other and, using a footballing analogy reminiscent of Argentina's controversial World Cup victory over Peru, he said 'the result will not be ten-nil' to either side. Galtieri then instructed officials to investigate the possibility of confiscating British-owned wealth and property in Argentina.

Galtieri and his Foreign Minister, Nicanor Costa Méndez, were now seeking to make their case at the United Nations. At least in the eyes of their supporters the Argentinians were putting forward 'constructive' ideas: a gradual, simultaneous withdrawal of both sides' military forces, the lifting of economic sanctions on Argentina, an interim UN administration for the islands accompanied by the flying of three flags over the Malvinas – those of Argentina, Britain and the United Nations – and negotiations at the UN to determine the issue of sovereignty. The Junta was also trying to insist that Argentinian civilians should be allowed to install themselves on the islands, something that would rapidly marginalise the small pro-British population. In his memoir, *The Malvinas: This is the Story*, Nicanor Costa Méndez would claim that on May 12th the Junta made a key concession in accepting the proposal of the UN Secretary-General Pérez de Cuéllar that negotiations about the islands could take place without the guarantee of a favourable end result.

It was at this juncture that Aníbal Gordon and his expert team waited in the leafy square in front of the Foreign Ministry for the opportunity to kidnap us. What seems certain, based on knowledge of other similar actions, is that they had some sort of high-level clearance to carry out an operation in that area and to move victims through the various security zones within the city, and our experiences on that terrible day bore this out. Our cameraman Ted Adcock was struck by the organised nature of his kidnapping in a separate vehicle. With his eye for detail, he remembers the smart suits and beneath them the polished leather holsters and ammunition belts of the men he describes as 'Gucci gunmen'. He too recalls being forced into the footwell of the car, in his case face-down, which then halted for some minutes in the car park of what appeared to be a large football stadium, with the rear of a stand looming over them, until the radio crackled into life with what seemed to be fresh orders. Years later, when democracy finally returned, a state prosecutor described the system as highly coordinated. There had been, he said, a 'mechanism of area release' to carry out kidnappings without interference from other branches of the security services. Under the system, 'the main coordinator was the Army, which was in charge of most of the territorial headquarters, and which carried out this task through the Tactical Operations Commands (COT), created at all levels of the territorial divisions.'

There is little information on how the gangs of state-sanctioned paramilitary thugs who were a key instrument of the Junta's domestic power were contributing to its war effort. The secret directive for the Falklands operation had said simply that such units should continue the fight against 'terrorism' and maintain 'control' of British residents in Argentina. Gordon was apparently regarded as a suitable person to do this. He may well have been part of the secret contingency plan which, according to the CIA report on April 12th, had been drawn up by his comrades in the 601st Intelligence Battalion to murder large numbers of British residents in the event of war. It is not known if this scheme ever progressed beyond vengeful fantasy or if it played any part in Gordon's actions on May 12th. However, the British government had soon learned of it and took it seriously. After our kidnapping a memorandum was circulated to key Ministers by the Foreign Secretary, Francis Pym, which, though the source of the information has been excised in the released version, spoke of a warning 'that in certain circumstances up to 500 members of the British community ... would be under threat of "removal" (i.e. murder) by Argentine special forces. The recent abduction of the "TV Eye" team', Pym said, 'illustrates the vulnerability of British subjects.'[12] It now appeared possible that launching the perilous operation to retake the Falklands would lead to the Junta's speciality: mass murder.

Other released American documents paint a picture of dissension in the Junta's ranks and shed some light on that crucial period and our own bit-part in the drama. One US Embassy report to Washington suggests that our kidnapping may have been staged by a faction within the Junta to try to damage the UN peace process. This document, based on information received 48 hours after we were seized, said that while the motive was as yet unknown it was possible that it was part of efforts by hard-line elements to prevent any negotiated settlement with Britain: 'It could have been designed to destabilize Galtieri because of his assumed concessions to the British or to force a breakdown in the talks with the British at the United Nations.'[13]

The same report emphasised General Galtieri's impotence in the face of such actions, which undermined his authority and the Argentine war effort. It dismissed Galtieri's claim, not least to us, that our kidnapping would be thoroughly investigated, providing a picture of the Junta's military-intelligence wing that more closely resembled the Cosa Nostra than an important branch of an army at war:

> Many people in the 601st Battalion know the names of the persons involved in the kidnappings, but the 'code of honour' of the 601st Battalion would not permit them to inform on their friends. In addition, there is divided opinion within the internal security section of the SIE that is doing the investigating. Some personnel are not seriously investigating at all, and those who are trying to do the investigation are considered outsiders and are getting no cooperation from their colleagues.

Aníbal Gordon was, of course, an important member of that Mafia-style unit and took his orders for such operations from highly-placed figures in the military regime. In retrospect it is perhaps significant that unlike some of his commercial kidnap victims, one of whom was asked bluntly, 'How much do you think your life is worth?', we were never asked to bargain for our survival. Thames Television paid no ransom and the only gains made by our captors were the dollars in my pocket which I had pathetically offered for my freedom and our television camera and equipment. These were never returned to us, and the Argentine police were later to claim that members of Gordon's gang had been overheard discussing how they could be disposed of profitably but, by his standards, this hardly constituted a motive for this very conspicuous crime.

What seems clear is that this curious and sinister event, which was accompanied during our subsequent meeting with General Galtieri by an unexplained bomb attack on the Buenos Aires branch of an American bank, which caused considerable damage to the building but no casualties, took place at a pivotal moment when the Junta was under great pressure. Whether or not, as rumour suggested, Galtieri was seeking solace in drink, the scales of illusion were now starting to fall from his eyes, while doubts about his leadership were spreading in the Junta's ranks. Whether Aníbal Gordon shared those doubts is unknown but it seems that our kidnapping was part of the turmoil inside a flailing Argentine regime that was blundering towards defeat.

Some in Buenos Aires regarded the contents of our interview with General Galtieri, which was broadcast on Argentine television, as a significant development in the crisis. They included the Swiss Embassy, which was now looking after British interests. This immediately reported to London Galtieri's statement that while his country would not give up the objective of sovereignty, 'we can talk with a view to achieving it in a reasonable time'. The Swiss Embassy commented that this 'is the most cheering news for a peaceful solution we have yet heard or seen in the Argentine media'.[14] However, this seeming concession made little impact in Britain or in the South Atlantic, where preparations to land British troops on the islands were gathering pace.

After the war, General Benjamín Rattenbach's official post-mortem lamented the fact that our kidnapping had damaged Argentina's position in the all-important forum of American opinion during attempts to negotiate a settlement at the United Nations:

> During this period, international public opinion, motivated by statements made by British and American authorities, insisted on showing Argentina's intransigence in the search for a negotiated agreement.
>
> Circumstances such as the kidnapping of journalists in Buenos Aires, caused, according to the comments of our Ambassador to the OAS [Organisation of American States], 'that the American press gave more importance to those events than to the negotiations taking place within the framework of the United Nations and to the war actions themselves.'[15]

I find myself recalling President Galtieri's slightly slurred explanation to me in our interview that the attack on us had been carried out by 'a very small group which is not contributing to the objective of peace'. Perhaps what he said was not too far from the truth and we had, as US diplomats speculated, been the victims of a faction within the Junta opposed to any last-minute concessions to Britain. There was, however, no possibility of any real investigation of what had happened. The Argentine Air Force, which its British opponents acknowledged fought courageously and well, privately voiced its concern at secret service activities which senior officers felt were undermining the war effort. Even in the middle of the war the Air Force apparently believed that the security services needed to be reined in but, as a CIA report made clear, they understood that the Junta was now a hostage to its own past crimes: 'Air Force officers realize, however, it will not be easy because the highest levels of the Argentine Army have been involved in incidents that they would not like to see publicized.'[16]

Thus, over-matched on the battlefield and fearful of the consequences of their own past actions, Argentina's Junta attempted to engage in diplomatic brinkmanship at the United Nations.

There the central question was whether the British government was really prepared to take a step back now that blood had been spilled and the task force was almost ready to strike. Again on May 12th, Britain's representative at the UN, Sir Anthony Parsons, warned London that the tide of opinion among the UN membership was in danger of turning against Britain:

> They believe (this includes a number of western delegations) that the Falklands should belong to Argentina provided that the interests of the islanders are safeguarded. At this stage, the dominant view here is that the Argentine position is becoming more moderate and that we should respond in order to bring to an end the hostilities which are creating increasing concern world-wide.

Sir Anthony warned that without British moves the UN talks could collapse, creating a dangerous 'diplomatic vacuum', with Britain widely seen as responsible. And he added a further crisp sentence to make sure his point got through: 'Right or wrong, this is how it is.'[17]

Thus for a few days Britain was compelled to engage in the manoeuvres at which her diplomats are so skilled. Amid deep and widespread scepticism that a negotiated settlement could be achieved, one key objective was to win time while the task force was being fully readied to disembark the troops. Sir Anthony Parsons was up to the task, as a now-released Foreign Office situation report explained:

> Sir A. Parsons employed delaying tactics successfully ... [he] took the line that because of the emergency debate [in Parliament] London had not been able to send definitive instructions ... The Secretary General and the Argentines accepted this.[18]

An Argentine diplomat in New York interpreted these manoeuvres as an attempt to extract further concessions from his country and, with unconscious irony, claimed that Britain was now practising 'extortion'. In fact, whatever British diplomats were saying, Margaret Thatcher was being frank about her intentions. When it was suggested by a radio interviewer that Britain would eventually hand over sovereignty of the islands, the Prime Minister responded in characteristic fashion: 'I beg your pardon. Did you really say that eventually Britain would leave these people to be under the heel of a Junta if they did not wish it? Those are words that I never thought to hear. We went to defend them. That's what we've gone for. We've gone to get the Argentines off the island.'[19] When Britain submitted her final proposals to the UN Secretary-General Pérez de Cuéllar on May 18th, they included what appeared to be concessions in the interests of peace. All military forces should withdraw and a

UN administrator should govern the islands pending good-faith negotiations. However, there was no guarantee that these would end with Argentinian sovereignty, and no hint of concession on Britain's insistence that the overwhelmingly pro-British islanders should enjoy self-determination. Asked to give a swift response at the UN, Argentina rejected the British proposals.

In his official post-mortem General Rattenbach suggested that to understand British wartime conduct Argentinian officials should be familiar with her behaviour in the Second World War and, in a surprising literary excursion, he recommended a piece of modern historical writing, Anthony Cave Brown's *Bodyguard of Lies*. The book describes British and US deception operations, in particular the methods used to conceal plans for D-Day. Its title derives from Winston Churchill's celebrated remark to Joseph Stalin at their conference in Tehran in 1943, where he told the cynically amused Soviet dictator that, 'In wartime, truth is so precious that she should always be attended by a bodyguard of lies.' However, Rattenbach's main target was the Junta which, he said, had failed to plan properly for war, squandered diplomatic opportunities, and had adopted 'unreasonable attitudes and procedures in the face of the reality of the situation and the magnitude of the opponent's comprehensive power.'[20]

In the end, however, there should be no underestimation of the risks that Margaret Thatcher and her government had determined they must take. As the final phase of the military campaign would demonstrate, Britain, for all the professionalism of her armed forces, was still suffering major disadvantages in an operation taking place 8,000 miles away in a different hemisphere, as the South Atlantic winter began to close in. Central among these was the frightening vulnerability of her surface ships, including those required to physically land the troops on the islands, to air attack. The task force commander, Admiral Sir John 'Sandy' Woodward, would later admit that he had not expected the Argentine pilots to attack at virtually wave-top height. The modern missiles which were supposed to protect the ships – Seacat, Sea Wolf and Sea Dart – while formidable, were shown to be unable to provide a complete defence against determined and courageous pilots flying at low level to deliver old-fashioned iron bombs, let alone against the technologically advanced Exocet.

The British cause was greatly assisted by the Junta's failure to plan in detail for the war they had chosen to launch. The fundamental challenge that Argentinian strike aircraft faced was the sheer distance between their bases on the mainland and the islands. The closest airstrip capable of taking combat jets was Rio Grande at Tierra del Fuego, 440 miles from Port Stanley, and others were further still. The distance was made still greater by Admiral Woodward's decision to frequently station his all-important aircraft carriers well out at sea a further 100 miles to the east. The result was that only the Argentinian aircraft capable of in-flight refuelling, the Skyhawks and Super Étendards, could be fully effective – and then only when supported by the two KC-130 tankers which were inadequate in number and inevitably slowed and complicated operations.

Argentinian Air Force officers had argued that after seizing the Malvinas urgent action should be taken to extend the runway at Port Stanley from its inadequate 4,000 feet to a length enabling it to handle bomb- and ammunition-laden combat aircraft. This might have allowed Argentine jets to establish air superiority over the islands and would certainly have greatly complicated the mission of the British task force. However, though the Junta conducted tests to establish whether its Super Étendards could operate safely from a

4,000-foot runway – they couldn't – it failed to ship in the necessary construction materials and equipment to lengthen it before the British naval exclusion zone effectively sealed off the islands. The extraordinary long-range air strike on the Port Stanley airfield by an RAF Vulcan flying from Ascension Island on May 1st also acted as a deterrent to extension plans. Argentine fliers were left to carry out their sea-skimming attacks at the end of their range with the constant threat of their fuel running out.

Their method of attack, though spectacular and of great concern to the British, also blunted the effectiveness of the Argentinian warplanes. On at least thirteen occasions British ships were hit by bombs which failed to go off – and in at least one case, HMS *Glasgow*, smashed straight through and came out the other side. A now-released study by the Argentine Air Force, entitled 'Why Our Bombs Didn't Explode', reveals that they were soon aware that the fusing mechanisms of bombs released out of necessity at very low level at 1,000 km per hour could not arm themselves in the split-seconds before impact. The result, it says, was that the pilots were launching with tremendous force large pieces of steel comparable to ancient cannonballs. According to the study, the Argentines embarked on a crash programme to manufacture new, more effective fuses, which came into service before the end of the war and led, among other successes, to the sinking of the British destroyer, HMS *Coventry*. But the true moral of this account must be that, once again, the Junta had failed to analyse fully the conflict into which it was entering and to assess properly in advance whether the varied and in some cases outdated arsenal in its possession was adequate for the task. It is also a powerful illustration of how its ruthless prosecution of the Dirty War, which had led to the US administration's arms embargo, had for years left it unable to access sophisticated military equipment and training which would have made its forces considerably more effective in the conflict with Britain.

The Junta's crude handling of relations with its close neighbour Chile – which, not without reason, saw itself as a future target of Argentine aggression if the Junta should emerge triumphant from the Malvinas conflict – also greatly weakened its strategic position. The Argentine Army, which routinely referred to Chile in its documents as the 'traditional enemy', felt forced to keep some of its best-trained units including many of its elite Marines on the mainland to guard against a possible Chilean 'stab in the back' on their 3,300-mile border, leaving poorly-trained conscripts to face the British professionals on the Malvinas. In the event there was no such Chilean assault, but there was aid to the British in the field of intelligence which proved immensely valuable and without which, in the words of Group Captain Sidney Edwards, the RAF officer responsible for securing it, 'we would have suffered many more losses to enemy air action and would almost certainly have lost the war.'[21]

Geography, which made Chile and Argentina virtual twins in the long southern cone of the Latin American continent, albeit with Argentina the larger and more muscular one, meant that Chile was an ideal location from which to spy on military movements next door. Above all, Chilean military radar, swiftly augmented by British radar equipment flown out and installed secretly on high ground near the southern town of Punta Arenas, was able to track the take-offs and initial directions of the Argentinian warplanes at four key airbases, including Río Gallegos where many of the Skyhawks were stationed. This information was immediately radioed to the task force where the signals served as early warnings of impending enemy air strikes. Thus the Argentinian cause was heavily damaged by the nation which had been her closest ally in the bloody struggle against 'terrorism', and in Operation Condor.

The Argentinian security services, which had clearly failed to maintain close relations with their Chilean counterparts, appear to have done very little about such intelligence threats if, indeed, they knew of them at all. There is no sign in the documents I have examined that they were aware of the radar-based information flowing to Britain from Chile, much less that they did anything to counter it. Aníbal Gordon would later state that the 601st Intelligence Battalion had identified an Argentine officer who had sold military codes to the British, but this 'identification' apparently took place after the war and the traitor was able to take refuge in Switzerland. Neither his identity nor the significance of his treachery are at present publicly known. At the time, the 601st was devoting much of its effort to producing propaganda for consumption by the Argentine public, an effort which actually made the eventual reality of defeat all the more painful.

In contrast British intelligence, with American assistance, generated almost more material than it could easily handle. Britain's military machine, long weakened by the country's economic condition and the thousand cuts forced upon it, had proved able to muster its strength and deploy it convincingly at the other end of the world. A US intelligence summary written just before British troops started to land on the islands even spoke of the danger of British over-confidence: 'Now that their mutual bluffs have been called, London and Buenos Aires are left with an immensely risky roll of the iron dice.'[22]

Britain rolled those dice on May 21st when, after skilled and successful moves to deceive the defenders, the task force began to disembark troops at San Carlos Water, distant from Port Stanley and considered by the Argentine command to be the least likely of several potential locations. San Carlos had been chosen because the surrounding high ground was thought to make air attack more difficult as well as providing suitable sites for Britain's land-based Rapier anti-aircraft batteries but, once again, the Argentine pilots flung themselves into the fray. A succession of low-level attacks by Skyhawks and Daggers hit a number of the British warships which had been deployed as an anti-aircraft screen. Several of the bombs again failed to explode but grievous harm was still inflicted. The frigate HMS *Ardent* was struck repeatedly and later sank. The destroyer HMS *Antrim* was badly damaged and put out of action, as was another frigate, HMS *Argonaut*. Two more frigates had suffered battle damage and a Harrier had been shot down. For their part the Argentinians had lost ten more combat jets with four pilots killed. It was tallies like these that led Admiral Woodward to declare later that the entire operation had been a close-run thing.

For all the losses, the task force had achieved its principal objective. In the six hours before the Argentines caught up with developments and the air strikes began, the fleet of landing ships had managed to enter San Carlos Water and disgorge many of the troops. Some support was denied them when the makeshift troop-carrier, the liner *Canberra*, and another civilian transport vessel were forced to withdraw to protect them from air attack later in the day. But critical Army and Marine units were now safely ashore and the hope was that with mobility provided by the all-important helicopters carried by the task force, British troops would now be able to attack key Argentinian strongpoints at a variety of locations and swiftly paralyse the enemy's defences. However, four days later on May 25th, Argentina's national day, further air strikes were to compel a dramatic reassessment of British plans.

First an Argentine Skyhawk carrying its maximum load of three 1,000lb bombs managed to put them all into the side of the destroyer HMS *Coventry*. This time they all exploded, inflicting massive damage, and within fifteen minutes the ship keeled over and began to sink. Determined rescue efforts saved the majority of the crew but nineteen men died and many more were injured.

Then, ten minutes after the *Coventry* went under, two more Argentine warplanes were detected approaching the task force. This time the attack was carried out by Super Étendards of Argentina's Naval aviation which carried the Junta's last three Exocets. The two planes successfully located the British ships, and briefly popping up from low level, managed to lock their missiles on to what appeared to be a substantial naval target. The pilots may have believed that this was one of the aircraft carriers but in fact it was the *Atlantic Conveyor*, a rapidly converted container ship, which was carrying vital equipment for the troops at San Carlos. Two missiles set the ship ablaze. Twelve men died, and when the ship sank under tow three days later, it took with it eleven helicopters including four giant Chinooks essential for any air-mobile strategy. Argentine strongpoints which could have been outflanked or even leapfrogged would now have to be taken one by one as winter threatened to close in. Out of necessity the legend of 'yomping' was born.

It is not my intention to provide another version of the much-written-about campaign which eventually led to the Argentine surrender. The fine narrative by Max Hastings and Simon Jenkins remains the classic account, while Hugh Bicheno's *Razor's Edge* contains invaluable intelligence and military expertise. Major General Julian Thompson's memoir, briskly and accurately entitled *No Picnic*, has the vivid authority of the man who was Commanding

Officer of 3 Commando Brigade of the Royal Marines which was at the forefront of much of the fighting.

What stands out of course is the series of assaults, most launched at night, in which British soldiers intensively trained for war against the Soviet Union set out to dislodge larger numbers of Argentine troops, most of them inexperienced conscripts. These young men, many of them part of the latest intake only months earlier, had been put through rapidly organised training courses and flown to the Falklands when the Junta finally recognised the likelihood of British military action.

The result was a patchy performance by Argentine forces in which some units displayed a willingness to defend their positions with determination while others showed a white flag at the first opportunity. Very often their units were static, sometimes almost paralysed, and failed to launch counterattacks at the San Carlos beachhead and other locations where the British might have been vulnerable. A number of episodes now have a special place in British military history, in particular the death of Lieutenant Colonel Herbert 'H' Jones, the Commander of 2 Para, killed at Goose Green, the target of the first significant British attack. He was cut down by an Argentine machine-gunner shortly after urging his men forward with a cry of 'Come on A Company, get your skirts off!' Though deprived of its commander, undersupplied and stretched to its limits, 2 Para emerged victorious, compelling an Argentine force more than twice its size to surrender. Lt. Col. Jones was awarded a posthumous VC. The victory won at a cost of eighteen British and 55 Argentine lives had provided the Argentinians with the clearest possible demonstration of British capability and resolve.

Two weeks later, after the historic 'yomp' across East Falkland, the series of decisive actions to take the hilltop positions guarding the approaches to Port Stanley began. In the interim the task force had suffered another air-inflicted disaster. The landing ship *Sir Galahad* carrying men of the Welsh Guards was hit by two 500lb bombs. Forty-six men died as fire engulfed the vessel. However, what was to prove the decisive British assault went ahead, with Mount Longdon as a central target. Major General Thompson describes his officers studying the plan on makeshift models of the battlefield made with 'lumps of peat, pieces of canvas, rifle slings and twigs',[23] but tactical surprise was lost when, as night fell, a British soldier suffered the misfortune of stepping on a landmine and the dug-in Argentines responded to the explosion with a blizzard of fire. There followed days of intense and sometimes savage fighting, with British troops using every weapon at their disposal from sophisticated and deadly Milan missiles to bayonets. As the British took control of their principal objectives, the winter weather which the Junta had prayed for moved in and it began to snow.

It was at this point that a desperate President Galtieri spoke on the telephone to the Argentine commander in Port Stanley, General Menéndez, claiming to have secret intelligence that the British were at breaking point and begging him to continue to resist for a few more days. Galtieri was by now a discredited figure and Menéndez was well aware that his army was disintegrating. In the hills the British could see groups of Argentinian soldiers abandoning their positions to surrender or retreat towards Port Stanley. Others were found curled up in their foxholes, hoping somehow to survive. Led by the light armoured vehicles of the Blues and Royals, British troops began to march into Stanley unopposed. Among the sights that greeted them, symbolic of the Argentine Army's collapse, was a field hospital with, near the entrance, the abandoned corpse of an Argentinian soldier lying in a wheelbarrow. The following day came the official surrender. The original plan set out in fine handwriting and intended to ensure the Junta's survival had failed.

From then until this day Argentinian journalists and historians, though most excoriate the Junta and its decisions, have struggled to come to terms with their nation's defeat. For many in Argentina the Malvinas campaign remains the noblest of causes and, in most cases, their writers do not make any attempt to explain how it fitted with and resulted from the Junta's years of murderous repression. Instead they emphasise what they portray as the David-and-Goliath nature of their country's struggle with Britain, a version which has undoubtedly resonated with Argentina's supporters in Latin America and elsewhere and continues to do so 40 years later.

Probably the most important published work to emerge from Argentina is the highly detailed and also highly partial account by the senior Air Force officer, Air Commodore Rubén O. Moro, who later served on the Rattenbach Commission which, as I have described, was appointed by the Junta to examine the causes and conduct of the war. The moral he draws in his book is that the Argentinian servicemen who fell, including the undeniably courageous officers of the Air Force, 'will be a shining example to generations of my countrymen yet unborn'. Far from exploring the Junta's blood-stained record and its real motivations for taking the gamble of confrontation with Britain, he is at pains to stress the chivalrous nature of his country's effort – stating for example that Argentinian aircraft never fired on British servicemen forced to abandon ship or bale out of their planes. He seeks to contrast this with alleged British behaviour on May 9th when British Harrier jets are said to have strafed lifeboats being lowered by the sinking Argentinian trawler, *Narwhal*. 'Let the record show for all to see,' the Air Commodore writes, 'that at no time did our forces ever attack or otherwise interfere with the enemy when he was engaged in any such humanitarian pursuit.'[24]

Moro notes that his country's first military action of what became a full-scale campaign was the landing on March 24th of a ten-man Naval commando team led by a Lieutenant Commander Alfredo Astiz at Stromness Bay, South Georgia. Completely unmentioned is that Astiz, who had already acquired the chilling nickname 'El Ángel Rubio de la Muerte' (The Blond Angel of Death), had achieved infamy by infiltrating the Mothers of the Plaza de Mayo posing as a sympathiser and then allegedly taking part in the torture and murder of the two French nuns and five mothers in December 1977. (Subsequently Astiz was one of the first to surrender to British forces and despite requests to question him by the governments of Sweden and France he was returned to Argentina by Britain after the war.) The Junta's decision to send Astiz on this vital mission when it was at the same time seeking to assure the world that it could be relied upon to protect the safety and interests of the Falkland islanders was an extraordinary but all too typical act of brutal insensitivity.

The Argentine conscripts, thousands of whom were left to face the attacks of the British Paras, Marines and Gurkhas, were well aware of the nature of the army in which they were serving. One of them, Miguel Savage who was conscripted in Buenos Aires, described how his unit had been starving in its trenches on Mount Longdon because of lack of supplies: 'We used to escape when the officers were asleep and go to Stanley and root through the bins.'

Savage said he knew that their officers and NCOs included men who had learned their skills torturing civilians during the Dirty War. 'Once, after I stole a tin of meat,' he said, 'a sergeant placed his rifle against my head. I knelt down and, crying, pleaded for him not to kill me. He pulled the trigger but the gun was empty.'

In recent years a democratic Argentine government has released documents containing other similar accounts showing that some officers mistreated and even tortured men under their command. Such mistreatment included beatings and mock executions. One Lieutenant described how 'another officer tied his hands and legs ... and left him face down on the wet sand of a cold Falklands beach for eight hours.' Others described how they were left without medical assistance in exposed defensive positions where trench foot and other damaging conditions proliferated.

Perhaps surprisingly in an operation ordered by a military government, one of the most telling failures was in logistics which had barely been considered before the invasion. A makeshift supply chain soon collapsed under British pressure, leaving many of the soldiers without rations or even, in some cases, supplies of ammunition. Some soldiers recalled their anger when, after the defeat, they saw warehouses in Port Stanley stacked with food which was supposed to have been sent to the defenders of outlying positions. According to a soldier called Guillermo, quoted in Daniel Kon's *Los Chicos de la Guerra*:

> We started to discover sheds and more sheds full of food up to the roof ... They were huge sheds, full to the ceiling, so full that in some cases we couldn't get in because there was so much food. And what made me most angry was that the English had to give us that food.[25]

Meanwhile the Junta was devoting its every effort to concealing the conditions in which the troops had fought and even the scale of the casualties from the Argentine public. As it did so, it relied heavily on its experts in 'controlling' the population, the security services that the military regime had spent years developing in its war against elements of its own people. Among the truths which could not be admitted was that these feared special units had made very little contribution to the Argentinian cause in a lost war which would now determine the fate of the Junta and the nation.

CHAPTER 17

Fall of the 'Dirty Warriors'

PRIME MINISTER Margaret Thatcher had not set out to topple the Argentine Junta but that is what she achieved. It took another eighteen months in which the reverberations of the military disaster made the Junta's hold on power unsustainable. General Galtieri himself was the first to go, three days later to be replaced, briefly, by the Minister who had tried to help us after our kidnapping, General Alfredo Saint-Jean, and then by another General, Reynaldo Bignone, who was seen as a more moderate figure and was thus immediately suspect in the eyes of hard-liners.

The Junta's immediate reaction to defeat was to try to hide the truth. Using the propaganda methods it had honed during the Dirty War – media control, censorship and threats – extraordinary measures were taken to conceal the return of the demoralised conscripts. These young men who later sometimes spoke warmly of the conditions in which they were held and transported by their captors, the British, landed back in Argentina to find themselves pariahs in the eyes of their own military. Men were transported to their bases in trucks with the rear tarpaulins closed, or buses with curtains drawn because, according to officers, they could be stoned by the population who were angry that they had lost the war. In fact when ordinary people had a chance to show their feelings, their response to the survivors of the defeat was often extraordinarily warm. Families besieged the barracks where conscripts were located, desperate to find out if their sons had come back alive. Nonetheless, officers warned the men not to talk about what they had experienced in the Malvinas and said that any who spoke to the press could be court-martialled.[1] The military intelligence apparatus of which Aníbal Gordon was a part had an important role to play. Even before the Argentine surrender, secret orders had been issued instructing intelligence officers to contact wounded soldiers in hospital so that 'greater control could be exercised to prevent the leakage of information'. Now they issued blunt warnings. 'You don't talk about this with anyone, this has to be forgotten,' a returning soldier was told. 'Remember that you have a family.'

The 601st Intelligence Battalion produced a booklet to be distributed to the conscripts before demobilisation. It included this exhortation:

Argentine ... You fought and repaid what the homeland gave you: the pride of being Argentine.

Now the homeland requires another effort from you.

From now on you must not be imprudent in your opinions. Do not give out information about mobilisation, organisation of the unit you belonged to and the support you had ...

Emphasise your deep knowledge and conviction in the cause you were defending ...

Do not talk about rumours or fanciful stories ...[2]

But no amount of propaganda could conceal the disillusion felt by many members of the armed forces after the trauma of the Dirty War and the shame of the Falklands surrender. One Army officer summed up his feelings:

> They ordered us to fight against the subversion, saying that we were defending society against the enemy ... We were not prepared for that type of fight and they made us do things that we never dreamed of as military men ... Immediately upon our return [from the Falklands], they treated us as criminals. They hid us as if we were lepers.[3]

However, the circumstances of the defeat were too great and far-reaching to be suppressed. Almost immediately the tabloid-style magazine *Gente*, which had been one of the most strident voices supporting the invasion of the islands and had run headlines claiming that Argentine planes were destroying the British fleet, published a special edition with a blood-red cover demanding answers to some of the big questions that the return of the troops was already raising:

> Did they have enough food?
> Did they have the right clothing?
> Did the weapons work?
> How many died?

It would take a long time for all these questions to be properly addressed but what was clear was that the standing of Argentina's armed forces and hence of the military government had been gravely affected by the Malvinas humiliation. If the Air Force had retained an heroic image in the eyes of the public, the Navy and, above all, the Army were heavily tarred with failure. Both of these services found themselves facing a growing current of anger over the atrocities carried out during a repression which a discredited regime found ever harder to defend. Shockwaves were running through the entire structure of military rule and bringing to the fore the fears that had helped to motivate the Junta's decision to launch the disastrous Falklands conflict in the first place. Behind the scenes, in what had been the secret bastions of the regime's power, there was apprehension over popular tumult erupting in the streets and real panic at the prospect of a civilian government organising war-crimes trials to expose and punish those who had tortured and murdered great numbers of their own people in the Dirty War. Commanders of the secret service ordered that records be destroyed. Thousands of case files with their records of arrest, kidnap and murder went up in smoke – something which would greatly complicate efforts to bring those responsible for atrocities to justice.

The principal concern of the dirty warriors was that they should not find themselves in the dock. The CIA reported regular mutterings of a fresh coup to bring more 'reliable' Generals to power and clear threats of armed violence if some sort of amnesty were not introduced. On August 4th, 1982, eight weeks after the Falklands surrender, a CIA dispatch reported a 'Possible attempt to remove the President and other government officials by 10 August.'

The fuse had apparently been lit by suggestions that a list might have been prepared of all military personnel who had participated in the anti-subversive campaign, and that new President Bignone and Army chief General Nicolaides were prepared to act on it.

Everyone who had any role in the anti-subversive campaign is very afraid of any investigation of those days … added to the fact that the heads of the intelligence services believe that Bignone and Nicolaides were prepared to permit an investigation of those days, would probably be sufficient justification, in the eyes of the military services, to remove Bignone and Nicolaides.[4]

This report was heavily redacted by the American vetting process before its release almost 40 years later, with more than two of its three pages obscured. It does not take too much imagination to conjecture that these concerned specific US efforts to try to assist the new Junta just weeks after Argentina's Falklands defeat, which had severely damaged Washington's policy and reputation in the region.

For a few months the new leadership enjoyed a truce with the political parties and trades unions after issuing a pledge that it would be a 'short-term transition government' which would soon restore civilian rule. But the politicians argued that the military had lost any right to rule after the Falklands fiasco, the economy remained in a state of collapse with inflation reaching 200%, and there was the unexplained revelation that Galtieri's earlier choice of the Dirty War commander, Carlos Suárez Mason, as chief of the state energy company had led to massive 'losses' amounting to billions of dollars. Still dominating negotiations between the military and civilians was the question of how the Dirty War atrocities were to be dealt with.

The CIA now reported direct threats to the government by the security services supposedly under its command. On May 3rd, 1983 it informed Washington that a secret meeting had taken place between Dirty War veterans from the Argentine Federal Police and the 601st Intelligence Battalion, the unit which had controlled Aníbal Gordon's killers.

The Federal Police described their willingness to carry out violent actions, if necessary, to impress the government with the
level of their concern over their perceived lack of protection
for actions during the 'Dirty War'. 601st Battalion agreed they
should re-establish the groups that operated during the 'Dirty
War'; they also agreed they should begin their own campaign of
violence if any member of a security or police service is called
to testify before a Judge ...[5]

According to another CIA document, this campaign of violence
would take place unless specific measures were taken to protect the
accused, and would include 'Assassinations and bombings against
the persons making the revelations, members of their families, and
federal judges investigating the activities being made public.'[6]

The military Junta, which had tried and failed to save itself by
launching the Falklands War, was now being threatened with its own
weapons: the death squads led by men like Aníbal Gordon.

The Junta tried to reassure its followers by banning the press from
publishing allegations of past atrocities in order, it said, to protect its
members from 'false statements' and 'slander'. Meanwhile, some in
the security forces took their own steps to try to halt the publication
of Dirty War revelations by newly emboldened newspapers: 'The
press officials were advised to cease publishing such stories in order
to avoid becoming the victims of any "accidents" that might occur.'

As the new post-Falklands Junta tried to cling on to power,
Gordon remained at its service. Six months after the war, demonstrations and strikes by an angry public given voice by civilian politicians
and trades unions threatened to topple the military regime. The US
intelligence structure included a 'Special Assistant for Warning', in
this case a certain H. Cochran, who cautioned that: 'In this highly

volatile atmosphere a misstep by the Government could trigger serious outbreaks of violence.'

A few days later on December 16th, 1982 Aníbal Gordon carried out what may have been instructions from hard-liners seeking to deepen the crisis and trigger another coup. As soldiers used tear gas to break up a big pro-democracy demonstration in the centre of Buenos Aires, a Ford Falcon drove into the fleeing crowd. A man in civilian clothes later identified as Gordon got out and fired a pistol at the demonstrators, including a young building worker called Dalmino Flores. 'Die, you son of a bitch!' Gordon is said to have shouted. Flores died on the spot.

As the Junta began visibly to expire and what passed for order broke down, Gordon and his men increasingly struck out on their own account. Their resources included the Falcon cars equipped with radios that could pick up police channels, uniforms, official identity documents and a veritable arsenal of automatic rifles and pistols. They also appear to have enjoyed the protection of Army commanders based in the town of Córdoba and the use of several outlying farms belonging to the 601st Intelligence Battalion. Thus equipped, they carried out a string of kidnappings for profit, often along or near the Pan-American Highway that links the capital to the north of the country, and rapidly became known as the *piratas del asfalto* (the asphalt pirates). Gordon, however, had his own favourite nicknames. He had taken to referring to himself as 'Comodoro Ezcurra', possibly taken in imitation of the founder of a neo-fascist terrorist group which had sprung up in Argentina after the Second World War. The original Ezcurra had inspired his followers to daub swastikas on houses owned by Jews after the kidnapping by the Mossad of the Nazi war criminal Adolf Eichmann near Buenos Aires in 1960. More light-heartedly, Gordon called his gang the 'Brigada Panqueque', a joke at the expense of his violent but apparently indecisive right-hand man Eduardo Ruffo. A *panqueque* is a pancake that spins as Argentine chefs throw it in the air before catching it on a plate. Such was the humour of the professional killer.

Among the numerous examples of 'asphalt piracy' cited in subsequent prosecutions of members of the gang and catalogued by Carlos Juvenal in *Buenos Muchachos* was the old-fashioned highway robbery they carried out on August 3rd, 1983 when, using a Ford Falcon and submachine guns, they halted traffic on the Pan-American and systematically robbed the backed-up drivers. But normally they were after bigger game. One successful operation was the kidnapping later in 1983 of Alberto di Nella, the owner of a car dealership. Di Nella had noticed that he was being trailed by a suspect vehicle but when he reported its licence number to the police was told that it was on official business. A few days later he was intercepted by four Falcons equipped with radio antennas, inside one of which was a man he identified as Aníbal Gordon. It was on this occasion that Gordon said bluntly: 'Let's talk straight. How much is your life worth?'

They settled on the equivalent of $100,000 in cash and jewellery which di Nella delivered to Gordon round the corner from his house. A month later di Nella was ambushed again while driving outside Buenos Aires and tried to outrun his attackers. They opened fire, di Nella lost control of the car and he and his son were wounded. This time Gordon and his men drove them to a medical centre in the town of Pilar.

A senior industrialist who was seized in his car was allowed to buy his freedom with a cheque for $50,000, which was duly cashed. Another case that exemplified Gordon's brazen criminal methods was the kidnapping in December 1983 of Riccardo Esposito, the son of a wealthy businessman. He was seized in a car park by Gordon and his son, Marcelo, who claimed to be policemen. While attempting to negotiate with the father by telephone, Gordon took the boy Riccardo first to a steak restaurant and then to a hotel 50 miles from Buenos Aires, where he checked him in to a room and handcuffed him to a bed. Apparently confident that he would be paid the ransom he was demanding, Gordon then released the young man with instructions on how to pay. Argentine newspapers later claimed that $100,000 had been handed over.

It is not known how much of these substantial sums was retained by Gordon and his gang and how much passed on to his military protectors. In later court cases it was established that Gordon was working in close concert with his long-time ally General Otto Paladino, the former head of the SIDE intelligence service. It is also clear that many in the military could see a day of reckoning approaching and were seeking to build up reserves of cash for future emergencies. Gordon told some of his victims that their money was going to fund a movement to keep the national flame alive. In its last days the Junta was doing everything it could to stave off retribution. In April 1983, it published its so-called 'Final Document on the War Against Subversion and Terrorism'. This conceded 'with the true sorrow of Christians' that mistakes may have been made in the struggle to protect Argentine society but said the time had arrived for 'national reconciliation'. Announced soon afterwards was the self-amnesty law, officially the 'Law of National Pacification'. This astonishing but, above all, desperate piece of legislation affected an even-handed approach by seeking to nullify the crimes committed both by subversives and by the military and paramilitary forces. Article 1 read:

KIDNAPPED BY THE JUNTA

The criminal actions arising from crimes committed with terrorist or subversive motivation or purpose, from May 25, 1973
to June 17, 1982, are declared extinct. The benefits granted by
this law also extend to all Acts of a criminal nature carried out
on the occasion or due to the development of actions aimed at
preventing, averting or putting an end to the aforementioned
terrorist or subversive activities, whatever their nature or the
injured legal asset. The effects of this law reach the authors, participants, instigators, accomplices or accessories and includes
related common crimes and related military crimes.[7]

In other words, the torturers and murderers of Automotores Orletti,
ESMA and the numerous other clandestine detention centres could
not be prosecuted or even, as Article 5 stated, questioned:

No one may be questioned, investigated, summoned to appear
or required in any way for accusations or suspicions of having
committed crimes or participated in the actions referred to in
Article 1 of this law ...

It was an attempt at a blanket amnesty against criminal and civil
prosecution both for those who had committed the crimes and also
for the senior officers who may have planned them, ordered them
and covered them up. In the shadows which still concealed them,
the men who had kidnapped, tortured and murdered thousands of
people they regarded as subversives were now deeply worried that
they would pay the price for their crimes.

The 'final' document and the self-amnesty law provoked widespread anger and contempt. Mass demonstrations erupted, climaxing
with a 24-hour March of Resistance in front of the Presidential Palace.

But now, for the first time in many years, this and other issues would be decided at the ballot box. The elections that finally took place on October 30th, 1983 pitted the Peronist Justicialist Party which promised to uphold the new self-amnesty law against the veteran social democrat politician Raúl Alfonsín who pledged to scrap it. Alfonsín had long trod a narrow line in what were called Argentina's 'Years of Lead', opposing both the Generals' murderous repression and the leftist insurgents. He also attacked both the Junta's and Britain's use of force in the Falklands War while upholding Argentina's claim to the islands. In the elections he scored a decisive victory with almost 52% of the vote, becoming Argentina's first civilian President since the mid-1970s and ending the seven dark years of military rule.

In the midst of political mayhem and his own frequent kidnap operations, Gordon apparently found the time to pursue his interest in art. In November 1983, just three days after Raúl Alfonsín's electoral victory, what was described as a heavily armed 'commando group' overpowered and gagged the security guards and staff of the Museum of Decorative Arts in Rosario, midway between Buenos Aires and Gordon's base in Córdoba. Displaying a degree of expertise, they headed for the French and Spanish rooms and stole a number of Old Masters including an El Greco and a Goya, removing them from their frames which they left scattered on the floor. This spectacular theft, thought to be worth more than $10 million, was linked to Gordon, who was said to have carried it out on behalf of a criminal syndicate which, as often happens in such cases, had difficulty in disposing of the artworks. In 2018, 35 years after the robbery and more than a decade after one of the missing paintings had been found in the possession of Gordon's former driver, a second work of art was discovered in a car in neighbouring Uruguay. This painting, a sublime, religiously-inspired piece by the 17th-century artist

Bartolomé Murillo, was being transported by five men with criminal records for drug trafficking. They claimed they were legitimate owners on their way to try to find a buyer.

But it was a kidnapping that Gordon claimed to have carried out on the orders of his military superiors in August 1983, while the Junta was still in power, which finally led to his downfall. The victim on this occasion was a colourful and mysterious figure of Irish descent who had long occupied an ambiguous, maverick role in the life of Argentina, the activist, journalist and suspected spy, Guillermo Patricio Kelly. He was a man known to everyone in Argentine politics and, it is fair to say, trusted by no one. Kelly had started his career as a neo-Nazi, frequently wearing a swastika on his sleeve. An extreme nationalist, he had been jailed in both Argentina and Chile, where in 1957 he had escaped from prison disguised as a woman. He had briefly established himself in the United States where he was investigated by the FBI under the Foreign Agents Registration Act for publishing a tabloid newspaper, seemingly funded by the Argentine government, attacking the human-rights policies of President Jimmy Carter. By then Kelly had made a volte-face on the question of Israel, cultivating links there which led to accusations that he was a Mossad agent. As the Junta weakened he published, in a magazine he now owned, what many thought were near-suicidal attacks on military figures he said were guilty of Dirty War abuse, in particular the dangerous Admiral Emilio Massera. The Admiral had been one of the Junta's original leaders and was hoping in 1983 to be a candidate in the scheduled elections. Now he found himself accused by Kelly of a string of crimes, including organising the murder of the diplomat Elena Holmberg, whose knowledge of his secret negotiations with the Montoneros had stood in the way of an earlier bid for power. Kelly also accused him of responsibility for the 'disappearance' of a businessman with whose wife Massera was having an affair. This accusation actually led to Massera's imprisonment pending an investigation. It was widely believed that Kelly could be an important witness in future trials of Junta figures. But Massera and the others had a potent ally in Aníbal Gordon.

According to later evidence,[8] Gordon organised the kidnapping of Kelly with particular care. Ford Falcons and a Chevrolet van were assigned to the task and a variety of weapons handed out. Gordon apparently told his men that they were seizing Kelly because of his work for Israel. They pounced in a Buenos Aires street as their target drove to his office. The kidnapping took place yards from a legitimate police patrol but Gordon, dressed as an Army Colonel and carrying a submachine gun, assured them that all was well and drove off with his victim. Shortly afterwards an unknown group calling itself 'Free Argentina' claimed that it had killed Kelly.

The kidnapping caused turmoil. The military Junta held an emergency meeting, hundreds of police patrol cars were sent out to comb the capital and police helicopters flew over suspect sites. Demonstrating Kelly's wide range of connections, there was a message from the Vatican calling for his safe return and, according to a later Argentine newspaper account, the Junta's last leader, General Reynaldo Bignone, personally telephoned Aníbal Gordon ordering him to release the politician. Twenty-four hours later Kelly appeared near a petrol station, shouting at the top of his voice that he needed the police. His face was cut and bruised and his clothes were covered in blood.

Kelly, who claimed that he had fought his way out of his kidnappers' car, declared that he knew who several of them were and said they were members of a mafia 'which has more power in this country than the armed forces'. Asked by a sceptical journalist if he had faked his own kidnapping, Kelly replied angrily: 'They beat me on the head and kicked me in the kidneys until I urinated blood. Then they broke one of my legs and bust my testicles ... What else do you want? Do you want me to show them to you?'[9] Kelly described his captors as 'psychopaths'.

This kidnapping – among the scores or even hundreds which Gordon had carried out, including our own – was the one that was to dog him. Indeed it made him a celebrity as his victim threw caution to the winds and openly accused him of carrying out the attack and numerous other crimes. Kelly's story and accusations were spread over the cover and half a dozen pages of Argentina's popular and frequently lurid magazine *Gente*, with Kelly re-enacting his kidnap and displaying his blood-stained shirt. Three weeks later an Argentine judge contacted Interpol to request an international warrant for the arrest of Gordon, his son Marcelo and three other men all allegedly members of the ultra-nationalist Triple A terrorist organisation. In fact the judge did not need to look so far. Gordon was comfortably ensconced, as he had been on and off for years, in the town of Córdoba west of the capital, where he continued to rely on the protection of the area's Army commander. So confident was he in his security that he paid a visit to a well-known nightclub and approached a table occupied by one of Argentina's most celebrated entertainers, Moria Casán, a woman already known for her beauty and talent. According to Casán's account, Gordon told her that he was a longstanding admirer and that if she wanted to greatly increase her earnings, he could help her to do that: 'We are ready to help you,' he told her, 'because you reach the people.' He then gave her the telephone numbers of various contacts in Buenos Aires.[10]

Asked who he was, Gordon said simply, 'Aníbal Gordon, the most wanted man in Argentina.' Casán's husband who had listened to the conversation shot back, 'And I am King Farouk.' But as they discovered, Gordon had told them no more than the truth.

However, Argentina was changing. The fall of the Junta and the election of Raúl Alfonsín had at a stroke toppled old power structures and installed new ones eager to demonstrate that they were responding to popular demands to create a cleaner, law-based democratic society. Patricio Kelly was demanding action to hunt down Aníbal Gordon, accusing him of being one of the most important criminals of the Dirty War and charging him with responsibility for more than 1,500 political kidnappings and murders on behalf of the armed forces. Two different judges were competing to bring charges against him. Meanwhile the new Argentine police chief, Antonio de Vietri, said Aníbal Gordon's group was also believed to have carried out 'acts of subversion' in the last three weeks against the recently elected democratic government. In fact de Vietri had immediately on appointment been given special orders to arrest Gordon, who was regarded as 'a destabilising element for Alfonsín's government, which he considered to be full of communists'.

Police were now tracking members of Gordon's family and not long afterwards, just two days after he had promised the beautiful Moria Casán that he would boost her career, he was found hiding in a small holiday house in the scenic hills of Córdoba province.[11]

Gordon had taken tourist accommodation with his wife and son and had in general done his best to be inconspicuous, spending much of his time in a deckchair with a box of cold drinks by the river. On February 10th, 1984 he was celebrating his birthday indoors with an Argentine favourite, the little meat pies called *empanadas*, when some 50 armed policemen surrounded the house. A police sergeant in civilian clothes but armed with a submachine gun jumped into the building through an open window and told Gordon to give himself up.[12]

'Stay calm, it's alright', Gordon is said to have told his 23 year-old son Marcelo, a fully-fledged member of the gang who had tried to get one of the two automatic weapons found in the house. 'Calm down, Tiger, we lost.'

As he was handcuffed Gordon sought assurance that this was a real police operation and not the sort of kidnapping and murder which he had carried out so often. 'Are you "sucking" me or is this a real arrest?', he asked, using the Dirty War slang for kidnapping. He seemed acutely aware that his extensive knowledge of the Junta's terrible secrets now made him a target for elimination. The officers showed him a marked police vehicle in an attempt to reassure him. Said Gordon: 'If you are from the Federal Justice Department I know I am alive.'

Ramón Salguero, the officer who had jumped through the window with his submachine gun, gave his own account, which says as much about the conflicted sympathies of some Argentinian policemen as it does about the operation itself:

I went there to arrest a legend, a very dangerous guy. I found a calm man who did not want to put his family's lives in danger ... You could see that he was a man driven by his beliefs, he was very Catholic. He had a white rosary. He told us that he was a good Christian and that people who were harmful had to be eliminated.

And the police officer expressed some empathy with the arrested man: 'He was tired of being in hiding. It was clear that a weight had lifted from his shoulders.'

On the military aircraft which flew him to Buenos Aires, Gordon declared that he was a patriot. 'Patriots are what this country needs,' he said.

Later, when questioned by a police doctor about a scar on his back, Gordon replied briskly: 'War wound.' Asked if he had been treated well since his arrest, he responded in military style: 'Propia tropa' – everything correct. For the record, the doctor answered an important question. He confirmed that Gordon had not been tortured.

In the house where Gordon had been staying and held his birthday party, police found a small assortment of weapons: an automatic rifle, a submachine gun and a pistol. In later raids on properties used by members or associates of the Gordon Gang, police found plastic explosives, more weapons including a rifle with a telescopic sight, Army and police uniforms, blank stationery from the office of the President of the Republic and a press card in the name Silva and carrying Aníbal Gordon's photograph. But Gordon would have no more use for any of that.

At the prison where he was incarcerated Gordon is said to have boasted to his guards that he would soon be free because his friend, the still-powerful Admiral Massera, would secure his release, but that was not to be.

CHAPTER 18

The Long Wait for Justice

G ORDON'S ARREST was just part of a far larger and more perilous effort by the new Alfonsín government to bring at least
some members of the fallen Junta to justice. It was a process that
some have compared to the Nuremberg war crimes trials, but this
was a case of a nation seeking to try its own leaders and military
commanders and many of their subordinates. In the end it has taken
almost 40 years and the often contradictory efforts of ten successive
governments, and is only just nearing some sort of conclusion with
the sentencing of a number of Aníbal Gordon's now elderly associates to prison 'in perpetuity'.

During his successful election campaign Raúl Alfonsín had promised that he would nullify the military's so-called 'self-amnesty law'
and prosecute both the Junta's various leaders and the people who
carried out their orders. Simultaneously members of the terrorist
groups that had carried out bombing and assassination campaigns in
Argentina would also be prosecuted in a process intended to punish both the 'two demons' which had brought unrestrained violence
to the country. As a first step the new President formed a National
Commission on the Disappearance of Persons (CONADEP),

which produced a 50,000-page report entitled *Nunca Más* (Never Again) and concluded that at least 8,961 people had been forcibly 'disappeared' under the military dictatorship.[1] Human-rights organisations said the true total was far larger. Meanwhile, supporters of the Junta maintained that its security forces, soldiers, policemen and civilian security officers had suffered some 6,000 casualties at the hands of the ERP, the Montoneros and other smaller groups.

Initially nine Junta leaders including General Videla, General Galtieri and Admiral Massera were named as legal targets for trial by the Supreme Military Council. Guerrilla leaders including Mario Firmenich, who would be extradited from Brazil where he had taken refuge, would be tried in the courts. But almost at once Alfonsín's efforts ran into legal and constitutional difficulties. Did the new government have the right to simply abolish laws passed by its predecessor? Could military officers and their men be prosecuted for following the orders of their superiors?

Two of the Junta leaders in particular reacted strongly to being charged and prosecuted. General Videla who had been President during the most violent 'Years of Lead' refused to even accept the term 'Dirty War' when he appeared in court: 'I absolutely refuse to accept that kind of terminology because it seems to imply that there are "clean wars" as opposed to "dirty wars". But war is war – just that.'[2]

During the key proceedings in the Federal Court of Appeals in April 1985, Videla refused to enter a plea or choose a lawyer. Instead he sat ostentatiously reading a book, usually a Christian catechism. Admiral Emilio Massera, who had also been part of the original Junta leadership and who had controlled the Naval secret service that ran the infamous ESMA torture and murder centre, initially displayed similar disdain for the court but then delivered a dramatic statement:

'I didn't come here to defend myself. No one has to defend himself for having won a just war and the war against terrorism was a just war ... But here we are, because we won the war of weapons and lost the war of psychology.'[3]

Such rhetoric was, however, outweighed by the deeply distressing testimony from survivors of what the military themselves called the *proceso*. A physicist and research assistant from the University of La Plata described how she had actually given birth blindfolded in the back of her kidnappers' car while being told that it didn't matter because both she and the child would soon be killed. Miraculously on this occasion they were both released. An Army General did much to undermine the defence when he described his attempt to recover the body of the murdered diplomat Elena Holmberg, only to be given the wrong corpse. 'What do you want,' he said he was told by the local police chief, 'You guys have thrown more than 8,000 bodies into that river.'[4] Evidence like this had an enormous emotional impact, with members of the audience weeping as they left the court. The chief prosecutor, Julio César Strassera, summed up his case in powerful fashion. It was necessary to punish the accused, he said, in order to establish 'That sadism is not a political ideology, nor a military strategy, but simply a moral perversion.' With that much of the audience rose to their feet and delivered a standing ovation with shouts of 'Assassins! Assassins!'

The hearing had lasted for 114 days, with more than 800 witnesses giving evidence. At the end of it two of the original Junta leaders, General Videla and Admiral Massera, were sentenced to life imprisonment; General Viola, the Junta's second President, got seventeen years and, to the shocked surprise of human-rights activists, the last three leaders of the Junta, General Galtieri, Admiral Anaya and Air Force General Lami Dozo, were acquitted. However, all three of these were already in prison, charged with the military crime of negligence in launching and losing the Falklands War.

Hopes that this trial would draw a curtain on past crimes and bloodshed were rapidly dashed. The Mothers of the Plaza de Mayo demonstrated against the acquittals. An increasingly powerful human-rights movement demanded that the Junta's subordinates, the men who had actually carried out the policy of torture and murder, be put on trial for their crimes. However, this prospect caused serious unrest inside the still-powerful armed forces. When the most notorious dirty warrior, Lieutenant Commander Alfredo Astiz, was brought before the Supreme Military Council on return from capture by British troops, that body deliberated for only one day before freeing him. The armed forces were also infuriated by apparently lenient treatment of former left-wing terrorists, some of whom, far from being put on trial, secured academic posts or even jobs in the new government. There was angry debate on the military's demand for laws protecting officers and men who had served in the Dirty War.

As the recently released American documents show, these turbulent events were being closely monitored by the US government, which was disquieted by what it saw as Alfonsín's leftist leanings and concerned by developments. A CIA report written while the trial of the Junta was in train reported that the military were waging 'psychological actions' against the new government and might consider 'direct action' attacks on the Argentine left.[5] The US National Security Council received reports of a plot by 'retired' Argentine Generals to establish 'a National Front with the goals, first to bring pressure on the Argentine government to end its efforts to prosecute armed forces personnel ... and, in the longer run, to remove the government of President Raul Alfonsín.' The method used would be 'a coup d'état if necessary' and the date chosen for the launch of the plan was to be April 2nd, 1985, the third anniversary of the Falklands invasion. One of the first steps would be the use of 'special operations action groups' to create incidents to embarrass and undermine the Alfonsín administration.[6]

The language describing the Generals' plans bore a strong resemblance to words used by Aníbal Gordon to his more recent kidnap victims when he told them that their ransoms would be used to fund a national movement to 'save' the country. Even in prison Gordon was still headline news. *Gente*, which had clearly decided that stories about the multiple murderer boosted sales, ran its own front-cover visualisation of him being escorted to his barred cell, suave in a brown sports jacket and surrounded by moustachioed and suitably menacing guards. The headline: 'This is how Gordon lives in jail.'

In fact Gordon was living in much better conditions than the many people he had kidnapped and tortured and he soon had the comfort of knowing that some of his associates were still close to power. As an American document described, one of the many challenges facing President Alfonsín was that he did not properly control his own intelligence services, which had been the mainstay of the military regime and the principal executors of its policy of torture and murder:

> The President is now trying to reorganize the intelligence community ... We believe, however, that military intransigence and civilian weakness will frustrate efforts at change and that the military intelligence services in all likelihood will continue to serve their own interests – rather than those of the elected government – for the remainder of Alfonsín's term.[7]

The democratic President's response, which would later be described by some Argentinian commentators as his 'Watergate', was to form his own parallel intelligence organisation inside the Ministries of Defence and Interior. One of its functions was to try to ensure Alfonsín's personal security, and occupying key positions were at least two men who had worked for Aníbal Gordon at the Automotores Orletti and after. One of them was Eduardo Ruffo, the violent veteran of many kidnappings and murders, and now seen as someone whose deadly expertise could help to protect the new regime as it faced another wave of instability. He was only fired when news of his appointment and past history became public.

Army units now staged a series of short-lived uprisings to protest at continuing moves to prosecute Dirty War veterans, and a wave of terrorist bombings, apparently designed to destabilise the government, once again afflicted the country. Several retired and active service officers were arrested for planning and carrying them out, but had to be released for lack of evidence. When Alfonsín attempted to visit an Army headquarters in the right-wing stronghold of Córdoba a bomb was discovered on his route. Military officials claimed that the incident was only a 'mildly dangerous prank'.

As this low-intensity civil conflict unfolded Aníbal Gordon was fighting his own battle against prosecutors who had begun by trying to pin hundreds of charges on him. Gordon represented a substantial challenge for the legal authorities, many of whose staff were still holdovers from the military dictatorship. The man who had been a valuable weapon in the arsenal of the security services had a vast store of knowledge of past crimes ranging from the ultra-nationalist assassinations of the Triple A, through Operation Condor to the torture and murders at the clandestine detention centres like Automotores Orletti and to the kidnapping and often holding for ransom of leading businessmen and politicians. He was a door to an ugly past which a number of still powerful people wished to keep shut. He was literally the man who knew too much.

Six months after his arrest Gordon and his former secret service boss and close collaborator, General Paladino, were remanded in custody on charges of having illegally imprisoned a number of people at Automotores Orletti including Carlos Santucho, the brother of the ERP guerrilla leader, who according to witnesses had died under torture. Gordon himself was directly implicated by a number of witnesses including the owner of the former car repair shop, who had rented it to him and had then been told by neighbours that screams could be heard coming from the building. Gordon was also identified by several surviving victims, among them the actor Alberto Brandoni and his wife Marta Bianchi who said she recognised Gordon as the man who made them take off their blindfolds because, he said, he was going 'to shoot them'. For his part, Gordon stated that he had served in the SIDE intelligence service until the day of his arrest in 1984, a period which, of course, included the date of our kidnapping in 1982. He said that he had held a rank equivalent to Army Colonel with the same salary and expenses. He claimed, however, that he had never carried out atrocities at the Automotores Orletti and that he had worked not in counter-subversion but in normal counter-intelligence protecting the state. This, he said, explained his possession of a diplomatic passport in a false name, which he had used on missions in a variety of countries including Nicaragua, China, Cuba and the United States. In a personal 'confrontation' of the kind favoured by some Latin justice systems, Patricio Kelly accused him of multiple crimes including the theft of children of his murder victims. Gordon denied it.

The many trials that followed in later years would contain hundreds of references to Gordon and provide a vivid picture of his murderous history but at this first stage his defence lawyers were assisted by the proposal, and eventual enactment, of the so-called 'Full Stop Law'.[8] When passed in 1986, it effectively halted the investigation and prosecution of people accused of political violence during the dictatorship and up to the restoration of democratic rule on December 10th, 1983. This paralysed hundreds of potential prosecutions including a large part of the case against Aníbal Gordon. In October 1986 Gordon was sentenced to sixteen years in prison for kidnapping Kelly with the use of violence. His son Marcelo received eight years as an accomplice in the same crime. Gordon's legal team openly congratulated themselves on what they called their efforts and achievements in watering down much of the case against him. Instead of large numbers of prosecutions, they said, there was just one guilty verdict and three other pending cases. Truly a triumph of the law.

Outside the prison where Gordon began to serve his sentence the pressure for more prosecutions of dirty warriors continued to build. Human-rights workers were collecting more witness statements and several mass graves were being excavated, including one containing hundreds of victims in one of Gordon's old stamping grounds, the town of Córdoba. Argentina's first forensic anthropology team was formed with the help of the American forensic scientist Clyde Snow, famed for his examination of the body of the assassinated US President, John F. Kennedy. With his help and advice, some of the remains would be identified, bringing closure to families and sometimes providing evidence for possible prosecutions. However, anger in the military also mounted. Unrest or short-lived uprisings took place at half a dozen military bases and the result was more legislation protecting the Dirty War perpetrators. While Gordon sat in jail the Alfonsín government, fearful of another coup d'état, passed the 'Law of Due Obedience' preventing the prosecution of officers and men for acts of violence including torture if they could demonstrate that they had been following orders.[9] This set the scene for the final dramatic chapter in Gordon's story. This professional killer for the secret service who, up to now, had been following a Mafia-style law of *omertà* (silence) with regard to his superiors, now made an eighteen-page statement detailing what he claimed had really happened in the Kelly case and why he qualified for release under 'Due Obedience'. What caused astonishment among people dealing with the case was that he confessed to the crime, at one point describing it as a *secuestro* (kidnapping), and that he named names.

Gordon stated that he had carried out the 'detention' of Kelly on the direct orders of the then head of the SIDE intelligence service, Rubén Visuara, and that because of his access to the Presidential Palace under the Junta, he knew that the then President, General Reynaldo Bignone, had been fully aware of it. He said that, following Visuara's instructions, a joint task force with men from SIDE, the 601st Intelligence Battalion and Police Federal Security was formed, with Gordon in command of it. This was provided with a variety of weapons, several Falcon cars and even the services of an Army helicopter to check that traffic was flowing freely in the areas the kidnap convoy would pass through. Gordon received further instructions and the keys of a property where Kelly would be held from an officer of the Second Army Corps, whom Gordon also named.

The purpose of this elaborate operation, Gordon claimed, was to seize and interrogate Kelly about his secret work on behalf of the state of Israel (though it has also been suggested that the real motive was fear that Kelly would testify against Junta leaders in any forthcoming trial). Gordon stated that Kelly's account of a 'psychopathic' assault was exaggerated. He claimed memorably that after an initial fracas in which the politician and journalist had attempted to defend himself with a pistol he had, in fact, been well cared for: 'Mr Kelly was well treated. During the trip ... compresses and bandages were applied to his wounds.'[10]

The questioning, said Gordon, was done 'energetically' but without 'physical aggression' and if Kelly feared for his life, this was because of his own apprehension, not the behaviour of his captors. The interrogation, Gordon said, was recorded, with copies given to officers of the various services whom he again named. Finally, Gordon said, he received orders by radio to free Kelly and did so, but not before the politician had hugged and kissed him in gratitude.

Gordon's statement, which he said he was making in the interests of 'national reconciliation', was remarkable. While heavily slanted in what he appears to have believed were his own interests and containing a variety of questionable details, it was the first account of a kidnapping by one of the Junta's leading practitioners, but even more important was the fact that to bolster his 'Due Obedience' case, Gordon had identified the officers who, he said, had ordered him to carry out the crime. This, however, carried evident risks. In the colourful if grim description of Carlos Juvenal in *Buenos Muchachos*, he had tried to save himself from drowning with 'a life-jacket made of reinforced concrete'.

Gordon made his statement on August 24th, 1987. Less than three weeks later, on September 13th, he was dead. The official cause of death given to the Argentine press was heart failure following an operation for cancer in a Buenos Aires hospital. Despite the timing and style of the announcement – which may have evoked for cynics the demonstrative punishment sometimes favoured by the Mafia – there were few doubters and even fewer who mourned. The claims made years earlier by the widow of a controversial trades union leader who had died suddenly of a heart attack in hospital after allegedly being injected with the Amerindian poison, curare, had long been forgotten. Only Gordon's tenacious victim, Patricio Kelly, spoke out. Whether motivated by headline-grabbing, a fear that Gordon might somehow still be alive or a genuine desire for truth, Kelly called for Gordon's buried corpse to be exhumed and given a full autopsy. His request was ignored.

Gordon's remains were scarcely cold when, perhaps coincidentally, President Alfonsín issued a secret decree concentrating control of the secret services in the hands of two officials on whose loyalty he believed he could count. This was followed by a new law that belatedly limited the function of military intelligence to the analysis of information about 'external threats'; however, these measures did little to prolong his rule.

CHAPTER 19

Open Wounds

IT WAS THE DEFENCE MINISTER of the Alfonsín government who had declared that 'The country cannot live forever with an open wound. A final full stop has to be put to this.'[1] It was to prove a forlorn hope. In 1989 Raúl Alfonsín was forced to give up the presidency because of the dire state of the economy and his successor, elected in a landslide, was Carlos Menem who embarked on a policy that he said was aimed at reconciliation. This quickly led to the release of policemen and Army officers who had rebelled against the previous government. But a year later Menem faced a serious uprising by troops known as the *Carapintadas* (painted faces), for the camouflage paint they wore. Unlike previous such rebellions this one led to bloodshed and gunfire could be heard in Buenos Aires. Menem's response was a broad amnesty for past crimes. The Montonero commander Mario Firmenich was freed and, most controversially, so too were all the imprisoned leaders of the military dictatorship. These included both the Junta leaders who had been found guilty of directing the Dirty War and those, like General Galtieri, who had been jailed for mishandling the Falklands conflict. Also pardoned was Aníbal Gordon's superior, General Carlos Suárez Mason, who had just been extradited from the United States where he had fled and faced 39 charges of murder.

The pardons caused uproar and not just in Argentina. Under the headline, 'Pardoning Mass Murder in Argentina', *The New York Times* wrote: 'For no good reason, President Carlos Menem ... has trashed his country's finest achievement of the last 60 years.'[2]

In Argentina itself voices were raised rejecting the very idea of reconciliation out of hand. They included veterans of the Mothers of the Plaza de Mayo such as Hebe De Bonafini, who had suffered the loss of her two sons under the 'repression' and declared frankly her continuing hatred for the Junta's torturers and killers: 'If I would say that I do not hate them I would be a hypocrite. I hate them from the bottom of my heart, and that's why I am not going to forgive and I'm not going to forget.'[3]

As the leader of the main faction of the Mothers, De Bonafini would prove highly effective in trying to ensure that the process of reconciliation was short-lived and that prosecutions of the dirty warriors would eventually resume.

Two issues now came to the fore in determining whether Argentina could come to terms with its past or if the process of legal retribution would have to be revived and continue. The first, which burst on the public in March 1995, was the public confession of a retired Navy Captain, Adolfo Scilingo, then in prison for fraud. In an interview, which could truly be described as 'exclusive', with the journalist and former Montonero militant Horacio Verbitsky, Scilingo confessed to having taken part in two of dozens of 'death flights' in which heavily sedated but still breathing victims were thrown from military aircraft into the South Atlantic. Scilingo said he had personally thrown 30 victims through an open hatch, almost falling to his death in the process. He said that up to 2,000 people had been killed in this way.[4]

The details of Scilingo's account were horrifying and were reported worldwide, along with his frank statement that he did not repent because he believed that he had been carrying out orders in a war. 'I'm not confessing to clear my conscience,' he said in the interview. 'I'm talking because I feel like the Navy has abandoned us, left us to the wolves, the very ones who were loyal and followed orders.'

President Menem and his allies attempted to play down the Scilingo revelations. Menem claimed that the retired Captain had invented the story to try to strike a lucrative deal in Hollywood. A gang of four unidentified men then kidnapped Scilingo and cut the initials of the three journalists he had spoken with on his face. Soon afterwards, he fled to Spain where he found himself caught up in a judicial investigation of the 'disappearance' in Argentina of Spanish citizens. He attempted to recant his confession but was eventually found guilty on 30 counts of murder and unlawful detention which in the verdict of Spain's Supreme Court constituted 'Crimes Against Humanity'.

Scilingo's appalling revelations set off popular protests and strident calls for justice from those who believed that prosecutions should resume. Individuals said to be responsible for Dirty War crimes were hunted down in their homes by demonstrators who used loudhailers to identify them to their neighbours and daubed accusations and slogans on their walls. And there was another telling issue to which Aníbal Gordon's violent deeds had contributed: the fate of the children of the 'disappeared'.

Ever since the Junta's lingering collapse and fall, the Mothers' emotive and well-organised offshoot, the Grandmothers of the Plaza de Mayo, had been using all available means to try to track down the babies and small children believed to have been taken by their parents' executioners. One case where identification had been possible and which had become well known was that of a one year-old baby, whose original name was Carla Rutila Artes. Carla was the child who had been given by Aníbal Gordon to his right-hand man Eduardo Ruffo and his wife after the 'disappearance' of her mother, Graciela Artes, at the Automotores Orletti, a victim of Operation Condor. Carla was renamed Gina and Ruffo's 'family' also included a small boy whom they called Alejandro but whose parentage and real name have never been established.

As I have related, Ruffo lived well under the dictatorship, taking part under Gordon's command in numerous operations both for the secret service and on their own account. He became chief of staff at the supposedly private Magister security agency owned by the former head of SIDE, Otto Paladino, and, even after the election which brought Alfonsín to power, he managed to retain a position in the secret service, apparently valued as a man who would carry out any job he was asked to do. The Ruffos lived in a succession of spacious houses and apartments with the children they had stolen. Men who Carla came to realise included Aníbal Gordon came to visit, and she remembered weapons, the tools of Ruffo's trade, being routinely kept there. She also recalled the angry violence of the man she had been brought up to believe was her father.

'I don't have any good memories of that man,' Carla would say later, describing Ruffo as nervous, aggressive and a heavy drinker who sexually abused her.[5]

The fall of the Junta and the faltering legal steps of the new democratic government brought a dramatic change in Carla's life. The Grandmothers of the Plaza de Mayo received a tip-off that she was alive and in the hands of a SIDE agent. The case had become a powerful symbol of what human-rights workers were trying to achieve and the Grandmothers put up posters seeking information. Ruffo was identified and Carla's real grandmother came to Buenos Aires where a judge ordered blood tests which confirmed her identity. But Ruffo was unwilling to give up his 'daughter' who was now ten years old, and tried to take legal action to keep her. Astonishingly, a member of the Argentine Supreme Court had spoken out in favour of those he regarded as the adoptive parents in such situations. Dr Augusto Belluscio declared that the child's relationship with the 'adoptive family' was more important than the biological connection. He said that demands for such children to be restored to their families of origin were a 'brainwashing operation worthy of the Muscovite psychiatric establishment'. The judge did not address the question of what should happen in cases like those produced by Aníbal Gordon's activities, where the child was adopted by a man who had carried out or contributed to the murder of his or her parents.

Carla's grandmother now had custody of Carla and the two of them were living under police guard in the Argentine capital. But the two new laws, 'Full Stop' and 'Due Obedience', had effectively saved Ruffo from prosecution for his Dirty War crimes and he succeeded in persuading a judge to ban the grandmother and Carla from leaving the country. Ruffo still had access to men and weapons and the threat of what had been Aníbal Gordon's gang continued to hang over them. However, the Carla case had now become a *cause célèbre*, and a group of Argentine journalists managed to get the girl and her grandmother by boat across the River Plate to Uruguay and then on to a commercial flight to Spain. It would be 25 years before Carla returned to Argentina, to testify against the man who had taken her at the Automotores Orletti.

There were other children whose survival would come to bring misfortune on the men who had appropriated them, such as Mariana Zaffaroni, who as an eighteen month-old child had been seized along with her parents in what Aníbal Gordon's men celebrated at the time as one of their most successful actions under Operation Condor, the destruction of Uruguayan 'terrorist' cells which had taken refuge in Argentina. So significant was this action seen to be that the US Department of Defense reported on it almost immediately using the name of the Uruguayan militants' military wing, the OPR-33.

> Members of the Argentine State Secretariat for Information (SIDE), operating with officers of the Uruguayan Military Intelligence Service carried out operations against the Uruguayan terrorist organisation, the OPR-33 in Buenos Aires. As a result of this joint operation, SIDE officials claimed that the entire OPR-33 infrastructure in Argentina has been eliminated.[6]

Unmentioned in this US cable, which appears to approve of the operation, is that at least one of those seized had committed suicide with a cyanide capsule at the moment of his arrest and that the others would be taken to a sordid former car workshop to be tortured and, in the case of Mariana's parents, 'disappeared', leaving just their small child alive.

Like Eduardo Ruffo, Mariana's 'adoptive father' Miguel Ángel Furci was highly valued by his secret service employers. His eventual charge sheets included dozens of crimes and stated that he was jointly responsible for the atrocities committed at the Automotores Orletti:

> Furci had joint control in carrying out the plan designed by his superiors, with perfect knowledge of everything that took place

inside the clandestine detention centre and of all the activities
carried out ... there was thus joint control of the act.

However, unlike Ruffo, Furci appears to have tried to bring up the
little girl he had rechristened Daniela with kindness and consideration. Mariana grew up cut off from the avowedly Marxist beliefs
of her murdered parents and was raised instead in the Christian
nationalist atmosphere of the Furci family. As an Argentine General
later claimed when asked about the 'adopted' children: 'We did for
them the best that we could; we gave them our own homes and
our own families.' Lying behind such statements was the belief that
children like Mariana were part of a noble cause. They would be
brought up as true citizens of Argentina rather than as servants of a
Marxist-Leninist creed intent on destroying the country.

In Mariana's case a real bond of affection was forged with the man
she at first believed to be her father. When democracy replaced military rule, Furci was another who managed to remain for a time in the
employ of the secret service, but in May 1984 the apparent tranquil-
lity of his family was shattered. A woman approached the now eight
year-old Mariana in the street outside her school and asked permis-
sion to take her photograph. The picture then appeared in posters
announcing that she was being searched for by surviving members of
her real family in Uruguay. She had been identified through the dedicated work of the Grandmothers of the Plaza de Mayo, who would
later say that they had traced some 50 children out of a total of more
than 200 known to have been stolen in this fashion. But for Mariana
the result of this work was not, initially at least, a happy one.

In June 1992 the girl, now seventeen years old, sat crying in legal
chambers in Buenos Aires. A judge had taken her identity card in the
name of Daniela Furci and ripped it up in front of her while ordering

her to apply for a new one in her real name, Mariana Zaffaroni. This was the culmination of years in which Furci had fled abroad with his wife and Mariana, moving to Brazil, Uruguay and Paraguay where the SIDE killer had received assistance from and continued to do work for the secret service while Mariana was sent to local schools. Four years later they returned to Buenos Aires. There a blood test confirmed that Mariana was a child of the Zaffaroni family and that Furci was not her father. The judge who presided over the case, Roberto Marquevich, was clear on his responsibilities:

> There is no precedent that I know of for this type of case – the secret police systematically stealing the fruit of the womb of the people they tortured and killed ... We owe it to these children to tell them the truth and punish the crime.[7]

Judge Marquevich ordered the arrest of Furci and his wife on charges of kidnapping, illegal imprisonment of a minor and falsification of the identity documents which had recorded Mariana as their child. Furci admitted receiving the child Mariana from Aníbal Gordon. He was sentenced to seven years in prison, the first of a series of ever-longer terms which he was to receive. His wife was sentenced to three years. Furci himself remained unrepentant, saying later: 'So I saved her life, therefore I am responsible for [her] life.'

But if the Grandmothers had succeeded in identifying Mariana and bringing her kidnappers to justice, they had not succeeded in reconciling her to her real family, in particular her maternal grandmother who lived in Uruguay, from where she had waged a vigorous effort to find her grandchild. While the Furcis were on the run, Mariana's real grandmother had received two hostile letters, purportedly from the little girl but probably inspired by Furci, accusing her of being an atheist and a member of the Communist Party. They said that her 'father', Furci, treated her with hugs and affection whereas the new grandmother was a harpy, a bird of prey. Now Mariana flatly refused to see her. Instead she insisted on visiting Furci in prison. It would take years before she came to terms with what had happened to her and who she really was.

There would, in the end, be no peace for the dirty warriors, and the stolen children would become their Achilles heel. The 'Full Stop' and 'Due Obedience' laws which had effectively protected them from charges of torture and murder provided no such protection for offences involving minors. Among the early targets was the Junta's first President, General Jorge Videla, who had led the 1976 coup and ruled during its brutal aftermath. In July 1998 Judge Marquevich ordered that the former President be arrested and held in custody pending trial for the theft of babies at the Automotores Orletti and two other clandestine detention centres. Specifically Videla was accused of five counts of theft and concealment of minors under ten years of age and five counts of 'suppression of the civil status of a minor'. Charged with him were a number of other senior officers including General Carlos Suárez Mason, the Commander of the First Army Corps, who had told a foreign diplomat that he had signed hundreds of death warrants per day. Suárez Mason had fled to the United States but was in the end extradited back to Argentina.

Starting in 2003 a new President, Nestor Kirchner, the sixth since the return of democracy, annulled both the pardons of the Junta leaders and the 'Full Stop' and 'Due Obedience' amnesty laws, opening the way for a new series of trials to go ahead. General Videla was first sentenced to life in a civilian prison for causing the deaths of 31 detainees, most of whom, according to official statements, had been shot 'while trying to escape'. Soon after, he was tried again and sentenced to 50 years for the systematic kidnapping of children during his rule. He was due to face yet more charges relating to the kidnappings and killings carried out under Operation Condor. The evidence for these relied heavily on accounts of the crimes committed by Aníbal Gordon at Automotores Orletti and highlighted Gordon's later claims that he had been carrying out the President's orders. But before another trial could take place, the now-elderly Videla came to an undignified end. While taking a shower in a prison bathroom, he slipped on a bar of soap and died of heart failure following the fall.

General Leopoldo Galtieri, the man who led Argentina into the disastrous war with Britain, was another whose appointment with justice finally arrived. He had been jailed for mishandling the war and then pardoned by President Menem. It was generally agreed that his conduct during the Dirty War had been less brutal than that of many others and that, unlike some, he did not appear to have used his senior position for personal profit. He was on his day an impressive figure and was remembered by me at least for his drink-fuelled cordiality. However in July 2002, new civil charges were brought against him alleging his command of units involved in the kidnapping of children and the 'disappearance' of eighteen leftist sympathisers in the late 1970s when he was chief of the Second Army Corps. Galtieri faced prosecution with 28 other officers and officials, but, due to his deteriorating health, was allowed to remain at home in Buenos Aires while lawyers prepared the case. In January 2003 he died in hospital of a heart attack aged 76.

Another who died before he could receive a final judgement was Admiral Emilio Massera, one of the members of the original three-man Junta and widely seen as responsible for some of its worst atrocities. It was Massera who in a meeting at Naval headquarters in

Buenos Aires was accused by US President Carter's human-rights envoy, Patricia Derian, of having a torture chamber beneath their feet, a reference to the Naval Mechanical School or ESMA where many detainees are known to have been tortured and murdered. Massera, who prided himself on his chiselled good looks, had lusted after the presidency, seeing himself as a strongman, a charismatic Caudillo, who would bring power and pride to Argentina. He had even tried to do a deal with what Junta members saw as the devil in the shape of the Montonero insurgents. These negotiations, which had involved the transfer of large sums in cash, were an effort by Massera to enlist their support and satisfy his ambition. He is also known to have employed the services of Aníbal Gordon. Now he saw his pardon by President Menem revoked and was again jailed pending investigations for the kidnapping of minors and the atrocities at ESMA, including the drowning of prisoners thrown sedated but alive from aircraft. According to Robert Cox, the former Editor of the English-language newspaper, *The Buenos Aires Herald*, Massera was a man who merited the description 'evil': 'He was corrupt from the start and he used corruption to increase his power,' said Cox. 'He turned the Navy into a criminal organisation. They stole, they raped, they murdered, they became malevolent, destructive gods.'[8]

In 2004 Massera suffered a severe stroke and was declared unable to face trial by reason of insanity. In 2010 a further stroke led to his death in the Naval Hospital in Buenos Aires. He was buried in secret with only a handful of people present.

His successor as Commander of the Navy and Junta leader suffered a similar fate. Admiral Jorge Anaya, known in Argentine fashion as 'El Negro' because of his dark complexion, had been the strongest advocate of invading the Falklands – he put great pressure on General Galtieri to carry out the plan – and then had to sit by impotently after the sinking of the *Belgrano* effectively drove the Argentine Navy out of the war. In 2006 he came under investigation for human-rights violations but the day before he was due to testify before a judge he suffered a heart attack. He died two years later without ever coming to trial.

The terrible crimes committed at the Automotores Orletti and at least some of the individuals responsible for them have been fully exposed in Argentine court rooms. Five successive court cases, Orletti I–V, have dealt with atrocities at the 'torture garage', with a number of Aníbal Gordon's former associates and gang members receiving lengthy prison terms. In what was probably the most emotional of these trials, dealing with the fate of 65 of the victims in 2011, the courtroom was packed with their families and shouts of '*Olé! Olé!*' and '*A donde vayan, los iremos a buscar*' ('Wherever they go, we will search for them') were directed at the accused – one of whom, a General from the SIDE command structure, responded with a military salute and kisses blown at his accusers. Many of the victims and survivors in the Orletti cases were Uruguayans seized under Operation Condor and the atrocities committed in that operation were further exposed in the Condor Trial which continued for three years between 2013 and 2016. The horrific events at Automotores Orletti were accepted by the court as representative of the entire Condor operation and in the end the Junta's last President, General Reynaldo Bignone, who had earlier been sentenced to 25 years for the abduction and murder of detainees at a military base, received a further twenty years for his overall responsibility for some of the Condor cases. He died in prison of heart failure in 2018.

The transcripts of all the trials are studded with references to Aníbal Gordon, the man who would have been a principal defendant but who now had the protection from prosecution afforded by death. Instead his former subordinates in what has increasingly become known as the 'Gordon Gang' have repeatedly stood in the dock to be sentenced for a succession of crimes, and in some cases their grinding struggles with the justice system of Argentine democracy continue to this day.

Eduardo Ruffo, Gordon's right-hand man and the appropriator and abuser of the child, Carla Artes, has been sentenced to a series of overlapping terms. In 2007 he received ten years for his part in Aníbal Gordon's series of kidnappings, attacks and robberies in the chaos following the Falklands War. In the 2011 trial Ruffo was sentenced to a further 25 years. It was on this occasion that his 'adopted daughter', Carla Artes, came back to Argentina from Spain where she was now living to testify against the man who had taken her.[9] Looking directly at Ruffo she told him: 'I have to assume that the person who took me must be the same person who murdered my mother.'

Carla recounted for the court the violence and sexual abuse she had subsequently suffered at Ruffo's hands and afterwards told the press that, while she gave evidence, he had been unable to look at her. Carla went on to meet and marry another victim of the 'repression', Nicolás Biedma, the son of a Chilean 'disappeared' in Automotores Orletti. It was a union Carla described as 'an act in defence of life'. Tragically she died of cancer five years later in 2017.

In 2020 Ruffo had to face justice again in a fresh trial of four of the key men who had worked under Aníbal Gordon at Automotores Orletti and later.[10] This time, because of the Covid pandemic, the trial took place virtually on Zoom, transmitted live on YouTube, and with Ruffo in the electronic dock was his former colleague, Miguel Ángel Furci, the man who had stolen Mariana Zaffaroni and who was already serving a 25-year sentence as one of those found guilty of crimes at Orletti during Operation Condor. In that trial Furci had been found responsible for 67 kidnappings and 62 cases of torture. In 2020, the charges included multiple cases of murder including the horrific killing of Carlos Santucho, brother of guerrilla leader Roberto, described in an earlier chapter. There was also the heart-breaking case of two more young children, a four year-old boy and an eighteen month-old girl, who were found wandering alone in Plaza O'Higgins, the main square in Valparaíso, Chile, 750 miles away from Buenos Aires. It was established that the children's parents were Uruguayans who had fled to Argentina and become the targets of a military operation in which armoured vehicles blocked the street where the family lived and troops opened fire with automatic weapons. The children's father is believed to have been murdered, though his body was never found. Their mother was 'disappeared' at Aníbal Gordon's torture centre at Automotores Orletti in Buenos Aires. No one could explain how the children came to be lost on the street in a different country, except that they appeared to be surplus to the requirements of Operation Condor.

These events were described as 'Crimes Against Humanity in a Framework of Genocide' and Ruffo, Furci, and two others were found guilty and sentenced to prison 'in perpetuity' – meaning, in reality, Argentina's maximum term of 25 years. These proceedings have shed great light on the Junta's methods in suppressing opposition and revolt and sentenced a number of the now-elderly perpetrators to terms which they cannot hope to outlive, though they are sometimes allowed to serve them under a form of house arrest. Throughout, however, there has been a sinister spectre in the background. The name Aníbal Gordon has been mentioned hundreds of times as the man who organised and led the murderers and torturers but he has long been beyond the reach of justice.

CHAPTER 20

The Struggle to Forget

I N RECENT YEARS, the man who snatched us off the street and threatened to execute us has achieved a macabre posthumous celebrity. Indeed for some he has become a source of fascination. Aníbal Gordon is recognised as perhaps the leading practitioner of the black art of kidnapping that played a key part in the Dirty War and became a money-spinning business in the period of chaos which followed the Falklands defeat. As the Argentine author Carlos Juvenal has written, kidnapping became an industry and Gordon was a kidnapper-in-chief.

That industry was recently the subject of a feature film which became one of the most popular movies in Argentine history. Called *El Clan* (The Clan),[1] it was based on the true and terrible story of a family which in the social and economic dislocation of the Junta's decline and fall turned to kidnapping their own wealthy friends and associates for ransom by their loved ones.

The clan leader was Arquímedes Puccio, an agent of the SIDE secret service who had worked with Aníbal Gordon. He was helped by two of his sons including Alejandro, a star player in Argentina's international rugby squad, known as 'the Pumas'. The film is set in the aftermath of Argentina's surrender in the Falklands War and in the opening minutes Arquímedes stares blankly at the television screen as General Galtieri delivers his angry but impotent statement announcing the defeat to a shocked population.

'Our soldiers,' Galtieri says, his rhetoric now sounding tired and empty, 'have made supreme efforts fighting for the dignity of the nation.'

Seemingly with the acquiescence of Gordon and the secret service, the Puccios begin their private kidnap business, starting with a friend of Alejandro's, a fellow member of the Argentine rugby team. He is dragged from his car and forced into a Ford Falcon in a scene recreated by director Pablo Trapero with such realism that, watching it while writing about my own experience, I felt my stomach turn over. The young victim is kept bound and gagged in the Puccios' house while a ransom in dollars is demanded and paid, but the ghastly logic of kidnapping people they knew meant that the victims could never be returned alive, lest they identify their captors. In the film as in fact, Alejandro's friend is murdered and the body dumped in a river outside Buenos Aires.

But with the advent of democracy Argentina is seen to be changing. The Army and secret service begin to lose their power to protect their members. Aníbal Gordon himself is arrested and Arquímedes Puccio visits the murderous sage in prison to take his advice on how to handle the new situation. He finds Gordon lamenting his arrest and saying it only happened 'because I let that useless idiot Kelly live'. His advice to Puccio: democracy won't last, things will get back to normal, kidnap people who have got something to hide and whose families can't make a fuss.

If such advice was given, it was not followed. The Puccios were finally arrested by armed police while holding a well-known businesswoman in a makeshift prison they had constructed in their basement. Both Arquímedes and his son were given lengthy jail terms and died after emerging from prison. For Argentinians, their story and the film made about it are less a reminder of an almost forgotten past than part of a dark shadow over their country which is still present. Not long after the film was released, one of the newly declassified American documents provided evidence of a secret basement prison used by Aníbal Gordon, of which the new Argentine authorities had been completely unaware. It was the CIA report describing the murder of Ambassador Hidalgo Solá, which stated that he had been held at 3570 Bacacay Street, an unremarkable suburban house screened from the road by bougainvillea and the scene of more terrible crimes. The layout of the building today is still as described by surviving victims. Beneath a hatch in the floor was a step-ladder leading to a cellar where the worst tortures are said to have been applied.

The property, which is around the corner from Automotores Orletti, is now owned by people unconnected with and until recently ignorant of these past events. However, on June 11th, 2020, 43 years after the Solá killing, Judge Daniel Rafecas issued a directive prohibiting any alterations to the property which, he said, needed to be preserved as evidence of the 'repression'.[2] The owners of the house now find themselves in possession of a macabre historical monument where, according to the judge, 'There are several existing clues regarding [the home as] an operational base of the personnel of the State Intelligence Secretariat (SIDE).' A lawyer working on the case says that for the survivors, locating the place where they were tortured 'has provided a catharsis'. It may also provide the basis for yet further prosecutions. 'After we identified the location,' says Judge Rafecas, 'new victims began to appear, who said they had been held there hooded and tortured. The work for the court has just begun.'

As the gulf in time to the Junta's crimes has lengthened, and the number of potential accused has inevitably dwindled, so the weight of the charges against them has grown and even the Covid pandemic has not impeded the legal process. In the 'Orletti V' trial concluded in November 2020, the fifth time events at Aníbal Gordon's torture garage came to court, the four former SIDE agents in the virtual dock were found guilty of actions 'In the Framework of a Genocide'. This is, of course, a controversial term in Argentina, which is a country undeniably built on acts of genocide against its native Amerindian population. However, in today's nation many in human-rights circles believe that only 'genocide' is a big enough word to embrace fully the Junta's crimes and to keep the flame of memory alive. Concern that recent events in Argentina, though terrible, do not meet the definition of genocide under international law is submerged in the conviction that only an acceptance of collective guilt which the term enables can truly expiate for the crimes of the 'repression'. In truth Argentina is still struggling to come to terms with the torture and disappearances almost 40 years after the end of military rule. Repeated calls for reconciliation by sympathisers of the military are seen by many as insincere and unacceptable, while the Mothers and Grandmothers of the Plaza de Mayo and the organisations which have stemmed from them have achieved a position that is close to unassailable in the new democracy. Immediately after the elections of 2015 the conservative newspaper *La Nación* called for the prosecution of military officers to be stopped – 'The hunger for revenge must be buried forever' – and the retired Bishop Jorge Casaretto spoke out to lament the failure to forgive: 'Reconciliation must be on Argentina's agenda in the near future,' he said.[3]

However, the Bishop was immediately slapped down by his episcopal superior, Archbishop José Arancedo, who declared: '[R]econciliation is not "wipe the slate clean" and, even less, impunity. What is needed is the commitment to search for the truth, the admission of what is deplorable, the repentance of those who are guilty, and the legal reparation of the damage done.'[4]

Of the hundreds of former officers who have been convicted, more than 300 are estimated to have died so far in jail, either serving their sentences or awaiting trial. But powerful voices insist that the legal process must continue. The main body of the Mothers is still led by its most formidable and uncompromising personality, one of the original founding marchers, the now wheelchair-bound Hebe De Bonafini. Although she has received the UNESCO Prize for Peace Education, she stands by her enduring and frank refusal to forgive:

> I ... cannot say that I do not hate those who tore more than 30,000 people to pieces, who raped them and who stole our children and grandchildren; who became God and master of life and death.[5]

Nationalists meanwhile point out that the crimes committed by left-wing terrorists have gone unpunished. Surviving bombers and assassins have been released in amnesties and the Montonero leader Mario Firmenich, author of one of the most successful kidnap and extortion operations in history and numerous other murderous actions, has been freed to become a history lecturer at the University of Barcelona in Spain.

There are nonetheless people who see the need for dialogue. They include at least one who herself suffered greatly, Mariana

Zaffaroni, the woman whose parents were 'disappeared' by Aníbal Gordon's gang and who was given, as a baby, to one of his men, Miguel Ángel Furci. For her and the other stolen children who have been found and had their true identities restored it has been a difficult, even heart-rending process to which they have responded in different ways.

Despite the trauma of a childhood disrupted by the revelation of her true origins and that the man she loved as a father may have been one of her parents' murderers, Mariana prospered at school and then successfully studied law, becoming a university lecturer. She has joined in several campaigns to try to locate similarly stolen children, including a brother she believes was born to her mother while she was in captivity shortly before her murder. But she has also maintained relations with her 'adoptive' parents, visiting Miguel Ángel Furci in prison and keeping in touch with him through Facebook. In a recent interview she said that the recovery of her real identity has been slow and progressive: 'Everything I thought was true was not as I believed ... But up to now I haven't felt hatred for my adoptive parents. Perhaps I will in the future, perhaps I never will.'[6]

In email correspondence with the author, Mariana expressed her support for the continuing legal process, however inadequate: 'I think that so many years after is not the kind of Justice that repairs all the damages that were made. But it's better than nothing.'

Other Argentines are still trying to come to terms with what happened in the war with Britain. While the Mothers and Grandmothers from the Dirty War continue to seek answers about the fate of the 'disappeared', a number of families of soldiers who served in the Falklands are still frustrated by contradictory and misleading information about their loved ones. Officially 649 Argentine servicemen died in the conflict, almost half of them in the warship *Belgrano*, but there remain doubts as to whether this is really an accurate final total. In the months following the conflict a British Army team led by Colonel Geoffrey Cardozo found and buried some 240 Argentine bodies, about 120 of whom could not be identified and were interred beneath the simple inscription, 'Argentine Soldier Known Only to God'.[7] Cardozo then wrote a full report with plans and drawings which would later be given to the Argentine government. It was never passed on to the families of the dead, many of whom were not officially notified of a soldier's death but were reduced, in the immediate aftermath of the war, to hunting for their family members by going to military barracks and shouting out appeals for information about them. Advanced DNA investigations have now established the identities of most of the dead buried by Colonel Cardozo, but the remains of another unidentified serviceman have just been found and the International Red Cross is now investigating reports of a further possible burial site perhaps containing as many as five more. Throughout, politics and semantics have impeded efforts to grant the dead a peaceful resting place. For some time Argentina's military-inspired Commission of Relatives rejected the 'repatriation' of the remains to the mainland as this would concede that the Malvinas are not Argentine territory. In the official view those who fell on the islands are Argentina's last bastion there and must remain. Meanwhile some families have been disturbed by suggestions that their loved ones are buried alongside officers who have been identified as murderers and torturers during the 'repression'. Here, as so often in Argentina, the ghosts of the past continue to torment the living.

Forty years later the 'Guerra de Las Malvinas' remains for many Argentines an open wound. Despite defeat, the Junta's propaganda and the statements of the governments which followed have convinced the majority of their people of the justness of their cause. Today, walls up and down the country are daubed with the crab-like outline of the islands and slogans such as 'The Malvinas Are Ours'. A law recently passed by the Argentine Congress has made it mandatory for all public transport to carry signs saying 'Las Malvinas Son Argentinas', and the politician who sponsored the move said it would reflect 'our undeniable sovereignty' over the islands. Another move is currently under way to have the words 'Malvinas Argentinas' embroidered on school uniforms in order to ensure that the young embrace the message. Schools have a legal obligation to include lessons about the Malvinas, and teachers at one kindergarten have announced their use of computerised 'augmented reality' to enable four and five year-olds to watch 3D images of the flora, fauna and geography of the islands. As one academic put it: 'There appears to be an imperative to keep on reminding Argentine children and young people of the "incomplete" nature of their national territory.'

Meanwhile the results of a plebiscite among the islanders themselves showing them voting to remain a British overseas territory by 1,513 ballots to three are rejected as an irrelevant vestige of colonialism. The recent findings of geographers that the islands may not be an ancient extension of the Latin American continent and hence part of Argentina's continental shelf, but are possibly linked in geological terms to southern Africa are likewise dismissed.[8]

There has been some diplomatic progress between Britain and Argentina, not least the signature of a £1 billion export initiative to boost trade between the two countries; however, the Malvinas issue refuses to die. Argentina continues to agitate at the UN Decolonization Committee and the recently elected President Alberto Fernández has declared that he will continue to 'shout' about the Malvinas. His obligatory address at a commemoration of the 1982 invasion used the language of a true believer: 'We must work very hard for Argentina to reaffirm its sovereignty rights over the Malvinas Islands on a daily basis. Once we have recovered the Islands, the lives lost there will regain sense for ever.'[9]

Britain has reinforced its presence on the islands, constructing soon after the war a new full-size airbase at Mount Pleasant, where four Typhoon combat jets are currently stationed. However, some in Argentina will doubtless have been encouraged by the sudden US decision to withdraw from Afghanistan in 2021, apparently without consulting its leading military ally and partner in the 'Special Relationship'. What this episode sadly illustrates is that Britain's stock in the world has fallen since Margaret Thatcher's triumph of will in the Falklands War and that the all-important Anglo-American alliance on which that victory was based may not be as dependable as in times past. The tectonic plates of international power and influence are shifting and not a few are watching the movements with a predatory eye.

As a military power, however, Argentina is greatly diminished. Attention was drawn to the state of the armed forces by the disappearance in November 2017 of the Argentine submarine ARA *San Juan*, lost with its entire crew of 44 in a training accident in the South Atlantic. A subsequent inquiry heard witnesses state that 'there are no seaworthy submarines, most aircraft are out of service and not a single combat plane is capable of flight'.[10] A senior prosecutor found that the armed forces were in a 'terminal state', disabled by obsolete or malfunctioning weaponry and with military budgets inadequate to replace it.

Some sympathisers with the military accuse a succession of civilian governments of continuing to 'punish' them for their Dirty War crimes. In fact, economic crises worsened by endemic corruption have resulted in shortages of hard currency, and an effective arms embargo by the British government has persuaded most western countries and, recently, South Korea, not to supply Buenos Aires with advanced equipment. The result is that, at the time of writing, the Argentine Air Force, which was one of the few branches of its armed forces to emerge with credit from the war, is virtually out of action. It is now reported that Argentina is seeking to buy twelve supersonic multi-role combat aircraft from Pakistan, a country which has emphasised its agreement with the Argentines on the issue of 'colonialism', i.e. the Falklands. The aircraft in question, the JF-17 Thunder, which, significantly, can be equipped to fire anti-ship missiles and is capable of in-flight refuelling, has been jointly developed by Pakistan and China. Such a purchase could open up new opportunities for Beijing in what, in terms of its natural resources, is still one of the most strategically significant areas of the planet, with globally important reserves of lithium, rare earths, oil, gas, fertile agricultural land and fresh water, a huge 'world jewel' in the words of one Argentinian writer.[11] This would clearly be of great concern to both the British and US governments, already disquieted by Beijing's success in establishing a 200-hectare space station in a remote part of Patagonia. The Argentinian government has claimed that this is solely for civilian research but admits that it has no physical oversight over the area, which is effectively controlled by the Chinese military. An Argentina nursing 40 year-old unhealed wounds may yet prove to be a point of vulnerability for the west, and it does not take a great deal of imagination to see the makings of another crisis lying in wait in the future.

The Argentine claim that it was and still is engaged in an anti-colonialist struggle may have resonance in Latin America and some other parts of the world – that is the penalty of Britain's past history. But the argument that the Falkland Islands along with the islanders should simply be handed over because of a highly contentious interpretation of 18th- and 19th-century history must still be undermined by the clearly recorded and much more recent past which I have described. The Junta's savage war against its own people and its attempt to seize the Falkland Islands by main force were not, as Argentine nationalists continue to claim, part of a noble struggle in which the highest motives predominated. The men who led and supported the Junta attempted to fashion for themselves an image of chivalry, finally exemplified by the Argentine Air Force pilots who flew dozens of near-suicide missions against the Royal Navy during the war, but this was in fact a façade concealing murder. Behind it, nightmare visions had become reality: corpses cemented into oil drums and thrown into rivers, other victims, still living, dragged to midnight Mass in hoods and chains, with the screams of the tortured audible behind religious incantations, Aníbal Gordon dangling his captives from steel girders and half drowning them in a vat before finishing them off with pistols. Delusions flourished: if the death squads truly 'disappeared' their victims, there would be no evidence that the crimes had taken place and the dead would not come back to provide evidence for the courts.

The investigators who examined many of these crimes in the bumpy years when democracy gradually re-established itself in Argentina were struck by the lack of remorse shown by most of the accused. The CONADEP commission, the National Commission on the Disappearance of Persons, though its hands were partly tied by restrictions placed on it by a still-fearful government, took witness statements from men who admitted having been members of the 'task forces' which had carried out torture and murder.

Rather than showing any sense of guilt or repentance, these statements expressed bitterness at having been 'abandoned by their leaders', and attempted to explain their actions by claiming that during their murderous work they had been tied by a 'pact of blood' which meant that any refusal to take part would have been punished by death. Those who carried out kidnappings for financial gain sought to justify them by claiming that they had been trying to establish a 'financial fatherland' to fund their nationalist crusade.

At the highest levels of the Junta when Galtieri himself came to power, there was a realisation that repression alone could not succeed and popular feeling had to be allowed to express itself. But the Dirty War had turned into a trap for the ruling elite. Stained with the blood of their own people, Galtieri and the Army leadership looked around for a way out and decided that asserting what they claimed were Argentina's historic rights over the Malvinas would rally a divided country behind them and distract it from the economic crises which continually threatened. Thus the invasion of islands hundreds of miles away at the very limits of its Air Force's range was launched by a nation equipped with just two air-to-air refuelling tankers, Mirage and Dagger jets which couldn't, in any case, use them, and only five potentially war-winning air-launched Exocet missiles, with little prospect of getting any more. That gamble failed and the resulting full exposure of what really took place in this crucial period of Argentine history is now the greatest obstacle to the fulfilment of her still-cherished ambition to possess the islands. A nation that for all its undoubted qualities and attractions has, in the words of its own judiciary, inflicted crimes against humanity and genocide on large numbers of its own citizens will continue to find it difficult to demand the handover of islands containing people who want no part of their rule.

Argentina is still paying the price of the military Junta's pact with the devil. To suppress its Marxist foes it allied itself with career criminals, used their methods and their uncompromising skills and, in the case of several leading figures, enthusiastically embraced the opportunities for self-enrichment. Our kidnapper, Aníbal Gordon, was emblematic of this regime. Recruited out of prison, he was a man who claimed to uphold patriotic and Catholic values. He demonstrated his commitment by his actions at the Automotores Orletti, and by blooding his young son, Marcelo, with a tour of that nightmare environment in his early teens. But he also displayed a lust for the financial gain that could be extracted from his victims, a system described by the French writer Olivier Rolin as '*Torture plus fric*' (torture plus cash).[12]

Even today judicial authorities are continuing to investigate what happened to the millions of dollars that Gordon and his gang are believed to have made from some of the people they kidnapped and did not immediately kill. One of those was Alberto Mechoso Méndez, who held much of the war chest of the extreme leftist Uruguayan group, The People's Victory Party. He was seized by Gordon on September 26th, 1976 as part of Operation Condor. His captors noted that he had been in possession of a cyanide pill but had failed to take it.

Gordon's men tortured Mechoso Méndez at the Automotores Orletti and as I have described earlier, tore his flat apart with demolition tools. Hidden inside the walls they found millions of dollars. Méndez was then murdered and dumped in an oil drum containing lime. The remains were finally identified in 2012.

Aníbal Gordon and his allies in the secret police had apparently intended to use the significant sums they had obtained from murder and extortion to build a luxurious yacht club, apartment and restaurant complex in the picturesque town of Chascomús near Buenos Aires, where they had bought more than 1,000 acres of land. Bulldozers had already started to reshape the property when the murderers fell out over their business arrangements and the Junta collapsed. The development never took place.

More than 40 years later, ownership of the land has been traced to the three daughters and a son of one of Gordon's close lieutenants, a now-dead secret policeman called Leonard Miguel Save. These people cannot be held responsible for the original murder of Mechoso Méndez, which took place when they were children or not yet born; however, in the eyes of the investigating magistrate the land can be classified as 'goods coming from a criminal offence considered to be a crime against humanity' and the four registered owners are being charged with 'asset laundering'. Meanwhile, human-rights organisations believe that hidden on the land is another mass grave of victims of the 'repression'.

The dream which Gordon seems to have entertained – that his family would join Argentina's property-owning elite as the owners of a luxury marina – will never be realised. And without the protection of a father who was widely feared when he was alive, Gordon's children have not prospered in the new Argentina. Five years after his death, his daughter Adriana suffered a somewhat ironic misfortune. As Argentina's economy nosedived once again and the kidnapping-for-ransom business made a comeback, she herself was kidnapped by a gang described as 'beginners', who were apparently initially unaware that they had seized the daughter of one of the country's most infamous criminals. The Gordon family paid a ransom of 55,000 devalued pesos, worth at the time some £20,000, plus $726 which they apparently had in cash. Unusually, the amateur kidnappers were then arrested by the police.

Gordon's son, Marcelo Aníbal Gordon, had initially been tried and sentenced to eight years in prison for his involvement in the Kelly kidnapping which had led to the arrest of his father, but was then released. In 2005 he was found guilty of being a full gang member and of taking part in his father's last series of criminal operations between 1982 and 1984, operations which were in the timeframe of our own kidnapping and mock execution in which he may well have participated. Marcelo Gordon was sentenced to twelve years in prison and has now apparently emerged. His present whereabouts are unknown.

There of course never was, and never could be, any recourse to justice for our terrifying treatment at the hands of the Gordon Gang and the elements of the Junta whose orders they were following. The principal actors in the operation are either dead or serving sentences that they are unlikely to survive. The journalist and former Montonero, Horacio Verbitsky, told me that they would never answer my questions because the law of *omertà* continues to prevail.

Looking back I can say that what happened on that day in Buenos Aires left an indelible mark on me. On instructions from London, fully justified as the now-released documents graphically show, we left Argentina a few days after the event and I took a holiday with my wife in the West Indies. There, in the middle of the night, I suddenly found myself crouching wide awake in the bedroom of our hotel in a fight-or-flight position. I had no recollection of how I got there but my wife told me that I had leapt out of the bed in one motion seemingly while still asleep. Less than a month later, in that age before PTSD diagnoses and specialist therapy, I was back at work on another story. Forty years on, I retain a strange sense of gratitude for the whole experience. I am one of those who went into journalism out of desire to be a witness to history – and this was history at its most raw. The Junta had already made all too clear its lack of respect, indeed antipathy, for journalism, which it frequently saw as an agent of Marxism. In Argentina such detestation went beyond abuse to violence and murder. Dozens of Argentine journalists were killed during the Dirty War, and the American diplomat 'Tex' Harris provided Washington with a graphic account of the threats that those trying to report on the 'repression' were facing:

> Journalists who wrote about this were beaten up. There was a famous case of several journalists who disappeared. There was one brutal case in which a fellow was hit with a set of brass knuckles as he was walking from his newspaper to his car. A car stopped, a man got out of the car, came up and slugged him in the face, broke his jawbone, and he has horrible scars across his face.[13]

In our case the worst had not happened but we had been given a unique insight into Argentina's wars and the methods of one of its principal dirty warriors. We had also seen the true nature of the regime that was claiming legal and historical justification for its Falkland Islands land-grab, and it was a glimpse that lent credence to the fears of the suddenly occupied islanders themselves. Our kidnapping showed a land where the last bastion of the regime's power was a murderous secret service unlike anything in recent British experience. It was and remains all too easy to imagine the terrible fate that so many others suffered at the hands of Gordon, a man who boasted of having personally killed hundreds of *subversivos* and who would, more than likely, have been given the job of disposing of dozens of British civilian prisoners if his battalion's secret wartime threat to 'disappear' them, as reported by the CIA in the document revealed earlier in this book, had been carried out. In that sense the Argentine people, wonderfully talented and attractive as they so frequently are, are still labouring under a burden from the past which they must somehow find a way to shake off.

As I write these words, I can see on the wall of my study a cartoon by Calman which appeared in *The Times* shortly after our kidnapping and which still evokes wry amusement. In it, a kidnap victim lies tied up on the ground with his news camera next to him. 'I've one last request,' he asks his unseen kidnappers, 'Can I use my camera?'

The cartoon contains what for me is a simple truth. Journalists can at times enjoy a privileged existence with a freedom and an access to people and information available to few others. But journalism is also a rough trade and we cannot afford to be surprised when the entity or individual we are pointing our cameras at or writing about bites back. In Argentina on May 12th, 1982 we did our best to cover the tide of events until they engulfed us in the way that violence in Argentina had engulfed so many others. In the end one can only be thankful that on that day Aníbal Gordon chose, or was instructed, only to terrorise and not to murder us and that we emerged alive to tell the tale.

Acknowledgements

Forty years after our terrifying, unforgettable kidnapping in Buenos Aires I would like to express my appreciation of the three members of the Thames Television team who were with me on that day. As I completed this book the sad news arrived that our sound recordist, Trefor Hunter, who behaved with great fortitude, had passed away in hospital. Also deceased is our producer, Norman Fenton, who succeeded in evading our kidnappers and raising the alarm. Still vigorous is our outstanding cameraman, Edward 'Ted' Adcock, who displayed great courage during our ordeal and has now kindly shared with me his recollection of events which is often more complete than my own. I am greatly in his debt.

I would also like to thank our film editor, Robert 'Bob' Oliver. It was his great professional skill that enabled our reporting to reach British television screens.

This book was triggered by a massive disclosure of previously secret documents by the US government. It may seem to be courting controversy to express thanks to the former US President, Donald Trump, for services to historical truth, however it was he who carried out the overwhelming bulk of the Argentina Declassification Project which made this account possible. The process was initiated by his predecessor, Barack Obama, but it was not until April 2019 that the majority of the disclosure, more than 43,000 pages, took place. The released material included for the first time reports by US security officials from the Department of Defense, the FBI and, crucially, the Central Intelligence Agency. It was among these that I found a cable identifying the man who had carried out our kidnapping.

This historic release owes much to the work of the American National Security Archive, a private non-governmental body which has performed extraordinary service by collecting, and sometimes augmenting through Freedom of Information requests, US government records going back to the Cold War. I would like to thank them for valuable initial advice on how to navigate what for me was a computerised swamp of files released by Declassification.

Thanks are also due to a number of individuals including Hugo Alconada Mon, senior journalist, and Juan Trenado, picture editor, at *La Nación* newspaper, Buenos Aires, Daniel Schavelzon whose book, which he sent me immediately, is an invaluable chronicle of the years of art theft and looting under the Junta, Mariana Zaffaroni Islas, the child of 'disappeared' parents brought up by a man now convicted of terrible crimes, who found the time amid her work as a professor of law to respond to my emailed questions, the journalist Nick Tozer for his valuable advice, and my old friend William Dowell who helped with research in the United States.

May I also express my appreciation of the work of Duncan Heath, Andrew Furlow and the small but highly effective team at Icon Books. Duncan applied an eagle eye to mistakes and possible improvements. I am indebted as well to my agent, Anna Power, an indefatigable promoter of her authors' efforts.

It goes without saying that any errors the reader may discover in this book are entirely my own.

Bibliography

Andersen, Martin Edwin, *Dossier Secreto: Argentina's Desaparecidos and the Myth of the 'Dirty War'* (Boulder, CO: Westview Press Inc., 1993)

Arditti, Rita, *Searching for Life: The Grandmothers of the Plaza de Mayo and the Disappeared Children of Argentina* (Berkeley, CA: University of California Press, 1999)

Basconi, Andrea, *Elena Holmberg: La mujer que sabía demasiado* (Buenos Aires: Random House Mondadori, digital edition, 2012)

Bicheno, Hugh, *Razor's Edge: The Unofficial History of the Falklands War* (London: Weidenfeld & Nicolson, 2006)

Burns, Jimmy, *The Land That Lost Its Heroes* (London: Bloomsbury Publishing, 1987)

CONADEP (National Commission on the Disappearance of Persons), *Nunca Más* (Never Again) (Buenos Aires: www.desaparecidos.org, 1984)

Costa Méndez, Nicanor, *Malvinas, Esta Es La Historia* (Buenos Aires: Editorial Sudamericana, 1993)

Cox, David, *Dirty Secrets, Dirty War* (Charleston, SC: Evening Post Publishing Company, 2008)

Dinges, John, *The Condor Years* (New York: The New Press, 2004)

Edwards, Sidney, *My Secret Falklands War* (Sussex: Book Guild Publishing, 2014)

Finchelstein, Federico, *The Ideological Origins of the Dirty War* (New York: Oxford University Press, 2014)

Freedman, Lawrence and Gamba-Stonehouse, Virginia, *Signals of War: the Falklands Conflict of 1982* (London, Faber & Faber, 1990)

Freedman, Lawrence, *The Official History of the Falklands Campaign*, Volumes 1 & 2 (Abingdon, Oxon: Routledge, 2005)

Glasman, Gabriel, *La Siniestra Triple A, Antesala del Infierno en la Argentina* (Miami: L.D. Books, 2009)

Guest, Iain, *Behind the Disappearances: Argentina's Dirty War Against Human Rights and the United Nations* (Philadelphia: University of Pennsylvania Press, 1990)

Hastings, Max, and Jenkins, Simon, *The Battle for the Falklands* (London: Michael Joseph, 1983)

Henderson, Sir Nicholas, *Mandarin* (London, Weidenfeld & Nicolson, 1994)

Hobson, Chris, with Noble, Andrew, *Falklands Air War* (Hinckley: Midland Publishing, 2002)

Hughes, Ben, *The British Invasion of the River Plate 1806–1807* (Barnsley: Pen & Sword Military, 2013)

Juvenal, Carlos, *Buenos Muchachos: La industria del secuestro en la Argentina* (Buenos Aires: Planeta, 1994)

Lewis, Paul H., *Guerrillas and Generals: The 'Dirty War' in Argentina* (Westport, CT: Praeger Publishers, 2002)

Middlebrook, Martin, *The Argentine Fight for the Falklands* (Barnsley: Pen & Sword Military, 1989)

Moro, Rubén O., *The History of the South Atlantic Conflict* (New York: Praeger Publishers, 1989)

Rattenbach, Benjamín, *Comisión de Análisis y Evaluación de las Responsabilidades del Conflicto del Atlántico Sur – Informe Final* (Buenos Aires: www.casarosada.gob.ar, published in full on March 22nd, 2012)

Robben, Antonius G.G.M., *Argentina Betrayed* (Philadelphia: University of Pennsylvania Press, 2018)

Rolin, Olivier, *L'Automne des Tortionnaires* (Paris: Nouvel Observateur, January 6th, 1984, republished in *Circus 1*, Seuil, 2011)

Schavelzon, Daniel, *El Expolio del Arte en la Argentina* (Buenos Aires: Editorial Sudamericana, 1993)

Shortland, Anja, *Lost Art* (London: Unicorn, 2021)

Sivak, Martin, *El Asesinato de Juan José Torres* (Buenos Aires: Ediciones del Pensamiento Nacional, 1997)

Thompson, Julian, *No Picnic* (Barnsley: Leo Cooper, 1985)

Yofre, Juan B., *1982: Los documentos secretos de la Guerra de Malvinas/Falklands y el derrumbe del Proceso* (Buenos Aires: Editorial Sudamericana, 2011)

Notes

Chapter 1: Swallowed

1. The destruction of the Cambodian Army battalion I was accompanying took place on November 23rd, 1970 near the town of Skoun, north of the Cambodian capital Phnom Penh. United Press International reported on the battle and my escape on November 24th.

Chapter 2: War

1. Sir John Nott autobiography, *Here Today, Gone Tomorrow*, Politicos Publishing, 2002.
2. *The British Invasion of the River Plate 1806–1807*, by Ben Hughes, Pen and Sword Books Ltd., 2013.
3. *The Fight for the Malvinas: Argentine Forces in the Falklands War*, by Martin Middlebrook, Viking, 1989.
4. US Defense Intelligence Agency report on 'International Terrorism' dated March 30th, 1980.
5. *The Guardian*, obituary, May 7th, 2013.
6. CIA intelligence information cable, August 25th, 1976.
7. Transcript of voice recording sent to US State Department by Embassy Human Rights Officer Allen 'Tex' Harris, May 31st, 1978 (released 2017). The name of the lady who was kidnapped and subsequently 'disappeared' was, in fact, Mrs De Vicenti, the error apparently being caused by faulty transcription of 'Tex' Harris's recorded voice message to Washington.
8. Telegram from US Ambassador Raul Castro to US State Department, March 30th, 1978 (released 2002).
9. *Dossier Secreto*, by Martin Edwin Andersen, Westview Press Inc., p. 187.

Chapter 3: End of the Road

1. 'Organizational Chart of 601', document apparently drawn up by the CIA during the presidency of Leopoldo Galtieri in 1982.
2. CIA information report, April 12th, 1982 (released 2018).
3. Christopher Jones, WNEW.
4. CIA information report, May 18th, 1982 (released 2018).
5. The Falklands War Oral History Programme, Centre for Contemporary British History, 2005, *inter alia*.

Chapter 4: Dictator

1. The Falklands War Oral History Programme, Centre for Contemporary British History, 2005.
2. Interview with the former Human Rights Officer of the US Embassy in Buenos Aires, Allen 'Tex' Harris. The Association for Diplomatic Studies and Training, Foreign Affairs Oral History Project, December 1999.
3. Profile of General Galtieri, *The Daily Telegraph*, March 13th, 2007.
4. 'Galtieri of Argentina: Decisive and Unyielding', CIA intelligence memorandum, May 17th, 1982 (released 2018).
5. 'Argentina Key Issues', Department of Defense paper, May 16th, 1977.
6. Falklands: NSC briefing for President Reagan ('Suggested Talking Points for Telephone Call to President Galtieri'), Margaret Thatcher Foundation.
7. Report from US National Security Advisor William P. Clark Jr to Secretary of State Alexander Haig, April 15th, 1982.
8. CIA information report, subject: 'Views of Brigadier Generals of the Argentine Army on the errors made by former President Leopoldo Galtieri', June 25th, 1982.
9. Interview with President Leopoldo Galtieri by the author on May 12th, 1982. Transmitted by Thames Television's *TV Eye* on May 13th, 1982. Available for viewing at the time of writing on YouTube: https://www.youtube.com/watch?v=kh_bCSE8y2g
10. CIA situation listing, Subject Category: 'File X, Situation Falkland report of May 17th, 1982'. 'Casual investigation of the temporary kidnapping of foreign journalists in Argentina'.
11. CIA National Intelligence Daily, May 17th, 1982.

Chapter 5: Dinner with the Junta

1. 'Target London – Inside a Soviet Nuclear Missile Base', Thames Television, *This Week*, 1991.
2. Rogelio García Lupo, *Diplomacia Secreta y Rendición Incondicional*, as quoted by Hugh Bicheno in *Razor's Edge*, Weidenfeld & Nicolson, 2006.
3. *The History of the South Atlantic Conflict*, by Rubén O. Moro, published in translation by Praeger, New York, 1989, p. 186.
4. *Razor's Edge*, by Hugh Bicheno, p. 50.

Chapter 6: Secrets

1. *The Washington Post*, 'The Intelligence Coup of the Century', by Greg Miller, February 11th, 2020.
2. Quoted by Hugh Bicheno in *Razor's Edge*, p. 79.
3. US internal briefing paper on Operation Condor, 'Counter-terrorism in the Southern Cone', dated May 9th, 1977.
4. Contained in CIA intelligence information report dated August 16th, 1977. Subject: 'Text of the Agreement by Condor Countries Regulating Their Subversive Targets'.

Chapter 7: Executioners

1. CIA information report no. 231283, dated May 21st, 1982. This report was marked 'WNINTEL', a since-discontinued classification meaning that it could identify or permit the identification of an intelligence source or method. Even after Declassification more than half the text is still withheld.
2. *The Buenos Aires Herald*, August 25th, 1983.
3. Quoted by Carlos Alfredo Juvenal in *Buenos Muchachos*, Planeta, Argentina, 1994, p. 176.
4. 'Jaque', Montevideo, February 24th, 1984.
5. Various Argentinian press reports including *El Cordillerano*, April 26th, 1971, 'They Looted the Bank and Escaped by Plane'.
6. Various Argentinian press reports including *Infobae*, February 3rd, 2019.
7. Carlos Alfredo Juvenal, *Buenos Muchachos*, p. 10.
8. Police reports on operations carried out by Aníbal Gordon, dated March 28th and September 26th, 1974.

9. *Nueva Presencia*, September 1983.

10. Press conference in Washington in March 1981 prior to his inauguration as President of Argentina.

11. 'La sociedad tiene ganas de empezar a hablar', by Alejandra Dandan, *Página 12*, February 5th, 2007.

12. *The Ideological Origins of the Dirty War*, Federico Finchelstein, Oxford University Press, 2014.

13. See the author's personal account in *The Fall of Saigon*, Rex Collings, 1975.

14. Interview with the former Human Rights Officer of the US Embassy in Buenos Aires, Allen 'Tex' Harris. The Association for Diplomatic Studies and Training, Foreign Affairs Oral History Project, December 1999.

15. Statement of arrest and torture victim Jorge Victor Martín, who was subjected to a mock execution and identified Aníbal Gordon as the 'chief' of his interrogators.

16. CIA Office of Political Research, 'Whither Argentina: New Political System or More of the Same?', February 1976.

17. *The Washington Post*, March 3rd, 2018.

18. Quoted in *Guerrillas and Generals: The Dirty War in Argentina*, by Paul H. Lewis, Praeger, 2002, p. 143.

19. Quoted in *Guerrillas and Generals*, by Paul H. Lewis, p. 108.

20. Priority cable from the US Ambassador in Buenos Aires, Robert C. Hill, to the US Secretary of State, Henry Kissinger, on May 20th, 1976.

Chapter 8: 'A world so terrible that it is difficult to imagine'

1. 'Un universo tan atroz que resulta difícil de imaginar', Attorney General Pablo Ouviña outlining charges against some of those accused of carrying out crimes at the Automotores Orletti as part of Operation Condor, May 30th, 2017.

2. Report by CELS (Centro de Estudios Legales y Sociales) in 2016.

3. Statement by Enrique Rodríguez Larreta to Amnesty International in March 1977.

4. From the introduction by Bernard Fall to *La Guerre Moderne*, by French counterinsurgency expert Roger Trinquier, published 1961.

5. Reports from US Embassy legal attaché and FBI representative Robert Scherrer to US Ambassador Robert Hill of September 3rd and

October 19th, 1976 as well as later Embassy summary of event, dated July 27th, 1985.

6. Report by US Embassy legal attaché and FBI representative Robert Scherrer on Argentinian operations against ERP guerrillas, dated August 3rd, 1976.

7. US Defense Intelligence Agency counterintelligence memorandum, 'The Terrorist Threat to US Nuclear Weapons', dated February 28th, 1977.

8. Statements of Luis Brandoni and Marta Bianchi during the trial of associates of Aníbal Gordon on charges of kidnapping, torture and homicide, May 2011.

9. Statements of PVP intermediary Washington Pérez during trial in 2010 of Aníbal Gordon's associate Orestes Vaello and others on charges of kidnapping and homicide, and to the Historical Research Team of the government of Uruguay in 2015.

Chapter 9: Americans Divided

1. Meeting between US Assistant Secretary of State Harry Shlaudeman and US Secretary of State Henry Kissinger on July 9th, 1976. *Foreign Relations of the United States, 1969–1976*, Volume E–11, Part 2, Documents on South America, 1973–1976.

2. Cable marked 'Immediate' from Secretary of State Henry Kissinger to US Ambassadors in Argentina, Chile, Uruguay, Peru, Brazil and Paraguay, dated August 23rd, 1976.

3. Memorandum of conversation between US Secretary of State Henry Kissinger and Argentine Foreign Minister Admiral César Guzzetti, June 6th, 1976. This key document was originally made public following a specific Freedom of Information request by Carlos Osorio of the National Security Archive.

4. Cable from US Ambassador to Argentina Robert Hill to US Secretary of State Henry Kissinger, October 19th, 1976.

5. Interview with the former Human Rights Officer of the US Embassy in Buenos Aires, Allen 'Tex' Harris. The Association for Diplomatic Studies and Training, Foreign Affairs Oral History Project, December 1999.

6. Testimony of Patricia Derian, Assistant Secretary of State for Human Rights from 1977 to 1981, during trial of former Junta member Admiral Emilio Massera on June 13th, 1985.

Chapter 10: Flight of the Condor

1. Department of Defense intelligence information report, dated October 1st, 1976.

2. 'Priority' cable from FBI representative at US Embassy in Buenos Aires to FBI Director in Washington, dated September 28th, 1976.

3. CIA intelligence information cable, dated September 8th, 1977.

4. CIA intelligence information cable, subject: 'CONDOR ... BASIC MISSION OF CONDOR TEAMS BEING SENT TO FRANCE', dated July 21st, 1976.

5. Report marked 'Secret', subject: 'Counter-terrorism in the Southern Cone', dated May 9th, 1977.

6. CIA intelligence information cable, subject: 'FIRST ATTEMPT OF CONDOR TO OPERATE AGAINST TERRORISTS [WORDS CONCEALED]', dated December 7th, 1976.

7. 'The Plot to Kill Ed Koch', by Christopher Ingalls Haugh, *Politico* magazine, February 17th, 2014.

8. Cable from CIA Directorate of Operations to [addressees withheld], subject: ' ACTIVITIES OF OPERATION CONDOR OUTSIDE CONDOR COUNTRIES', dated January 25th, 1977.

9. Cable from CIA Directorate of Operations to [addressees withheld], subject: 'VISIT OF REPRESENTATIVES OF WEST GERMAN, FRENCH AND BRITISH INTELLIGENCE SERVICES TO ARGENTINA TO DISCUSS METHODS FOR ESTABLISHMENT OF AN ANTI-SUBVERSIVE ORGANIZATION SIMILAR TO "CONDOR"', dated April 7th, 1978.

10. 'The escape of a married couple that led to the closure of the Automotores Orletti clandestine center', by Eduardo Anguita and Daniel Cecchini, *Infobae*, March 2nd, 2019.

11. Orders from Carlos Guillermo Suárez Mason, General de División, 'Orden de Operaciones 9/77 (Continuación de la ofensiva contra la subversión durante el período de 1977)', dated June 13th, 1977.

12. CIA Directorate of Operations intelligence information cable, subject: 'KIDNAPPING AND ASSASSINATION OF ARGENTINE AMBASSADOR TO VENEZUELA BY A GROUP ASSOCIATED WITH ARGENTINE STATE INTELLIGENCE SECRETARIAT (SIDE) WITHOUT SIDE KNOWLEDGE OR AUTHORIZATION', dated September 8th, 1977.

13. *The New York Times*, 'Carter Aide Again in Argentina For Assessment of Human Rights', August 9th, 1977.
14. US State Department Bureau of Intelligence and Research, 'INR Weekly Highlights of Developments in Human Rights', dated July 26th, 1977.

Chapter 11: Weapons for Lives?

1. CIA memorandum, 'Impact of the US Stand on Human Rights', dated May 11th, 1977.
2. Cable from General Dennis P. McAuliffe, Commander-in-Chief Southcom, to US Department of Defense, dated May 5th, 1978.
3. US Embassy telegram to Secretary of State Cyrus Vance, prepared by M. Chaplin and signed by Ambassador Raul Castro, dated January 17th, 1979.
4. Memorandum of conversation, President Carter/President Videla Bilateral, The White House, dated September 9th, 1977.
5. Cable from US Secretary of State Cyrus Vance to US Secretary of Defense Harold Brown, dated May 1st, 1978.
6. Cable from the Defense Intelligence Agency to the US Secretary of Defense Harold Brown, the US Secretary of State Cyrus Vance and others, dated October 25th, 1979.
7. Action Memorandum from the Director of the Bureau of Politico-Military Affairs Leslie H. Gelb to Secretary of State Cyrus Vance, dated September 15th, 1977. Interestingly the signatory, Leslie Gelb, had been a journalist – the Diplomatic Correspondent of *The New York Times* – before joining the State Department as a senior official only weeks before signing this document.

Chapter 12: Follow the Money

1. CIA information cable, subject: 'FEDERAL POLICE INVESTIGATION OF THE DEATH OF ELENA HOLMBERG', dated January 18th, 1979.
2. US State Department background document, 'How the Montoneros Struck It Rich', dated July 27th, 1977.
3. Cable from US Embassy, Buenos Aires to US Secretary of State Edmund Muskie, subject: 'THE TACTIC OF DISAPPEARANCE', dated September 26th, 1980.

4. US State Department, 'Memorandum for the Record', dated April 1st, 1977.

5. Carlos Juvenal, *Buenos Muchachos*, pp. 156–68.

6. 'El Fantasma de Aníbal Gordon', by Susana Viau, *Página 12*, August 30th, 2005.

Chapter 13: Children of the Disappeared

1. Evidence in 'Operation Condor' trial, 2013.

2. Statement by Miguel Ángel Furci to 'Operation Condor' trial in 2013.

3. Order from Secretaria de Inteligencia de Estado to Comando 1er Cuerpo. – jef. 1. ICIA – 601, 'Tupamaro –Agente Activo – Uruguayos', dated September 8th, 1976.

4. Statement by Miguel Ángel Furci to 'Operation Condor' trial in 2013.

5. *The Post-Dictatorship Generation in Argentina, Chile and Uruguay*, by A. Ros, Palgrave Macmillan, 2012.

6. 'El Acoso Sexual del Apropriador', by Eduardo Tagliaferro, *Página 12*, March 28th, 1999.

Chapter 14: Hubris and Fear

1. 'The heavy weight of recalling the seventies', by Andrew Graham-Yooll, *The Buenos Aires Times*, September 2nd, 2019.

2. Memorandum from US Deputy Secretary of State Patricia Derian to Secretary of State Cyrus Vance, subject: 'Next Steps in Argentina', dated January 26th, 1979.

3. *The Economist*, May 23rd, 2013.

4. 'Immediate' cable from US Embassy, Buenos Aires to Secretary of State, Washington DC, September 26th, 1980.

5. CIA Directorate of Intelligence, 'Insurgent Success and Failure: Selected Case Studies', May 1983.

6. Report from US Embassy, Buenos Aires to US Secretary of State Cyrus Vance, July 21st, 1978.

7. Report from US Embassy, Buenos Aires to US Secretary of State Cyrus Vance, subject: 'EFFORTS TO ACCOUNT FOR THE DISAPPEARED', dated May 10th, 1979. The same report stated that the government of Argentina could not account for a 'long list of disappearance cases'. According to an 'army intelligence source',

investigations had enjoyed limited success because 'security forces have destroyed records which served as evidence that there had been contact between a disappeared person and that particular branch or unit.'

8. Carlos Juvenal, *Buenos Muchachos*, p. 318.

9. 'Civil War in El Salvador', Thames Television, *TV Eye*, March 12th, 1981.

10. 'The Deadly Patriots', series on El Salvador conflict by Craig Pyes, *Albuquerque Journal*, December 18th–22nd, 1983.

11. Letter from Argentine Ambassador in El Salvador, Victor Bianculli, to Salvadoran Army, dated October 14th, 1981, inviting senior officers to a SIDE intelligence course in November.

12. *Inner Circles: How America Changed the World: A Memoir*, by Alexander M. Haig, Warner Books, New York, 1992.

13. Memorandum by US Embassy political officer Townsend B. Friedman, subject: 'Hypothesis – The GOA As Prisoner of Army Intelligence', dated August 18th, 1980.

14. Memorandum by US Embassy political officer Townsend B. Friedman, subject: 'HUMAN RIGHTS: a Military View', dated September 11th, 1979.

15. 'Argentine Rights: One Issue Settled, Many Remain', by Charles A. Krause, *The Washington Post*, September 27th, 1979.

16. 'Informe Rattenbach': 'El Informe Final de la Comisión de Análisis y Evaluación de las Responsabilidades del Conflicto del Atlántico Sur.' Finally published in what is said to be an uncensored form on March 22nd, 2012.

17. 'The Malvinas/Falklands Affair: A New Look', by Enrique Cavallini, *International Journal of Intelligence and Counterintelligence*, November 23rd, 2006.

Chapter 15: Murderer Turns Art Lover

1. *Lost Art*, by Anja Shortland, Unicorn, 2021.

2. *El Expolio del Arte en Argentina*, by Daniel Schavelzon, Editorial Sudamericana, Buenos Aires, 1993.

3. Trial of members of the 'Grupo Gordon' including Gordon's son Marcelo, April 2005.

4. Statement of Julio Bárbaro during trial of Aníbal Gordon's associate Eduardo Ruffo, June 2012.

5. On February 25th, 1982, five weeks before Argentine troops landed on the Falkland Islands, the Australian government announced that it had agreed the purchase of HMS *Invincible*.

6. *1982*, by Juan B. Yofre, Random House Mondadori, 2011.

7. Embassy Counsellor David Joy to Robin Fearn at the Foreign and Commonwealth Office in London, TNA: FC07/4073.

Chapter 16: The Gamble That Failed

1. 'Directiva de Estrategia Militar Nro 1/82 (Caso Malvinas)'. Annex to 'Informe Rattenbach'.

2. *1982*, by Juan B. Yofre, Random House Mondadori, 2011.

3. 'Los documentos secretos de Malvinas: el día que la flota argentina cortó su comunicación con el continente y se preparó para la guerra', by Juan B. Yofre, *Infobae*, March 31st, 2019.

4. Record of a telephone conversation between President Galtieri and Foreign Minister Costa Méndez at 10pm on April 6th, 1982. Annex to 'Informe Rattenbach'.

5. Record of second meeting between President Leopoldo Galtieri and US Secretary of State Alexander Haig at 9.30pm on April 10th, 1982. Annex to 'Informe Rattenbach'.

6. Cable from US Secretary of State Alexander Haig to President Ronald Reagan. Marked 'Immediate' and dated April 12th, 1982. The cable was sent from Haig's aircraft as he flew to London from Buenos Aires.

7. Jeanne Kirkpatrick, television interview, *CBS Face the Nation*, April 11th, 1982.

8. Quoted in 'US Envoys "may have talked the Generals into invasion"', by Jack Malvern, *The Times*, December 28th, 2012.

9. Foreign and Commonwealth Office Sitrep, May 14th, 1982.

10. Cable from US Ambassador to Argentina Harry Shlaudeman to US Secretary of State Alexander Haig, April 30th, 1982.

11. 'Immediate' message from Director of the FBI to Director of the CIA, dated May 7th, 1982.

12. 'Falkland Islands: Consequences for British Interests and British Subjects in Latin America', dated May 14th, 1982.

13. Cable from US Embassy, Buenos Aires to US State Department, dated May 15th, 1982.

14. Cable from British Interests Section, Swiss Embassy, Buenos Aires to the Foreign and Commonwealth Office, London, May 13th, 1982.

15. 'Informe Rattenbach', para 481.

16. CIA information report, dated May 17th, 1982.

17. Cable from Britain's Ambassador to the United Nations, Sir Anthony Parsons, to the Foreign and Commonwealth Office, dated May 12th, 1982.

18. Foreign and Commonwealth Office Sitrep, dated May 14th, 1982.

19. Margaret Thatcher Foundation Archive, 'Prime Minister's Interview with Independent Radio News, Monday, May 17th, 1982'.

20. 'Informe Rattenbach', para 722.

21. *My Secret Falklands War*, by Sidney Edwards, Book Guild Publishing, 2014.

22. Memorandum from 'Special Assistant for Warning', US Department of Defense Intelligence, to Chairman, National Intelligence Council, dated May 20th, 1982.

23. *No Picnic*, Major General Julian Thompson, Leo Cooper, 1985.

24. *The History of the South Atlantic Conflict*, by Rubén O. Moro, Praeger, New York, 1989.

25. *Los Chicos de la Guerra: hablan los soldados que estuvieron en Malvinas*, by Daniel Kon, Galerna, Buenos Aires, 1982.

Chapter 17: Fall of the 'Dirty Warriors'

1. Statement by Ernesto Lorenzo, head of the Commission of Ex-Combatants, La Plata.

2. Quoted by Francisco Abelenda and Valeria Villalba, in 'Guerra de Malvinas: un análisis de los documentos de archivo del Ejército', *Aletheia*, October 2017.

3. Captain Breide Obeid, quoted in *Felices Pascuas! Los hechos inéditos de la rebelión militar*, Planeta, Buenos Aires, 1988, pp. 224–5.

4. CIA information report, 'POSSIBLE ATTEMPT TO REMOVE THE PRESIDENT AND OTHER GOVERNMENT OFFICIALS BY 10 AUGUST', dated August 5th, 1982.

5. CIA intelligence information cable, 'FURTHER ACTIONS BY SECURITY AND POLICE PERSONNEL TO TRY TO PREVENT FURTHER REVELATIONS OF EXCESSES DURING THE "DIRTY WAR"', dated May 3rd, 1983.

6. CIA intelligence information cable, 'RENEWED CONCERN WITHIN THE FEDERAL POLICE OVER REVELATIONS OF EXCESSES DURING THE "DIRTY WAR". CONSIDERATION OF CARRYING OUT VIOLENT ACTIONS TO IMPRESS THE GOVERNMENT WITH THE LEVEL OF CONCERN', dated April 29th, 1983.

7. 'Ley de Pacificación Nacional' (Law no. 22.924), passed September 22nd, 1983.

8. Prosecution of Gordon associate Eduardo Ruffo, C. N° 45.757, 'RUFFO, Eduardo Alfredo s/asociación ilícita', Buenos Aires, June 28th, 2012.

9. *The Buenos Aires Herald*, August 26th, 1983.

10. *Clarín*, February 24th, 2017, et al.

11. 'Most Wanted Criminal is Seized in Argentina', *The New York Times*, February 11th, 1984.

12. 'A 31 años de la detención del represor Aníbal Gordon en Córdoba', *El Diario de Carlos Paz*, March 24th, 2015, et al.

Chapter 18: The Long Wait for Justice

1. Comisión Nacional sobre la Desaparición de Personas (CONADEP), created by President Raúl Alfonsín on December 15th, 1983.

2. Preliminary hearing of the Supreme Military Council which opened on December 29th, 1983.

3. *El Diario del Juicio*, 1985, 20:25.

4. *Guerrillas and Generals*, by Paul H. Lewis, p. 214.

5. CIA analysis, subject: 'COMMENTS [withheld] ON ADMINISTRATION ARMED FORCES RELATIONS', dated November 9th, 1984.

6. US National Security Council Secretariat, subject: 'Claims that two retired Army General Officers have a plan to bring pressure on and ultimately to remove the government of President Raúl Alfonsín', dated March 5th, 1985.

7. CIA analysis, 'Argentina: Grappling With Intelligence Reform', dated September 12th, 1986.

8. 'Ley de Punto Final' (Law no. 23.492), passed December 24th, 1986.

9. 'Ley de Obediencia Debida' (Law no. 23.521), passed June 4th, 1987.

10. Aníbal Gordon, statement in Federal Court No. 5, Buenos Aires, on August 24th, 1987, as quoted in *Buenos Muchachos* by Carlos Juvenal, p. 137.

Chapter 19: Open Wounds

1. Argentine Defence Minister Raúl Borras, quoted in *Argentina Betrayed*, by Antonius C.G.M. Robbin, University of Pennsylvania Press, 2018, p. 212.
2. *The New York Times*, 'Pardoning Mass Murder in Argentina', January 3rd, 1991.
3. Quoted in *Argentina Betrayed*, by Antonius Robben, p. 214.
4. *El Vuelo*, by Horacio Verbitsky, Planeta, Buenos Aires, 1995. Adolfo Scilingo was eventually sentenced to 1,084 years in prison for the murder, illegal detention and torture of 30 people by Spain's Supreme Court, which said he was guilty of 'Crimes Against Humanity'; however, he is unlikely to serve more than 25 years because of Spain's statute of limitations.
5. 'Desde Madrid, Carla Cuenta Su Infancia Con Ruffo; El Acoso Sexual del Apropriador', *Página 12*, March 28th, 1999.
6. US Defense Intelligence Agency report, subject: 'Special Operations Forces', dated October 1st, 1976.
7. 'Stolen Childhoods: A special report; Argentines Contend for War Orphans' Hearts', by Nathaniel C. Nash, *The New York Times*, May 11th, 1993.
8. Admiral Emilio Massera obituary, *The Guardian*, November 10th, 2010.
9. Causa nº 1.627 caratulada 'GUILLAMONDEGUI, Néstor Horacio y otros s/privación ilegal de la libertad agravada, imposición de tormentos y homicidio calificado'. Sentenced May 31st, 2011.
10. 'Orletti V: nuevas condenas a perpetua para cuatro represores son represores que estaban imputados en el quinto juicio por delitos de lesa humanidad cometidos en el centro clandestino de detención Automotores Orletti.' Argentina.gob.ar, Monday, November 30th, 2020.

Chapter 20: The Struggle to Forget

1. *El Clan*, directed by Pablo Trapero, released in Argentina, 2015.
2. 'Bacacay 3570: Floresta family home identified as dictatorship torture site', *Buenos Aires Times*, July 15th, 2020.
3. 'Un Pedido de Explicaciones a la Iglesia', *Página 12*, August 22nd, 2015.
4. 'La Justicia es el Primer Paso', *Página 12*, September 5th, 2015.

5. Hebe De Bonafini, quoted in *Argentina Betrayed* by Antonius Robbin, p. 214.

6. 'Je m'appelle Mariana', documentary programme broadcast by France 24, October 11th, 2016.

7. 'El militar inglés que les devolvió su nombre a los argentinos caídos en Malvinas', *The New York Times* Spanish Edition, April 2nd, 2018.

8. *Revisiting the Falklands-Malvinas Question*, edited by Guillermo Mira and Fernando Pedrosa, Institute of Latin American Studies, University of London Press, 2021.

9. Ministry of Foreign Affairs, Government of Argentina, Information for the Press, N°: 103/21, March 31st, 2021.

10. 'La Justicia Desnuda al Deterioro de las Fuerzas Armadas', *La Nación*, June 18th, 2018.

11. Jorge García Mantel, former National Director of Planning and Strategy of the Argentine Ministry of Defence, *Infobae*, July 22nd, 2019.

12. 'L'Automne des Tortionnaires', Olivier Rolin, *Le Nouvel Observateur*, January 6th, 1984.

13. Transcript of voice recording sent to US State Department by US Embassy Human Rights Officer Allen 'Tex' Harris, May 31st, 1978.

Index

309